Financial Structure and Stability

Contributions to Economics

Giuseppe Gaburro (Ed.)
Ethics and Economics
1997. ISBN 3-7908-0986-1

Frank Hoster/Heinz Welsch/
Christoph Böhringer
CO_2 Abatement and Economic Structural Change in the European Internal Market
1997. ISBN 3-7908-1020-7

Christian M. Hafner
Nonlinear Time Series Analysis with Applications to Foreign Exchange Rate Volatility
1997. ISBN 3-7908-1041-X

Sardar M. N. Islam
Mathematical Economics of Multi-Level Optimisation
1998. ISBN 3-7908-1050-9

Sven-Morten Mentzel
Real Exchange Rate Movements
1998. ISBN 3-7908-1081-9

Lei Delsen/Eelke de Jong (Eds.)
The German and Dutch Economies
1998. ISBN 3-7908-1064-9

Mark Weder
Business Cycle Models with Indeterminacy
1998. ISBN 3-7908-1078-9

Tor Rødseth (Ed.)
Models for Multispecies Management
1998. ISBN 3-7908-1001-0

Michael Carlberg
Intertemporal Macroeconomics
1998. ISBN 3-7908-1096-7

Sabine Spangenberg
The Institutionalised Transformation of the East German Economy
1998. ISBN 3-7908-1103-3

Hagen Bobzin
Indivisibilities
1998. ISBN 3-7908-1123-8

Helmut Wagner (Ed.)
Current Issues in Monetary Economics
1998. ISBN 3-7908-1127-0

Peter Michaelis/Frank Stähler (Eds.)
Recent Policy Issues in Environmental and Resource Economics
1998. ISBN 3-7908-1137-8

Jessica de Wolff
The Political Economy of Fiscal Decisions
1998. ISBN 3-7908-1130-0

Georg Bol/Gholamreza Nakhaeizadeh/
Karl-Heinz Vollmer (Eds.)
Risk Measurements, Econometrics and Neural Networks
1998. ISBN 3-7908-1152-1

Joachim Winter
Investment and Exit Decisions at the Plant Level
1998. ISBN 3-7908-1154-8

Bernd Meyer
Intertemporal Asset Pricing
1999. ISBN 3-7908-1159-9

Uwe Walz
Dynamics of Regional Integration
1999. ISBN 3-7908-1185-8

Michael Carlberg
European Monetary Union
1999. ISBN 3-7908-1191-2

Giovanni Galizzi/Luciano Venturini (Eds.)
Vertical Relationships and Coordination in the Food System
1999. ISBN 3-7908-1192-0

Gustav A. Horn/Wolfgang Scheremet/
Rudolf Zwiener
Wages and the Euro
1999. ISBN 3-7908-1199-8

Dirk Willer
The Development of Equity Capital Markets in Transition Economies
1999. ISBN 3-7908-1198-X

Karl Matthias Weber
Innovation Diffusion and Political Control of Energy Technologies
1999. ISBN 3-7908-1205-6

Heike Link et al.
The Costs of Road Infrastructure and Congestion in Europe
1999. ISBN 3-7908-1201-3

Simon Duindam
Military Conscription
1999. ISBN 3-7908-1203-X

continued on page 250

Alexander Karmann
(Editor)

Financial Structure and Stability

With 16 Figures
and 27 Tables

Physica-Verlag
A Springer-Verlag Company

Series Editors
Werner A. Müller
Martina Bihn

Editor
Prof. Dr. Alexander Karmann
Technische Universität Dresden
Fakultät Wirtschaftswissenschaften
Lehrstuhl Geld, Kredit und Währung
Mommsenstraße 13
01062 Dresden
Germany

ISSN 1431-1933
ISBN 3-7908-1332-X Physica-Verlag Heidelberg New York

Cataloging-in-Publication Data applied for
Die Deutsche Bibliothek - CIP-Einheitsaufnahme
Financial structure and stability: with 27 tables / Alexander Karmann (ed.). - Heidelberg; New York: Physica-Verl., 2000
(Contributions to economics)
ISBN 3-7908-1332-X

Physica-Verlag Heidelberg New York
a member of BertelsmannSpringer Science+Business Media GmbH

Softcover Design: Erich Kirchner, Heidelberg

SPIN 10779392 88/2202-5 4 3 2 1 0 - Printed on acid-free paper

Preface

This book is intended to cover the issue 'financial structure and stability' in an epitome way. It reflects the contributions to a workshop on this subject held in Dresden on May 21st, 1999. The workshop was supported by Dresden University of Technology, DaimlerChrysler AG Research and Technology, and Sachsen LB what is gratefully acknowledged.

The workshop was starting point of the research project 'stability of the financial sector: theoretical analysis and an empirical cross-country study' which is financially supported by Deutsche Forschungsgemeinschaft. As research assistants, Oliver Greßmann and Christian Hott did helpful supportive work during the editing process. Michael Graff has made a great contribution to the book by detailed comments and criticisms. I am grateful to all of them as well as to the participants of the workshop for their stimulating discussion. Last, but not least, I am very indebted to the authors having contributed to this book by their substantial work.

Alexander Karmann　　　　Dresden/Figino, June 2000.

Table of contents

Financial systems: What can we learn from the past? Introduction to the book

Alexander Karmann

Dresden University of Technology, D-01062 Dresden, Germany

1 On financial systems

What can we learn from empirical as well as theoretical analysis of financial systems, differing cross-sectionally and changing structurally over time, with respect to the issue of stability of financial systems? This is the basic question underlying the contributions to this book.

In historical perspective, two generic types of financial systems can be identified, which we observe today in different multifaceted mixtures: banking-oriented and market-oriented systems. Both prototypes provide their own institutional answers for a number of issues like economies of scale (branches versus funds), informational asymmetries (information acquisition versus external rating; incomplete contracts: delegated monitoring versus voting rights). So, the question arises which system is more appropriate in a specific environment, at a specific stage of development in a specific environment. The issue touches on a number of present today features like globalization, crises and bubbles, transition economies or bank restructuring. The answers to this question are given in terms of efficiency and in terms of stability. More precisely, we can focus on cost aspects (technological efficiency), on the allocational outcome (Pareto efficiency), on the informational content of prices (informational efficiency). And/or, we may think of asset price dynamics (stability of prices) or intertemporal risk sharing (stability of contractual relationships). Having specified the economic terms in which the analysis shall be carried out, the solution to the problem of an 'optimal' financial structure typically depends on the weights in the social welfare function attached to the parties involved, reflecting shareholder's protection or stakeholder's protection. Standard results, as shown in BOOT AND THAKOR (1997) e.g., suggest that market-oriented financial systems provide better short term cross-sectional risk sharing and a higher degree of informational efficiency, whereas bank-oriented systems provide better intertemporal risk sharing and a superior resolution to moral hazard behaviour of debitors. Both types of systems have their weaknesses. While the first is strongly exposed to (changes in) expection dynamics, the latter is vulnerable to contagion resulting from informational asymmetries. The potential deficiencies of any of these systems are the starting point in the discussion on regulation of financial institutions and markets.

The book is divided into four sections. The first one deals with stability issues in a globalizing financial world and addresses topics of convergence, domestic policy, financial bubbles, crises and international coordination. The second section is on banking systems. Country specific adoption and restructuring of (universal but also separation) banking systems are key problems for the industrialized economies, while catching-up is of major concern for the economies in transition. Feeble regional economies and subsidized banking is at the heart of the vivid dispute on public sector banking being taken up in the third section. The last section is devoted to resource-oriented approaches in quantifying financial development and risk of sovereign default. We summarize the main findings and their relation to the ongoing debate on international coordination and regulation in the next subsections.

2 On stability, globalization, and coordination

The effects of globalization are far reaching. Expanding the global market system influences the evolution of bank-oriented as well as market-oriented financial systems, questions existing monetary policy rules, may enforce the separation of asset price formation from real development, and demands for redirection of policy as well as co-ordination rules to react on political, economic or financial risk and contagious financial turmoil.

In her contribution, NEUBERGER (this volume) focuses on the evolution of financial systems characterized as highly path dependent in reflecting national preferences. But there are significant signs of convergence due to growing international capital mobility, increased competition of legal environments including regulation and harmonization of rules. On the one hand, tendencies towards convergency to market-oriented financial systems can best be illustrated by securitization instruments. Asset backed securities, for example, allow to transform non-tradeable bank credits to marketable financial claims. On the other hand, there is a certain convergence towards universal-bank-oriented systems by harmonizing prudential rules and banking supervision. Closer analysis indicates that this convergence improves allocation efficiency of financial markets, but at the cost of weaknesses inherent to market-oriented systems, as described by terms like non-conforming asset price dynamics, and thereby threatens the second goal, stability. NEUBERGER takes a skeptic view whether harmonization in terms of uniformly regulated systems is a good advice to enhance stability.

WAGNER (this volume) takes a more optimistic view concerning the effectiveness of national monetary policy in a world of growing economic interdependencies. Not withstanding to admit weaker abilities for traditional stabilization policy due to looser links in the monetary transmission mechanism, he emphasizes the disciplining effect of globalization to prevent inflation. In a Barro/Gordon-type of model, the result of a lower inflation bias follows, among others, from policy maker's increased risk aversion responding to increased cost of inflation. And as coordination incentives should grow to prevent capital flights, the perceived lower inflation bias will help to reduce output volatility, too.

In his discussion, FUHRMANN (this volume) questions the appropriateness of the framework chosen and asks for a multinational modelling to endogenize the mechanism of coordination pressure and to reflect different degrees of internalization and different institutional arrangements in their responses to shocks.

In a nonstandard approach, FAND (this volume) explains the simultaneous coexistence of stock market bubble and price stability, as being observed throughout the 1990s in the market-oriented US financial system. Criticizing the New Paradigm explanation of a more sophisticated management, he bases his arguments on combining a truly quantity-theoretic approach for the domestic (US) economy and a Keynesian-type of rationed world-supply model. The ongoing rapid growth of monetary (as will as broader financial) aggregates is accompanied by a rapid growth of stock prices at spectacular rates in the second half of the 1990s and a stimulated (post-1995) US-boom – but without inflation. According to FAND, the last can be explained by idle resources in post-Maastricht Europe and idle capacities in the emerging market world, resulting in a flat world-economy AS curve. The first observation is a direct consequence of money-stock to asset-price relation in the presence of CPI targeting of a Fed handcuffed by its commitment to inflation targeting. This is even more aggravated in a CAPM integrated system where lending in Japan at low rates allows financing in bubbling US markets.

WIESMETH (this volume) comments on whether low US inflation is rather a result of Keynesian idle capacity, to be accompanied by Keynesian unemployment, than a consequence of European sticky (above equilibrium) wages, producing unemployment, and of strict EMU price targeting in the presence of free trade.

The issue of crises and consequences is tackled by the remaining contributions of this section. In a short-term perspective, the Asian crisis can be explained in a KRUGMAN (1998)-type of modelling, as done by FRENKEL (this volume) who emphasizes the ambivalent role of implicit government guarantees of a currency peg. Capital inflows result in growing demand to collateralize the peg, accompanied most likely by an ongoing decline of net reserves for interventive actions. The collapse occurs when it is known that net reserves just would cover – in form of foreign currency – the drop in domestic money holdings as expected to follow from higher post-collapse interest rates.

In contrast to this financial risk-oriented modeling, DEVINNEY (this volume) takes a socio-political risk-oriented analysis of the Asian story, beginning with rapid growth and ending in an aftermath of weathering the 1997 storm quite differently. He combines neo-institutional reasoning, to reflect regional differences but not sudden changes, and neo-classical arguments, to reflect patterns of existing growth but not its emergence. DEVINNEY identifies growth impulses from well-liberalized Singapore/Hongkong economies spreading over the region, driven by increasing labor force participation and capital imports, and collapsing after factor input realignments (similarily as described above). While right institutional settings allowed for quick resuscitation in the Anglo Saxon capitalist economies, mismatch in relational capitalism and non-openness for arm's length ownership control did considerable harm to crony capitalist economies.

Institutional reforms beyond the scope of the IMF discussion on fragility and re-regulation are also at the heart of FILC's (this volume) analysis, though from a different point of view: informational efficiences as a prerequisite for asset price stability may not be assured by market mechanism, as Asian financial markets have shown. And bank-oriented systems may have failed to experience severe turbulences only due to stable macro conditions in the post-Bretton Woods era. Therefore, FILC asks for a managed USD-Yen-Euro exchange rate system guided by a Macro Forum of experts.

In his commenting remarks, ECKWERT (this volume) first clarifies to separate between (the multiplicity of) price dynamics and erratic fluctuations which are either insurable risk or subject to self-regulation. With regard to the cure side, he doubts on the ability of the proposed Forum to credibly disseminate reference values for exchange rates without enforcing speculative attacks.

3 On banking systems, restructuring, and catching-up policies

Banks are often characterized as optimal institutional solution to problems of liquidity transformation, risk sharing and monitoring under asymmetric information, but at the cost of inherent instabilities since the realizable values of a bank's financial assets may depart from their nominal values (see, e.g., VIVES (1991)). As the informational advantage of bank-oriented systems is of particular importance for economies in transition, as for any backward regional economy, in their strategy to overcome the issue of informational heterogeneity, the debate on universal banking and its historic protagonist, the German banking system, is of everlasting interest.

The more recent discussion questions the ability of continental European banks to use efficiently their specific characteristics of intertemporal relationship lending and diversified all-purpose banking. In their conclusion, EDWARDS AND FISCHER (1994) attribute missing evidence for superiority of German universal banks to the nonexclusiveness of housebank relationships – though nonecxlusiveness typically enforces contestability, hence competitiveness – and to the (indeed) large number of individual banks believed to be too small to exert delegated monitoring – though the vast majority of German banks profits from membership to one of the two banking networks, Savings Bank Association and Cooperative Bank Corporation sharing information among their members. A popular empiricism is to cite return-on-assets (ROA) or return-on-equity (ROE) figures of universal versus separation banking systems. But, keeping credit claims in their own accounts, as continental European banks do, or directly selling securities to ultimate lenders, as Anglo Saxon banks do, has completely different impact originating from one and the same business, to ROAs and ROEs. Hence, the mere race to higher numbers of relative return on the sake of the shareholders is a rather shortsighted view. Admittedly, there is a difference in the allocation of risk which may be reflected by differing growth of bank share values and, finally, result in increasing asset transfers out of banks through asset-backed-security instruments allowing universal banks to lower their balance of account volumes and, thus, to increase their return-to-equity numbers. And there are numerous other technological issues leading to commodization of products and a variety of socio-political issues like the diminishing role of state or the aging of population with the need to sustainably finance pension funds, which alltogether drive universal bank-oriented systems towards higher market orientation (see also WHITE (1998) or NEUBERGER (this volume)).

Two tendencies in the strategies to restructure continental banks seem to prevail: the first is disintegration of banks' ownership stakes in nonfinancial firms; the other is focused merging. The focus may be on niche strategies to serve SMEs or local customers, on retail supermarkets including fund activities and, most prominently, on crossborder or worldwide investment activities. This also means that universal banks will separate in part by building their specific multichannel networks for the specific needs of their clientele.

In his more historic reconsideration, TIMMERMANN (this volume) points out the success of German universal banks by two features: the first one is relationship lending and long term investment which helped prominent manufacturers like Krupp, Thyssen, Bayer to survive in uneasy periods of time. The recent Holtzmann example highlights the ambivalence between today's rescueing act and tomorrow's profitability. The second constituant is unsecured personal loan and local knowledge which is, at another place, particularily claimed to hold in public sector banking (see MILBRADT below). Path-dependent adaption rather than imitation of the German bank system led universal banking to establish elsewhere, as the Japanese example demonstrates.

In his study of the Italian banking system, GOISIS (this volume) identifies uncompetitive and deficient institutional features, like bad recovery policies or political pressure on public sector banking, as the main determinants of (cost-) inefficiency. Moreover, interregional imbalances within one jurisdiction are shown to end in higher credit rationing for the backward Southern regions and induce profitable saving transfers to the more advanced North through the acquisition of Southern banks by Northern group-leaders. This, in return, calls for redirection of restructuring policies in Italian banking.

LOCAREK-JUNGE (this volume) emphasizes in his comment the relevance of disaggregated statistics and size specific analysis of country related bank studies. He suggests to rank country specific bank systems according to their abilities to respond to future challenges.

The obviously difficult way for economies in transition (EIT) to follow a stable transition path from a state-owned to a fully privatized banking system is described by ENKHZAYA (this volume). In order to supplement the new formal rules, as characterized by privatization, property rights and prudential laws, informal rules have to be established which allow to overcome the problem of incentive mixture between old opportunistic behaviour and new selfishness. Path-dependent solutions, in terms of a well-measured liberalization, explicitly involve the disengagement of the state from bank governance.

SOLARZ (this volume) adds that shock therapy is a necessary first step to overcome the old command structure. Adequate sequencing to gain stable transition is a far more important, though complex, issue than searching for short-term liberalization policy.

HÖLSCHER (this volume) concentrates on monetary policy guidelines for EIT. Starting with the dilemma to stabilize capital imports by high lending rates and thereby to enforce moral hazard and adverse selection of borrowers, EIT's central banks will, thereafter, have to induce decreasing spreads in order to stimulate investment activities by lower lending rates. Setting standards of regulation and, even harder, maintaining them may turn out to be a task more difficult to perform than in real markets. But the process of catching-up with developed economies seems to be of striking success for EU accession candidates which import stability through a credible peg to the Euro.

4 On public sector banking, regional policy, and distortion

The discussion on public sector banking centres on the existance of services of public interest not being provided by private banks and the privileges given herefore by the legislator.

According to today's conventional arguing there is a full range of financial services offered by private banks to meet cross-sectional and cross-regional needs. Hence, there is no justification for legislatory preferential treatment resulting in distorted competition. It is claimed that the state guarantee impairs refinancing conditions, that hidden infusion of equity capital allows to expand cross border activities, which is not in the ultimate interest of domestic taxpayer, and that 'unlimited backing' of liabilities favours managerial moral hazard behaviour.

MILBRADT (this volume) emphasizes the specific feature of public sector banking for regional development policy in the presence of feeble economic regions in transition, as it holds for Germany's New Bundesländer. The risk of business relocation, exaggravated in case of remote financial decision making from outside regions, demands for resident banks supporting local investment activities regardless of available collateral as long as there is public commitment of the project's creditworthiness. Close relationship with customers thereby helps to bridge the informational gap typically arising in newly established economic environments. These lines of arguments strikingly resemble the feature of unsecured, personal loans as described by TIMMERMANN. Apart from preventing relocation, public sector banking functions as conduit of financial information for policy decisions related to economic development, as MILBRADT adds to his agenda of a 'two stages of growth'-policy. That means: establishing public sector banking first, transforming it to private credit institutions second.

WEISS (this volume) supplements on the need of restructuring stand-alone practice towards financial network solutions in order to co-share fixed costs and to cope with decreasing margins.

In his brief review of past debates on European public sector banking, SCHIPS (this volume) concludes that the aim of procuring information for policy making through public sector banking may enforce detrimental developments outside of taxpayer's direct control. Cooperative banks, as the Swiss example stands for, have similar features in common with public sector banks, but they are lacking the temptation of intervention which finally may lead to financial repression.

5 On resource orientation and new architecture

As the above reasoning suggests, weathering of financial storms seems to be highly resource depending. Human resources invested in building up a sound institutional framework is a prerequisite for 'immunisation' strategies, as DEVINNEY's analysis outlines. The acceptance of this view is underlined even in the more radical, on restricting bounds oriented MELTZER report of the CONGRESSIONAL ADVISORY COMMISSION ON INTERNATIONAL FINANCIAL INSTITUTIONS (2000) by recommending the introduction of 'institutional reform loans'. A more short-term oriented policy guide is the accumulation of foreign currency reserves by central banks of developing countries, seen by IMF representatives as a main determinant to pre-qualify for IMF credits.

The aspects of real and financial resource orientation are both reflected in two quantitative explorations closing our volume. GRAFF (this volume) employs the idea of resources a society devotes to run its financial institutions and traces the finance-growth nexus since 1960 in a cross-country study. He comes up with a causal relation switching over times between supply-leading finance and detrimental financial repression.

KARMANN's (this volume) sovereign risk analysis illuminates the predominant role of financial resources, materialized by foreign exchange reserves. Within a Black-Scholes type of approach, information on spreads has to be supplemented by estimation of the economy's ability to accumulate currency reserves in order to infer default probabilities.

Besides resource orientation, as a basic principle in the process to stabilize financial systems, there are organisational principles to be met in the design of a new financial architecture. In terms of Industrial Economics, a well designed structure should rely on the principles of separation of different tasks and of clear division of responsibilities. So, long-term development, short-term emergency activities, including a quasi lender-of-last-resort option for developing countries, international prudential standards and liquidity provision (in developed countries) should be attributed separately to the institutions of World Bank, IMF, BIS and central banks (of the developed economies). As the debate on 'Contingent Credit Lines' for pre-qualified IMF members exemplifies, a narrow cooperation between the institutions is still an important task.

The international harmonization of rating standards is fostered by the Bank for International Settlements as a financial standard setter. Reflecting the discussion on path dependence of market- versus bank-oriented systems, the former relying on external rating, the latter relying on internal rating, we have to conclude that a nonequivalent treatment of any of the two rating approaches would directly impair the financial system relying on the other approach and, thereby, distort the former 'optimality' of the respective institutional arrangement. This means that laying down external rating as the exclusive requirement would hamper continental banking and impede, among others, the process of financing SME in continental Europe. A simultaneous coexistence of external and internal rating, on the other hand, should be treated along the 'one business, one law' argument implying both practices to be under the surveillance of one and the same institution.

The evolution of bank-oriented systems towards more market orientation is already described (see NEUBERGER). In addition, we observe a splitting-up into either international banking or local banking activities. Moreover, public sector banking seems to be an element of contestability of financial markets, at least for less developed regional economies. In the New Bundesländer of Germany, credit banks have reduced their supply of credit, as the sharp –3,5 % drop down of their 1999 lending activities in Saxony indicates while public sector banking expanded at the same time by some 6,5 %.

What are the consequences for banking supervision when the evolution of banking systems splits, in part, towards internationally operating and locally operating groups? In general, the coverage of banking supervision and central bank policy should coincide geographically, which asks for redirecting financial supervision within the EMU from a nation-wide to a supranational level. On the other hand, and similarly to the US, locally based banking groups may be subject to prudential laws differing from those applicable to internationally operating intermediaries. To reflect the observable convergence towards market orientation, the financial supervisory agency should be designed in a consistent way to target the full range of banking, insurance and financial market activities.

References

Boot, A. W. A. and A. V. Thakor (1997), Financial System Architecture, Review of Financial Studies 10, 693-733.

Congressional Advisory Commission On International Financial Institutions (2000), Report (Meltzer Report), http://phantom-x.gsia.cmu.edu/IFIAC/Report.html.

Edwards, J. and K. Fischer (1994), Banks, Finance and Investment in Germany, Cambridge: Cambridge University Press.

Krugman, P. (1998), What happened to Asia?, MIT mimeo.

Vives, X. (1991), Banking Competition and European Integration, in: Giovannini, A. and C. P. Mayer (ed.), European Financial Integration, Cambridge: Cambridge University Press, 9-31.

White, W. (1998), The Coming Transformation of Continental European Banking, Basle: Bank for International Settlements.

Part I:

Financial stability and globalization

Evolution of financial systems: Convergence towards higher or lower stability?

Doris Neuberger[1]

Lehrstuhl für Volkswirtschaftslehre – Geld und Kredit, Wirtschafts- und Sozialwissenschaftliche Fakultät, Universität Rostock, Parkstraße 6, D-18057 Rostock, Germany

Abstract. Financial systems evolve as different mixes of markets and intermediaries to provide financial services and risk sharing opportunities to households and firms, supplemented with regulations to protect them against systemic risk. The present paper reviews the research on comparative financial systems to discuss their determinants, stability properties and evolution. Although convergence towards a uniform financial system can be excluded, there is a tendency of evolution towards an arm's length-cum-market-oriented financial system with intermediation by institutional investors and universal banking with harmonized prudential regulation and qualitative supervision. The stability effects depend on the kind of stability aspired, on short-term and long-term relations between efficiency and stability and on the pros and cons of harmonizing regulations on an international scale. In the long run, instability tends to rise.

1 Introduction

During the course of history, a variety of financial systems has developed in different countries, containing different ways in which savings are mobilised from surplus units and channeled to deficit units to finance real capital investments. The historical development reflects the response of financial markets and institutions to the progress of technology, the openness of markets, particular government restrictions and fundamental factors of the cultural and legal framework. Studies of comparative financial systems have categorized different financial systems and seek to explain their origins and implications for economic welfare. They use different classifications according to different functions of financial systems. Those which focus on the intermediation function differentiate between bank-oriented or intermediated finance on the one hand and market-oriented finance on the other hand (e.g. Allen/Gale 1995, Schwiete 1998). Those which focus on corporate fi-

[1] I would like to thank Martina Eckardt, Solvig Räthke and Markus Hennig for helpful comments.

nance and corporate control functions use the dichotomy between control-oriented finance and arm's length finance (Berglöf 1997, Fischer 2000).[2] While the Anglo-Saxon financial systems of the US and the UK are considered as prototypes of market-orientation or arm's length finance, the financial systems of Germany and Japan are typically bank-oriented or control-oriented.[3] According to different banking regulations, these systems go along with a universal banking system or with a separation of commercial from investment banking.

While the financial systems have evolved independently from each other for a long time, they face heightened competition due to financial liberalization, globalization and innovation since the last two decades. Increasing openness of financial markets to international competition has pressured governments to deregulate or harmonize financial systems towards the most efficient type. Since financial capital is very mobile, it can be easily and quickly transferred to a system which provides the highest return on investments. Thus, the interest in the relative efficiency of financial systems has rekindled, inspiring many theoretical and empirical studies on the comparative advantage of different designs of intermediation, corporate finance and corporate control.[4] They focus on the efficiency goal of a financial system to minimize transaction costs and costs of asymmetric information in principal agent conflicts and, from a dynamic point of view, to promote innovation and growth. While there is no conclusive result concerning the relative overall efficiency of a single system, some studies find a tendency of financial systems to converge (e.g. Baums 1996, Moerland 1995b, Allen 1999).

Another goal of a financial system is stability, i.e. protection of retail investors, firms and of the economy as a whole against systemic risk. Theoretically, there are many possible technologies to produce stability, ranging from 'free banking' without state intervention to highly regulated financial systems with banking and/or securities market supervision. In the last two decades, many advanced countries have experienced increased instability in the financial sector, with volatile asset prices and financial stress or crises in banking. The underlying factors are cyclical and structural, caused by deregulations in the light of heightened competition (Davis 1992, Nakajima/Taguchi 1995). While governments obviously competed for the most efficient financial system, they may have been less concerned about provid-

---

[2] Compatible with this are the dichotomies between network-oriented and market-oriented financial systems (Moerland 1995a, 1995b) and between insider and outsider systems of corporate control (Franks/Mayer 1995).

[3] See e.g. Allen/Gale (1995), Berglöf (1997), Schwiete (1998). The classification into bank-oriented and market-oriented financial systems has been critized for not taking into account that bank credits are the most important source of external finance also in Anglo-Saxon countries (Fischer 2000).

[4] For surveys see Allen (1999), Allen/Gale (1995, 1999), Shleifer/Vishny (1997), Thakor (1996).

ing the public good of stability[5], or they were unaware of potential conflicts between efficiency and stability. The globalization of financial markets forces them to harmonize banking and securities market regulations to ensure a minimum level of stability in the changing environment.

The present paper asks in which way financial systems can be expected to converge, and whether convergence would lead to higher or lower stability. The answer depends on the kind of stability to be reached, on the relations between efficiency and stability of a financial system and on the stability effects of harmonizing regulations. A harmonization of regulations neglects that the demand for financial stability may differ between nations, due to different risk aversion and different traditions of risk sharing arrangements. Since the financial system of a country depends on history and has been shaped by its legal system, preferences and culture, the effects of a partial reform are path-dependent and welfare-reducing effects on efficiency and stability are likely.

Chapter 2 reviews the determinants and stability properties of financial systems by resorting to theories of financial intermediation in unregulated markets (2.1) and theories of regulations to provide stability (2.2). Chapter 3 reviews the evolution of financial systems and their tendencies of convergence (3.1) to discuss implications for stability (3.2). The conclusions are summarized in chapter 4.

2 Theories of financial systems and stability

2.1 Unregulated financial markets and intermediaries

"A 'financial system' can be defined as institutional arrangements designed to transfer savings from those who generate them to those who are willing to make use of them, above all wishing to invest, on terms and conditions inclusive of the degree of risk mutually acceptable to both parties" (Rybczynski 1984, p. 276). Such arrangements provide financial services to households as main providers of funds and to firms as main users of funds. On the household side, they comprise the collection and transfer of savings by banks and other depository institutions, the provision of marketable and transferable securities by capital markets and of risk sharing opportunities by intermediaries and markets. On the firm side, they comprise arrangements of corporate finance and governance to mitigate agency costs of external finance.

Theories of the new institutional economics and financial intermediation explain the evolution of financial institutions by market imperfections such as transaction and information costs. In their absence, there would be no role for intermediaries

---

[5] Possible explanations are that internationally active investors which shall be attracted have low risk aversion or that negative externalities by spillovers of instability are not internalized. As to the concept of institutional competition with stability as a public or merit good, see Siebert/Koop (1990, p. 442).

(Fama 1980b). Three main theories of intermediation explain the emergence of financial institutions: theories of economies of scale and insurance, information asymmetry and incomplete contracts.[6]

Economies of scale due to indivisibilities in transaction technologies restrict diversification and risk-sharing under direct financing via securities markets. Here, the role of intermediaries consists in risk pooling and diversification, providing a *liquidity insurance* to risk-averse depositors and exploiting economies of scale in lending and payments services (Gurley/Shaw 1960). This theory applies to banks and other intermediaries such as mutual funds, which differ in the extent of risk sharing. While mutual collective investment funds issue deposits with uncertain value, the value of bank deposits is nominally fixed. The special role of banks to provide a riskless deposit rate while holding long-term risky and illiquid assets makes them vulnerable to runs (Diamond/Dybvig 1983).

Information asymmetries between borrowers and lenders further explain this uniqueness of banks. They are delegated to screen and monitor borrowers to avoid adverse selection and moral hazard, exploiting economies of scale and scope within ongoing credit relationships (Diamond 1984). Since banks thus acquire private information, their loans are typically non-marketable. The costs of delegation are minimized by portfolio diversification of banks which ensures an almost riskless deposit rate. In a multiperiod context, moral hazard problems can be further reduced by the establishment of reputation by the borrower. A firm which can be relied on not to exploit its lenders may avoid the costs of being monitored by banks and access the securities markets (Diamond 1989, 1991). This gives rise to the role of rating agencies to offer monitoring services to investors in securities markets.

Banks solve *incomplete contract problems*, which result from imperfect observability or verifiability of outcomes. The longer the term of the contract, the greater is the scope of the borrower to exploit the lender or vice versa and the more likely a renegotiation of contract terms becomes profitable. Banks may have a comparative advantage in resolving these problems, if they obtain special control rights and provide commitment devices which prevent the exploitation of one partner by the other (see Neuberger 1994, pp. 79, 1998, pp. 39). In the event of the borrower's default, it is efficient to delegate the control to banks, to bundle the creditors' claims and reduce costs of free-riding by bondholders. In non-default states, corporate control by financial intermediaries may be efficient to prevent actions of firm managers against the interests of creditors and/or shareholders, e.g. by voting rights from equity holdings, proxy voting rights or representations on the supervisory boards of companies. Equity holdings by banks reduce their incentives to pose creditor over shareholder interests (see Stiglitz 1985, p. 148). Alternative mechanisms of corporate control are provided by the markets, i.e. the capital mar-

---

[6] For surveys see Bhattacharya/Thakor (1993), Freixat/Rochet (1997), Neuberger (1994, 1998), Davis (1992, pp. 16).

ket with takeovers, the product market and the market for management (see Jensen/Ruback 1983, Hart 1983, Fama 1980a). The relative efficiency of these different arrangements is an empirical question. As an alternative to control in long-term credit relationships, commitments are implicit contracts which cannot be specified formally (Mayer 1988, Hellwig 1991). Devices of committing banks not to exploit their borrowers are the establishment of reputation and equity participation by banks (Sharpe 1990, Neuberger 1997). Commitments cannot be provided by capital markets and rest on imperfect competition between financial institutions.

These theories thus explain financial systems as mixes of institutional arrangements and markets which are shaped by the prevailing information and investment technology (see Allen/Gale 1997), competition, preferences (with respect to risk and time) and legal rules and their enforcement. Since these factors differ between countries, are interdependent and time-variant, different systems have evolved (see chapter 3.1). The main types we observe can be classified into bank-oriented or market-oriented financial systems according to the dominant institutions of intermediation and risk sharing, and into control-oriented or arm's length-oriented financial systems with respect to the dominant corporate control mechanisms. As illustrated in figure 1, bank-oriented finance typically goes along with control-oriented finance, while market-oriented finance goes hand in hand with arm's length finance. Therefore, we will differentiate between two financial systems: *control-cum-bank-oriented (CB)* and *arm's length-cum-market-oriented (AM)*. In CB systems, banks play a dominant role in the allocation of capital and risk sharing and they are heavily involved in the control of firms with which they form long-term relationships. They face little competition from financial markets, which are relatively unimportant. Households have access to a narrow range of financial products and there is little publicly available information about firms. In AM financial systems, financial markets play an important role in providing opportunities for direct financing and controlling firms. They allow a wide variety of financial products and of non-bank intermediaries, such as mutual funds and consumer finance companies, to provide risk-sharing arrangements. The public availability of information makes possible an active market for corporate control, where firms are controlled by external investors at arm's length. The categories of universal banking versus separation of commercial and investment banking concern both corporate control and intermediation functions. Although it is often the case, universal banking need not be part of a CB system, and the separation of commercial and investment banking need not go along with an AM system.

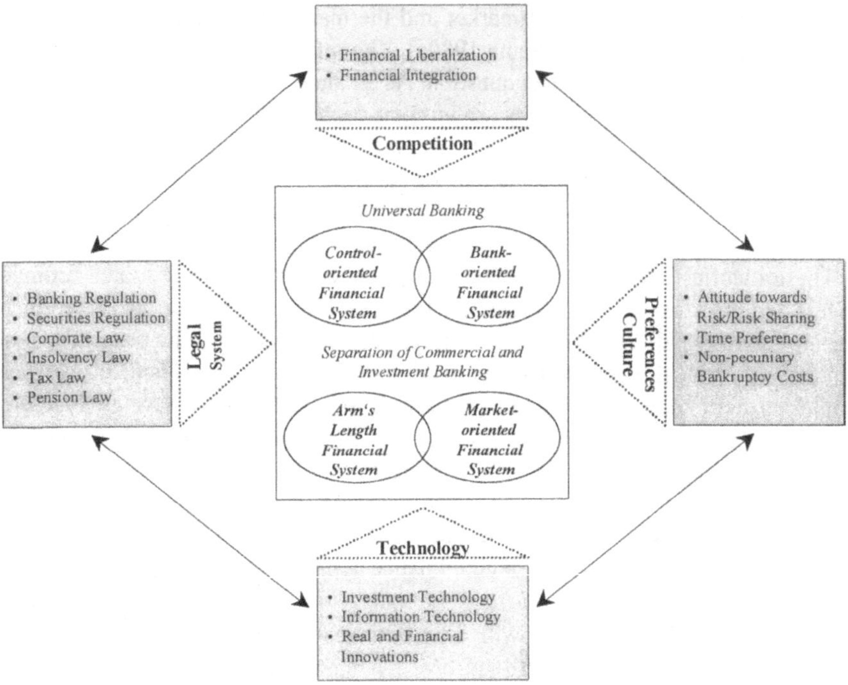

Figure 1 Financial systems and their determinants

An important determinant of financial systems are government interventions, which are justified by market failures that cannot be resolved by the development of private institutions. If financial systems fail to provide stability as a public good, banking or securities regulations become necessary as part of the legal system.

2.2 Stability of financial systems and regulations

The stability of a financial system depends on its ability to curb *systemic risk.* "'Systemic risk' ... or 'instability' are used to describe a disturbance in financial markets which entails unanticipated changes in prices and quantities in credit or asset markets, which lead to a danger of failure of financial firms, and which in turn threatens to spread so as to disrupt the payments mechanism and capacity of the financial system to allocate capital" (Davis 1992, p. 117). Systemic risk should be distinguished from the macroeconomic risk of business cycles, interest rate and exchange rate changes, although they usually coincide (Hellwig 1998). From the point of view of an individual investor, stability means to be protected against unanticipated changes in asset values. From the point of view of an entrepreneur, it means that he or she can rely on long-term relationships with financiers or stable financing conditions. The ability of a financial system to provide these kinds of insurance is closely related to its risk-sharing arrangements, which differ fundamentally between AM and CB systems. In an AM system, cross-sectional risk sharing is the dominant arrangement, i.e. different individuals are exchanging risks at a given point in time. This is possible because markets provide many instruments to diversify portfolios, hedge idiosyncratic risk, and adjust portfolio risk to suit their risk preferences. The investors bear asset price or liquidity risk, even if they hold deposits in mutual funds. A CB system, on the other hand, is based on intertemporal smoothing by banks. Banks can provide insurance against asset price swings by averaging gains and losses over time (intergenerational risk sharing) or by accumulating assets as reserves (Allen/Gale 1995). However, bank depositors are not fully insured against liquidity risk, because the risk-sharing deposit contract may give an incentive for runs of depositors to withdraw their funds, even if the bank is solvent. According to Diamond and Dybvig (1983), a run may be caused by any random event, including an observed run at some other bank. If fears of insolvency at one bank raise concerns about insolvency at other banks, runs are contagious and result in a '*banking panic*', where many depositors run on many banks at once.

Thus, the probability of bank runs creates an instability inherent to a bank-oriented financial system. Two arguments call for state regulations to reduce it: market failure by negative externalities and asymmetric information. Externalities arise, because bank managers or depositors do not take into account the social costs of a contagious bank run which may result from their risk-taking decisions or withdrawals of deposits in a run. While the run on a single bank may be socially advantageous to select good from bad banks, contagious bank runs are likely to impose huge costs on the economy as a whole (Burghof/Rudolph 1996, pp. 21). They mainly consist in an interruption of production when assets are prematurely liquidated (hurting especially small firms which depend on bank lending), a disturbance of risk-sharing and a disruption of money supply and the payments mechanism (Davis 1992, pp. 119). The probability of a contagious run rises by asymmetric information, if depositors cannot distinguish between risky and less risky banks. The moral hazard problem is especially severe for banks which are by their nature less capitalized than non-bank firms. The lower the bank's capital ratio, the higher are the bank managers' incentives to increase risk in order to raise the value of equity at the expense of bank creditors. This makes depositors vulnerable to bank capital reductions and explains why they should react very sensible to signals about a crisis and need to be protected (Burghof/Rudolph 1996, pp. 32, Dewatripont/Tirole 1994, pp. 141).

Public policy may counteract runs and panics by *'protective regulations'*, i.e. provision of a 'safety net' by deposit insurance and lender-of-last-resort facilities, and by *'preventive or prudential regulations'* to control risk-taking (e.g. by capital standards, liquidity norms, diversification norms, prohibition of certain businesses).[7] Both types of regulations should be combined because they are complementary: protective regulations have preventive effects by enhancing depositors' confidence, while preventive regulations are necessary to reduce the costs of protective regulations. A system which relies only on provision of liquidity by the lender of last resort and/or risk-insensitive deposit insurance[8] would be vulnerable to excessive risk-taking by banks, imposing heavy burdens on the regulator and taxpayers.

Since regulations imply monitoring costs and costs of adverse incentives, they are only efficient as long as they are able to provide stability at lower marginal cost than the '*free banking*' laissez-faire alternative. According to the free banking theory, banks need no state control because the market mechanism provides enough self-regulation to ensure stability at lower cost. If depositors observe that their bank takes too much risks or maintain too little capital to absorb risks, they would demand a higher risk premium. "If bank customers want safe banks, market forces will ensure they get them" (Dowd 1996, p. 681). Competitive pressures would also prevent contagious bank runs, because good banks should have a strong incentive to distance themselves from bad ones. Any state intervention would weaken the market forces and imply higher costs. This theory neglects the arguments of market failure by asymmetric information, externalities and control costs that can be reduced by delegating the supervision of banks from depositors to a regulatory agency (Burghof/Rudolph 1996, p. 38). An empirical test of free banking is not possible for the current banking systems, because all rely on state regulations.[9] Evidence rather supports the asymmetric-information hypothesis that depositors tend to run on banks when adverse economic conditions lead them to doubt the value of bank assets (Benston/Kaufman 1995). On the other hand, the claim that protective regulations encourage more risk-taking by banks is borne out by evidence (Benston 1995, Kaufman 1991, see Benston/Kaufman 1996, Dowd 1996). Therefore, there is a trade-off between market and state control and the free banking theory is a suitable reference model to question the appropriateness of existing regulations. They should correct market failures without undermining market control when it is more efficient. The solution of the trade-off also depends on equity considerations: if the social welfare function poses much weight on the protection of small investors and firms, a government safety net (by government

---

[7] For surveys on the economics of bank regulation see Burghof/Rudolph (1996), Benston/Kaufman (1996), Bhattacharya et al. (1998), Dewatripont/Tirole (1994).

[8] Means of relating deposit insurance premiums to risk in order to prevent an implicit subsidy to bank shareholders are difficult to devise (see e.g. Kane 1986, Baltensperger/Dermine 1987, Bhattacharya et al. 1998).

[9] Historical evidence indicates that free-banking was mostly stable (Dowd 1996, 1992), but since it refers to periods without a central bank, the issues of bank supervision and note-issuing privilege cannot be disentangled (Burghof/Rudolph 1996, p. 38). The Scottish experience of stability during free-banking cannot be generalized, because it shows the evolution of private institutions in a small, cohesive community, where the potential for strong social sanctions prevented self interest and moral hazard (Dow 1996, pp. 704).

deposit insurance or state banks) may be preferable to market control with a limited capacity of private insurers. Its higher moral hazard costs are then borne by the taxpayers.

Although the provision of banking stability plays the key role in a CB financial system, it is also important for AM systems, which, too, rely on banks as providers of credits and payment facilities.[10] But also non-bank financial intermediaries may be vulnerable to runs, to the extent that they rely on short-term financing, have a mismatch between assets and liabilities, and that there is imperfect information about the quality of their assets (Davis 1992, p. 121). As a form of market control, credit agencies have developed to assess the risk of individual fund portfolios and prevent contagious runs. The key instability of an AM financial system is, however, not the fragility of financial firms, but the volatility of asset prices with the possibility of bubbles and crashes. A large theoretical and empirical literature points to *excess volatility of asset prices*, i.e. they are more volatile than changes in payoff streams and discount rates can account for (for a survey see Allen/Gale 1995, p. 195). Excess volatility is the higher the more information about firms is released to the public, so it is highest in an AM system where the allocation of capital relies on public information. The phenomenon of booms and crashes has been explained by irrational speculation ('manias' or panics', see e.g. Kindleberger 1978, De Long et al. 1990) as well as by rational bubbles or sunspots (for a survey see Blanchard/Fischer 1989, Chapter 5). Recent explanations focus on asymmetric information and informational dynamics. Asymmetric information, e.g., explains why a small supply shock can create a large fall in prices, provoking a stock market 'crash'. It rests on the observation that typically only a small proportion of investors actively gather information on future market values, while the others form expectations about future prices by looking at current prices. When these 'uninformed' investors do not observe the hedging activities of the informed investors, hedging can destabilize a market, leading to greater volatility and ultimately to a crash (Gennotte/Leland 1990). Informational dynamics can lead to booms and crashes by 'informational overshooting': if market fundamentals change for an unknown period of time, prices experience a boom, which ends in a crash. This is likely when the market expands to a new capacity, due to increased productivity or to entry of new investors to the stock market, which implies that financial liberalizations tend to be followed by booms and crashes (Zeira 1999). Runs with externalities also impair risk-sharing by stock markets. If doubt arises about the future liquidity of the market, it is rational for an investor to sell first, before the market crashes (Davis 1992, p. 121). Policies to minimize excess volatility are reduction of incomplete information by transparency rules and dissemination of knowledge about the actions of informed investors. Since the volatility of asset prices also affects the stability of non-bank financial intermediaries, public

---

[10] As to the theoretical alternative to substitute banks by mutual funds with payment facilities, see Goodhart (1993).

regulations such as capital adequacy rules are justified to reduce also their credit and market price risks (see Burghof/Rudolph 1996, pp. 168).

3 Evolution of financial systems and stability

3.1 Evolution and tendencies of convergence

The evolution of the financial systems in the Anglo-Saxon countries to AM systems and in countries of Continental Europe and Japan to CB systems took place along different growth paths, reflecting the response of financial markets and institutions to different investment opportunities, information technologies, preferences and legal systems. In the Anglo-Saxon countries of the US and the UK, the main factors conducive to an AM system have been: non-state-assisted industrialisation with financing of firms by retentions and simultaneously developing capital market instruments, rapid income growth with concentration of wealth accompanied by willingness to take risk, a favourable tax climate and a legal system with a corporate law in favour of arm's length financing.[11] In the UK, an informal regulatory framework was conducive to the specialisation of banks on the provision of working capital and of capital markets and non-bank intermediaries on the provision of risk and long-term capital. In the US, on the other hand, banks have been severely regulated by a safety net in response to the bank failures of the 1930s, to prevent risky behaviour. Its key elements were: lender of last resort, federal deposit insurance, regulations on bank assets, bank structure (separation of commercial and investment banking, prohibition of interstate banking), and interest rates. This resulted primarily from a strong fear of concentration of economic power in individual banks and the banking system. The prohibition of large shareholdings by financial institutions was crucial to the development of the Berle-Means corporation with its fragmented share ownership (Roe 1991, 1994).

In Continental Europe and Japan, on the other hand, CB financial systems developed along with an actively state-assisted process of industrialisation, with special policies and rules to foster the provision of long-term bank loans to industry and ensure stability of the financial and non-financial sector. The main factors have been: promotion of close business ties between industry, financial institutions and government, encouragement of banks to hold risk capital by way of participations, creation of special investment banks, limiting public disclosure of business information, limiting competition in banking and finance and poor protection of minority investors' rights (Davis 1992, p. 25, Rybczynski 1984, pp. 281, Modigliani/Perotti 1999).

---

[11] See Rybczynski (1984); as to effects of the legal system on corporate finance and interdependencies between corporate law and corporate finance see Berglöf (1997), La Porta et al. (1997, 1998) and Modigliani/Perotti (1999).

A fundamental reason for the different arrangements of corporate control are deep-rooted differences in legal frameworks. Within Europe, Anglo-Saxon common law systems have company-based systems, where the focus is on the relationship between the firm as a legal entity and its investors, and legislation aims to maximize shareholder value. Civil law systems of the French, German and Scandinavian type, on the other hand, have traditionally enterprise-based systems which take a broader view of the stakeholders of an individual plant, going along with legislation to protect their interests (e.g. codetermination laws, creditor-oriented insolvency laws) (Berglöf 1997, Baums 1996). The AM and CB groups of financial systems are, however, not homogeneous. For example, the separation of commercial and investment banking existed only in the US, Japan and (until 1984) in France, and control-oriented financial systems differ according to the role of banks versus other intermediaries, families or the state in controlling industries (Moerland 1995b).

In the wake of technological advances, growing international capital mobility has increased financial market integration (Gischer 1999) and stiffened competition between financial systems, inducing deregulations in both CB and AM systems during the last two decades. Some signs seem to indicate that this system competition will gradually lead to convergence, i.e. evasion of differences. Two *tendencies of convergence* can be distinguished:

(i) convergence towards an AM financial system with preponderance of intermediation by institutional investors

(ii) convergence towards a universal banking system with harmonized prudential regulation and qualitative supervision

Concerning (i), there is a trend towards securitization, defined as 'matching up of borrowers and savers wholly or partly by way of the financial markets' (Cumming 1987, see Davis 1992, p. 21). The main stimulating factors have been financial innovations and increasing price competition which have improved the efficiency of capital market finance while reducing the banks' ability to provide relationship lending with implicit contracts (Davis 1992, p. 21, Burghof/Rudolph 1996, pp. 7). Relative costs of securities market financing are further reduced by economies of scale due to an increasing demand from institutional investors such as life-insurance companies and pension funds. This is a response to changes in relative transaction costs as well as to the privatisation of pension systems in aging populations (Baums 1996, p. 10, Davis 1991). In almost all European countries, institutional shareholders have become more important at the expense of private individuals, although there are differences in the types of institutions and their possible exercise of corporate control (Berglöf 1997, p. 102). To further increase the role played by capital markets in the channeling of savings and provision of risk capital, countries of Continental Europe and Japan have improved securities markets regulations or liberalized financial markets. Within the EU, securities market law has been harmonized (Burghof/Rudolph 1996, pp. 198) and the recent Action Plan of regulatory changes shall further boost the integration and market-driven development of the European securities markets (Duisenberg 1999).

The trend towards securitization is, however, limited by the comparative advantage of banks in the provision of private-information loans, small-business loans and high-risk transactions such as project credits (Collin 1997, Burghof/Rudolph 1996, p. 8, Davis 1992, p. 22). Moreover, it is not uniform across countries. In contrast to the convergence hypothesis, a comparative study on France, Germany and the UK finds that the general trend towards securitization does not imply a trend towards a loss of importance of banks, nor towards a general transformation from bank-based to market-based financial systems. Instead of a simple shift from banks to capital markets there is a trend towards increased specialization of banks in lending operations, while the intermediation chain is lengthened via a growing portion of savings mobilized by non-bank financial intermediaries (Schmidt et al. 1999).

The trends towards securitization and institutionalizing of savings imply a trend towards arm's length-oriented corporate control. Increasing competition between large publicly held companies for international capital market funds and between performance-oriented asset managers for mobilizing savings puts pressure on managements to increase shareholder orientation and improve investor relations, especially by accounting policies and by the release of more public information. Since the professional institutional investors hold internationally diversified portfolios, the performance of which is periodically evaluated against international yardsticks, their activities have induced an international standardization of investment policies and performance measurement (Moerland 1995b, p. 460). This puts the control-oriented financial systems with their reliance on insider control, long-term implicit contracts and stakeholder-orientation under pressure. In Germany, e.g., increasing shareholder orientation of the big banks has led them to untangle themselves from industrial firms, selling their stakes or managing them more actively by new subsidiaries. Unlike the traditional German banks, these subsidiary investors "...will invest at arm's length and badger poor managers; purchases will be carefully selected to add value to the existing holdings; and compared with old stakes,...investments will be fleeting punts. Most will be held for no more than four years" (Economist, August 14th, 1999, p. 61). Despite this transformation, one can exclude that Germany will fully adopt the Anglo-Saxon AM system for several reasons: it is unlikely that debt finance reaches a similar degree of securitization as in the US, ownership concentration of German companies should remain higher, the importance of listed companies is still lower, and banks still possess special control rights, may it be from shareholdings, from custody business (proxy-voting rights) or from representation on supervisory boards (see Schröder/Schrader 1997, Baums 1996). Nor is it likely that European corporate governance systems will converge as a consequence of competition between national legislators or of centralized rule-setting (Baums 1996, Neuberger 1999). The US system of arm's length control may move opposite to these tendencies, because there is growing scope for financial intermediaries to intensify their relations with business firms. The excessive functioning of the market for corporate control with practices such as corporate raiding, crude hostile takeovers or junk bonds has lost importance, having been replaced by active investors' diplomacy and persuasion as disciplining mechanisms (Moerland 1995b, p. 460, Roe 1994).

Concerning (ii), in many advanced countries, competition between banking regulations and technological shifts have led to the removal of structural regulations such as regulations segmenting financial markets (functionally or regionally), regulations restricting establishment of foreign institutions, interest-rate controls or cartels that fixed rates and direct controls on credit expansion (Davis 1992, p. 26, Lewis/Pescetto 1996). With the removal of separations between commercial and investment banking in the US and in Japan, there is a general trend towards universal banking.[12] It can be precluded that competition between banking systems will ultimately lead to the 'zero-regulation' case (see Siebert/Koop 1990, pp. 446), because international capital market interdependence forces countries to harmonize regulations to the provision of a minimum safety level. Since regions of different stability put a threat to the stability of the system as a whole, regulations which provide a minimum level of system stability are a condition to participate in the international capital market (Burghof/Rudolph 1996, p. 38). Hence, banking supervision law has developed to a primarily international law, where national legislation and rule-setting by national supervisory authorities are more and more restricted to the adoption of agreements by the EU or the Basle Committee of Bank Supervisors. However, only minimum financial regulation is harmonized within the EU or the countries subscribing to the Basle agreements, leaving single states free to adopt stricter rules than others.

The harmonization policy is based on prudential regulations tied to risk-based capital requirements. Internationally agreed weights are imposed on different types of risk, including off-balance-sheet risk, to reach financial stability, competitive equality and a level-playing field for banks and non-bank intermediaries. In banking supervision, there is a trend towards more reliance on qualitative elements and the use of internal quantitative risk management models. Since financial innovations such as derivatives have increased the scope of banks to increase rapidly the risk of their portfolios, a misuse of these instruments can no longer be controlled only by ex post supervision of quantitative norms (Burghof/Rudolph 1996, pp. 112). The need for deposit insurance is reduced by the improved asset liquidity in the capital market and the evolution of banking into an off-balance-sheet business (Bhattacharya et al. 1998). According to country-specific traditions, different protective regulations and mixes between government and private deposit insurance

---

[12] In the US the Glass-Steagall Act, which separates commercial from investment banking, is finally scrapped (Economist, October 30th 1999, pp. 89). Previous trials to abolish it did not pass the U.S. Congress, because the fear of financial crises resulting from too much banking power had been still stronger than the fear of loosing competitiveness of the U.S. banking sector (Zwätz 1999). For Japan see Nakajima/Taguchi (1995).

prevail.[13] In view of the deregulation that has occurred and the moral hazard induced by commitments to rescue banks and their depositors, there should be a greater willingness to accept bank failures and develop private deposit insurance systems (Witherell 1995, p. 107, Meister 1999).

3.2 Implications for stability

How will the word-wide trend towards an AM system with growing institutionalization of savings, universal banking and minimum harmonization of financial regulations affect stability? The answer depends on three aspects:

(i) What kind of stability is the aim?
(ii) Is there conflict or harmony between efficiency and stability?
(iii) Will harmonization of regulations enhance stability?

Concerning (i), we know that financial systems have evolved to provide different kinds of stability, which may partly be due to different preferences for risk-sharing or different time preferences: on the one hand, stability of banks with intertemporal risk-sharing and long-term relationship lending, and on the other hand, stability of asset prices with cross-sectional risk-sharing and more short-sighted capital market finance. Although preferences and cultures may change in response to changes in the financial system, we cannot rule out that the investors of a traditionally CB financial system will suffer welfare losses by the transformation to an AM system. For them, stability inherent in a CB system will be lost.

As to (ii), the trend towards securitization and intermediation by institutional investors might reflect an economically sound development, i.e. an increase in the efficiency of the entire financial system, and thus not give rise to problems of stability of the banking sector. Benefits which have clearly been realized are the extension of the scope of financial services, reduced cost of services due to improved efficiency of financial markets and improvement in resource allocation due to reduced credit rationing (Davis 1992, p. 27). On the other hand, this development puts banks under stress by increasing costs of funding. In the case of France, there are signs that the stability of the banking system is threatened by the profound change in its financial system (Schmidt et al. 1999). Also the bank disruption which many industrialized countries (especially Japan, the US and Nordic countries) experienced in the 1980s can be explained by a sharp squeeze on banks' profit margins in the wake of heightened competition and deregulations. The banks responded by increasing the provision of credit to profitable but riskier projects related to real estate and investments in financial assets. Such aggressive lending

[13] While in the US, the lender of last resort and federal deposit insurance play a large role, European countries rely more on self-insurance by the banking groups, to minimize moral hazard (see Baglioni/Marotta 1993, Burghof/Rudolph 1996, p. 45, pp. 73). Within the EU, there is controversy about a directive which poses minimum harmonization of deposit insurance systems (Weber 1994).

contributed to a sharp rise in the prices of property and other assets and hence to an asset price bubble which collapsed worldwide at the end of the 1980s. Governments and central banks then were called upon to prevent banking failures (Nakajima/Taguchi 1995). In the US, the problem has been exacerbated by the moral hazard induced by inappropriately priced and overly extended deposit insurance and by the Fed's policy of bailing out insolvent banks (Benston 1991, Bordo 1991). Some deregulations, on the other hand, had favorable stability effects. In the United States, the removal of functional and regional regulations of banking activities has improved bank efficiency and the ability of banks to diversify risks.[14] The conflicts between efficiency and stability which occur during the transformation from one system to the other are only short-run, if the regulatory system and internal risk management procedures adapt in a way to ensure stability in the long-run.

The key question then is whether in the long-run, the 'new' financial system will produce more or less stability than the 'old' ones. It is unlikely that the banking instability we have witnessed during the transition period is a long-term characteristic of the liberalized financial environment. Recently, strains in the banking sector of most OECD countries have been significantly eased as evidenced by lower loan losses, higher profitability and a rise in bank share prices. Bank managers are now more concerned with efficient use of capital and risk management than with asset growth (Witherell 1995, pp. 105, N.N. 1999a). The improvement of prudential regulation with risk-based capital norms and qualitative supervision should support banking stability in a market-oriented financial system. The proposition that financial innovation in derivative securities has increased the volatility of securities markets was not supported by evidence (Tiniç 1995). On the other hand, there is the risk that the deregulationist approach to control instability will not work, because financial firms are pressured to pursue short-run non-value maximizing goals in imperfect capital markets (Coggins 1998, see also Mayer 1999). US banks with lower charter value due to increased competition assumed significantly more risk even in the 1990s (Galloway et al. 1997). There is also growing concern about financial market failure to correct market expectations with respect to asset prices that do not conform to economic realities. The liberalization of financial markets in OECD countries has led to increased asset price inflation and volatility, with asset prices occasionally deviating sharply from 'fundamentals'. The trend towards more financial fragility and systemic risk is aggravated by an increased use of credit to purchase assets and finance consumption, resulting in lower saving, and by changes in the effectiveness of monetary policy (Davis 1992,

---

[14] The restriction of interstate banking by the McFadden Act of 1927 and numerous state laws has been blamed for many failures of US banks in the 1980s (Lewis/Pescetto 1996, pp. 190, Greenbaum/Thakor 1995, pp. 548). The Riegel-Neal Interstate Banking and Efficiency Act of 1994 put an end to this geographical restriction by permitting interstate banking and branching. The evidence shows that this fostered economic growth by improving the quality of bank lending (Jayaratne/Strahan 1996).

pp. 27, Borio et al. 1994).[15] The financial market turbulence of 1998 has shown how rapidly shock waves propagate geographically and grow due to high debt finance (N.N. 1999b). The stock market crash of October 1987 can be explained by informational overshooting after a massive entry of new investors to the stock market (Zeira 1999) and the use of dynamic hedging strategies in the presence of asymmetric information (Gennotte/Leland 1990). The growing intermediaton by institutional investors is likely to contribute to the rise in instability, if they are better informed than small investors. Large foreign investments of hedge funds, mutual funds and other big financial institutions have been blamed for recent financial crises in emerging markets, because they were suddenly withdrawn. The evidence about whether foreign institutions actually move markets is, however, inconclusive. On the one hand, it has been found that in most of the financial crises during the past five years, foreign institutions did not in fact pull out large amounts of money: "Institutional money is lukewarm, not hot" (Economist, 21st August 1999, p. 64). On the other hand, foreign institutional investors display strong herd instincts in reaction to global factors, with increasing correlation of their charges in and out of countries over the past five years (Froot et al. 1999, see Economist, August 21st 1999, p. 64). The South-East Asian financial crisis in 1998 may have been caused or at least aggravated by the incompatibility of different corporate control mechanisms: while East-Asian countries had developed control-oriented financial systems with a dominant role of banks and the state, they liberalized their securities markets to attract arm's length capital from abroad. However, they failed to provide the control rights to foreign investors that would have been necessary for long-term commitments to finance their growth (Fischer 2000, Neuberger 2000.

Whether an arm's length-oriented financial system is superior to a control-oriented financial system in terms of stability, is an open question, and its answer depends on whether we consider protection of firms or investors. Control-oriented systems should provide more stability to firms which need long-term commitments, which has been supported by evidence for Japan and Germany. Japanese firms that are members of keiretsu, a specific form of control-oriented finance, have less variability in cash flows, and their investments are less sensitive to variation in cash flows (Hoshi et al. 1990, 1991). German firms with close bank ties have been found to be less liquidity constrained in their investments than independent firms (Elston/Albach 1995). However, comparative evidence for Germany, Japan and the United States shows that there are no significant differences in the probability that the management of a corporation is replaced when a firm is experiencing problems (Kaplan 1994a, b). The differences in the corporate control systems do not necessarily imply differences in the correction of managerial failure or investor protection, if the various rules and institutions substitute and comple-

---

[15] As to the controversy about whether central banks should pay more attention to asset-price inflation, see e.g. Goodhart (1995, 1996), Kindleberger (1995), Kloepfer/Tigges (1999), Economist (September 25th, 1999, pp. 15, survey pp. 78).

ment each other so as to produce the same outcome.[16] Evidence on the level of investor protection in different countries shows that shareholders are better protected in Anglo-Saxon common law countries than in civil law countries, but creditors in Scandinavian and German civil code countries are at least as well protected as their counterparts in the Anglo-Saxon countries. Shareholders and creditors are most vulnerable in French civil code countries (La Porta et al. 1998). However, more investor protection is not always better with respect to efficiency, and its optimal value remains an empirical issue (Berglöf 1997, p. 114).

Concerning (iii), harmonizing banking and securities market regulations will further increase the level of globalization of the financial services industry. This serves to diversify world economies from domestic problems or failures and to diffuse losses caused by major financial disasters across many nations (Lewis/ Pescetto 1996, p. 191). On the other hand, an equalization or overly harmonization of banking regulations removes the possibility to diversify regulations and the freedom of nations to choose their preferred regulatory systems. It creates the regulatory risk that a weakness of the uniform financial system poses a threat to the stability of the whole world economy, which can no longer be eliminated by competition between different systems (Burghof/Rudolph 1996, p. 207).

While minimum harmonization is necessary to ensure stability of the system as a whole, harmonization is likely to have unfavorable effects on efficiency and stability, unless it goes along with fundamental changes in both legal and economic systems. Because of the interconnection between legal system, financial system and cultural framework, corporate governance and finance systems are composed of complementary elements which should not be dismantled by partial reforms (Berglöf 1997). As has been shown by Burghof (1999), capital adequacy rules have different impact on efficiency and stability because of differences in the cultural and institutional frameworks and they are not neutral to competition between banking systems. Capital rules work together with other mechanisms to bind bank managers who would otherwise take excessive risks at the expense of depositors. Such complementary and substitutive mechanisms are given by the banks' charter value (dependent on competition), insolvency law, compensation policy and non-pecuniary bankruptcy costs to bank managers. Only in CB financial systems as in Germany, they have developed in a way to enable long-term financing relationships, calling for strict capital rules as a complementary instrument to prevent bank runs. A uniform regulation of banks pertaining to different financial systems therefore is likely to produce too much or too less stability. To reach a uniform level of minimum stability, it would be optimal to construct a regulatory system which sets different norms according to different institutional frameworks. This requires flexibility in the international harmonization of banking supervision law. The in-

---

[16] See Berglöf (1997, p. 109), Kaplan/Minton (1994). For further studies on the efficiency of different corporate control mechanisms see Edwards/Fischer (1994), Franks/Mayer (1990), Schwiete/Weigand (1997), Schmid (1996) and the survey by Shleifer/Vishny (1997).

formal Basle Committee of Bank Supervisors is better suited to reach this aim than the legislative procedure of the EU Directives with its formal coordinating mechanisms (Burghof 1999, p. 286).

4 Conclusions

The present paper reviewed theories and empirical studies on comparative financial systems to tackle the questions whether and how financial systems will converge, and whether convergence would lead to higher or lower stability. Two tendencies of convergence have been found: (1) convergence towards an arm's length-cum-market-oriented (AM) financial system with preponderance of intermediation by institutional investors, (2) convergence towards a universal banking system with harmonized prudential regulation and qualitative supervision. These tendencies are mainly induced by technical progress in information technology and growing international financial integration, which have increased competition between regulatory systems. However, financial system competition is limited by the interconnectedness between financial arrangements, legal systems and cultural factors. The control-cum-bank-oriented (CB) financial systems of Continental Europe and Japan have reacted differently to the changing environment and maintain country-specific arrangements of corporate control and finance. In the United States, the abolishment of the Glass-Stegall Act may not completely remove the separation between commercila and investment banking. Convergence towards a uniform financial system can thus be excluded.

The stability effects of financial system transformation depend first on the kind of stability to be reached, which differs between CB and AM systems. The tendency of CB financial systems to develop towards more cross-sectional risk-sharing, short-sighted market control and shareholder-orientation is likely to induce welfare losses to its investors by conflicting with preferences for intertemporal risk-sharing and long-term relationship lending in a culture of stakeholder orientation. They may thus find themselves in a 'globalization trap' (see Neuberger 1999). Secondly, we differentiated between short-term and long-run relations between efficiency and stability. In the short run, the transformation of financial systems to more efficient arrangements is likely to conflict with stability, as evidenced by the bank disruptions which many advanced countries experienced in the 1980s. In the long run, regulations should develop to enhance stability of the transformed financial systems, which may be higher or lower than before. While the evidence is inconclusive about the relative overall efficiency and investor protection of a single financial system, several arguments point to a tendency towards increasing instability: increasing asset price inflation and higher probability of booms and crashes with rising financial market integration, paired with a trend of institutional investors to enhance the volatility of asset prices. Whether this trend towards higher capital market failure can be compensated by an improvement in the regulatory system, has to be seen. The trend towards more prudential regulation with risk-based capital rules and qualitative banking supervision is an appropriate response, but it relies increasingly on market control which is itself imperfect. Third, and ultimately, the international harmonization of these regulations may have unfavorable effects on financial system stability. There is a trade-off between diversification and specialization of regulations, and uniform regulations are likely to produce suboptimal levels of stability because they do not take into account the different private institutions that have evolved in different financial systems to provide stability. Therefore, the international harmonization of banking supervision law should allow enough flexibility to set different norms according to different institutional frameworks. To draw more concrete policy conclusions, more research is needed about the comparative stability of different financial systems and relations between financial regulations and private arrangements.

References

Allen, F. (1999), The Design of Financial Systems and Markets, Journal of Financial Intermediation, 8, 5-7.

Allen, F. and D. Gale (1995), A Welfare Comparison of Intermediaries and Financial Markets in Germany and the US, European Economic Review, 39, 179-209.

Allen, F. and D. Gale (1997), Financial Markets, Intermediaries, and Intertemporal Smoothing, Journal of Political Economy, 105, 523-546.

Allen, F. and D. Gale (1999), Comparing Financial Systems, Cambridge (forthcoming).

Baglioni, A. and G. Marotta (1993), Deposit Insurance: Implications from Financial Intermediation Theory, in: Conti, V. and R. Hamaui, eds., Financial Markets' Liberalization and the Role of Banks, Cambridge, 337-364.

Baltensperger, E. and J. Dermine (1987), The Role of Public Policy in Ensuring Financial Stability: A Cross-Country, Comparative Perspective, in: Portes, R. and A. Swoboda, eds., Threats to International Financial Stability, Cambridge.

Baums, T. (1996), Corporate Governance Systems in Europe - Differences and Tendencies of Convergence, Crafoord Lecture, University of Lund/Sweden, May 13, 1996.

Benston, G. J. (1991), Does Bank Regulation Produce Stability? Lessons from the United States, in: Capie, F. and G.E. Wood, eds., Unregulated Banking. Chaos or Order?, Houndsmills, 207-232.

Benston, G. J. (1995), Safety Nets and Moral Hazard in Banking, in: Sawamoto, K., Z. Kakajima and H. Taguchi, eds., Financial Stability in a Changing Environment, London, 329-377.

Benston, G.J. and G.G. Kaufman (1995), Is the Banking and Payments System Fragile?, Journal of Financial Services Research, 9, 209-240.

Benston, G.J. and G.G. Kaufman (1996), The Appropriate Role of Bank Regulation, The Economic Journal, 106, 688-697.

Berglöf, E. (1997), Reforming Corporate Governance: Redirecting the European Agenda, Economic Policy, April, 93-123.

Bhattacharya, S., Boot, A.W.A. and A.V. Thakor (1998), The Economics of Bank Regulation, Journal of Money, Credit, and Banking, 30, 745-770.

Bhattacharya, S. and A.V. Thakor (1993), Contemporary Baning Theory, Journal of Financial Intermediation, 3, 2-50.

Blanchard, O. and S. Fischer (1989), Lectures on Macroeconomics, Cambridge.

Bordo, M.D. (1991), Comment on Chapter 6, in: Capie, F. and G.E. Wood, eds., Unregulated Banking. Chaos or Order?, Houndsmills, 233-240.

Borio, C.E.V., N. Kennedy and S.D. Prowse (1994), Exploring Aggragate Asset Price Fluctuations Across Countries, BIS Economic Papers, No. 40, Bank for International Settlements, Basle.

Burghof, H.-P. (1999), Eigenkapitalnormen in der Theorie der Finanzintermediation, Berlin.

Burghof, H.-P. and B. Rudolph (1996), Bankenaufsicht. Theorie und Praxis der Regulierung, Wiesbaden.

Coggins, B. (1998), Does Financial Deregulation Work? A Critique of Free Market Approaches, Cheltenham, U.K., and Northampton, MA.

Collin, S.-O. (1997), Financial Intermediation through Markets and Organizations: An Information-Boundary Argument for Financial Organizations, Scandinavian Journal of Management, 13, 175-189.

Cumming, C. (1987), The Economics of Securitisation, Federal Reserve Bank of New York, Quarterly Review, Autumn, 11-23.

Davis, E.P. (1991), The Development of Pension Funds: An International Comparison, Bank of England Quarterly Bulletin, 31, 380-390.

Davis, E.P. (1992), Debt, Financial Fragility, and Systemic Risk, Oxford.

De Long, B., Shleifer, A., Summers, L. and R. Waldeman (1990), Noise Trader Risk in Financial Markets, Journal of Political Economy, 98, 703-738.

Dewatripont, M. and J. Tirole (1994), The Prudential Regulation of Banks, Cambridge (Mass.).

Diamond, D.W. (1984), Financial Intermediation and Delegated Monitoring, Review of Economic Studies, 51, 393-414.

Diamond, D.W. (1991), Monitoring and Reputation: The Choice Between Bank Loans and Directly Placed Debt, Journal of Political Economy, 99, 689-721.

Diamond, D.W. and P.H. Dybvig (1983), Bank Runs, Deposit Insurance, and Liquidity, Journal of Political Economy, 91, 401-419.

Dow, S.C. (1996), Why the Banking System Should be Regulated, The Economic Journal, 106, 698-707.

Dowd, K. (1992), ed., The Experience of Free Banking, London/New York.

Dowd, K. (1996),The Case for Financial Laissez-Faire, The Economic Journal, 106, 679-687.

Duisenberg, W.F. (1999), Developments in the Financial Sector in Europe following the Introduction of the Euro, in: Deutsche Bundesbank, Auszüge aus Presseartikeln, No. 38, Frankfurt/Main, 6-8.

Edwards, J. and K. Fischer (1994), Banks, Finance and Investment in Germany, Cambridge.

Elston, J. A. and H. Albach (1995), Bank Affiliations and Firm Capital Investment in Germany, Ifo-Studien, 41, 3-16.

Fama, E.F. (1980a), Agency Problems and the Theory of the Firm, Journal of Political Economy, 88, 288-307.

Fama, E.F. (1980b), Banking in the Theory of Finance, Journal of Monetary Economics, 6, 39-57.

Fischer, C. (2000), Corporate Governance – Implikationen für die Systemstabilität, in: Conrad, C. A. and M. Stahl, eds., Risikomanagement an internationalen Finanzmärkten, Stuttgart, 293-306.

Franks, J. and C. Mayer (1990), Capital Markets and Corporate Control: a Study of France, Germany and the UK, Economic Policy, 5, 191-231.

Franks, J. and C. Mayer (1995), Ownership and Control, in: H. Siebert, ed., Trends in Business Organization: Do Participation and Cooperation Increase Competitiveness?, Tübingen, 171-195.

Freixat, X. and J.-C. Rochet (1997), Microeconomics of Banking, Cambridge (Mass.)/London.

Froot, K., O'Connell, P. and M. Seasholes (1999), The Portfolio Flows of International Investors, Harvard Business School Working Paper, August.

Galloway, T.M., Lee, W.B. and D.M. Roden (1997), Banks' Changing Incentives and Opportunities for Risk Taking, Journal of Banking and Finance, 21, 509-527.

Gennotte, G. and H. Leland (1990), Market Liquidity, Hedging, and Crashes, American Economic Review, 80, 999-1021.

Gischer, H. (1999), Kapitalmarktintegration, Zinsvolatilität und gewerbliche Kreditnachfrage, in: Berg, H., ed., Globalisierung der Wirtschaft: Ursachen – Formen – Konsequenzen, Berlin, 183-206.

Goodhart, C.A.E. (1993), Can We Improve the Structure of Financial Systems?, European Economic Review, 37, 269-291.

Goodhart, C.A.E. (1995), Price Stability and Financial Fragility, in: Goodhart, C.A.E., ed., The Central Bank and the Financial System, Houndsmills, 263-302.

Goodhart, C.A.E. (1996), Financial Globalization, Derivatives, Volatility, and the Challenge for the Policies of Central Banks, in: Siebert, H., ed., Monetary Policy in an Integrated World Economy, Tübingen, 61-90.

Greenbaum, S.I. and A.V. Thakor (1995), Contemporary Financial Intermediation, Fort Worth.

Gurley, J.G. and E.S. Shaw (1960), Money in a Theory of Finance, Washington.

Hart, O.D. (1983), The Market Mechanism as an Incentive Scheme, Bell Journal of Economics, 14, 366-382.

Hellwig, M. (1991), Banking, Financial Intermediation and Corporate Finance, in: Giovannini, A. and C. Mayer, eds., European Financial Integration, Cambrige U.K., 35-63.

Hellwig, M. (1998), Systemische Risiken im Finanzsektor, in: Duwendag, D., ed., Finanzmärkte im Spannungsfeld von Globalisierung, Regulierung und Geldpolitik, Zeitschrift für Wirtschafts- und Sozialwissenschaften, Beiheft 7, Berlin, 123-151.

Hoshi , T., Kashyap, A. and D. Scharfstein (1990), The Role of Banks in Reducing the Costs of Financial Distress in Japan, Journal of Financial Economics, 27, 67-88.

Hoshi, T., Kashyap, A. and D. Scharfstein (1991), Corporate Structure, Liquidity and Investment. Evidence from Japanese Industrial Groups, Quarterly Journal of Economics, 106, 33-60.

Jayaratne, J. and P.E. Strahan (1996), The Finance-Growth Nexus: Evidence from Bank Branch Deregulation, Quarterly Journal of Economics, 111, 639-670.

Jensen, M.C. and R. Ruback (1983), The Market for Corporate Control: The Scientific Evidence, Journal of Financial Economics, 11, 5-50.

Kane, E.J. (1986), Appearance and Reality in Deposit Insurance: The Case for Reform, Journal of Banking and Finance, 10, 175-188.

Kaplan, S.N. (1994a), Top Executive Rewards and Firm Performance: A Comparison of Japan and the United States, Journal of Political Economy, 102, 510-546.

Kaplan, S.N. (1994b), Top Executives, Turnover and Firm Performance in Germany, Journal of Law, Economics, and Organization, 10, 142-159.

Kaplan, S. N. and B.A. Minton (1994), Appointments of Outsiders to Japanese Boards: Determinants and Implications for Managers, Journal of Financial Economics, 36, 225-257.

Kaufman, G.G. (1991), Lender of Last Resort: A Contemporary Perspective, Journal of Financial Services Research, 5, 95-110.

Kindleberger, C.P. (1978), Manias, Panics, and Crashes, Houndmills et al.

Kindleberger, C.P. (1995), Asset Inflation and Monetary Policy, BNL Quarterly Review, 192, 17-37.

Kloepfer, I. and C. Tigges (1999), Aktienkurse sind keine Zielgröße für die EZB, Frankfurter Allgemeine Zeitung, August 19th, in: Deutsche Bundesbank, Auszüge aus Presseartikeln, No. 56, Frankfurt/Main, 8-9.

La Porta, R., Lopez-de-Silanes, F., Shleifer, A. and R.W. Vishny (1997), Legal Determinants of External Finance, Journal of Finance, 52, 1131-1150.
La Porta, R., Lopez-de-Silanes, F., Shleifer, A. and R.W. Vishny (1998), Law and Finance, Journal of Political Economy, 106, 1113-1155.
Lewis, A. and G. Pescetto (1996), EU and US Banking in the 1990s, London.
Mayer, C. (1988), New Issues in Corporate Finance, European Economic Review, 32, 1167-1188.
Mayer, C. (1999), Book Review on Coggins, B., 1998, Journal of Economic Literature, 37, 681-682.
Meister, E. (1999), Allow Banks to Fail!, in: Deutsche Bundesbank, Auszüge aus Presseartikeln, No. 7, Frankfurt/Main, 7-8.
Modigliani, F. and E. Perotti (1999), Security versus Bank Finance: the Importance of a Proper Enforcement of Legal Rules, FEEM Working Paper No. PRIV 37.99, Fondazione Eni Enrico Mattei, Milano.
Moerland, P.W. (1995a), Alternative Disciplinary Mechanisms in Different Corporate Systems, Journal of Economic Behavior and Organization, 26, 17-34.
Moerland, P.W. (1995b), Corporate Ownership and Control Structures: An International Comparison, Review of Industrial Organization, 10, 443-464.
Nakajima, Z. and H. Taguchi (1995), Toward a More Stable Financial Framework: Long-term Alternatives – an Overview of Recent Bank Disruption Worldwide, in: Sawamoto, K., Nakajima, Z. and H. Taguchi, eds., Financial Stability in a Changing Environment, London, 41-108.
Neuberger, D. (1994), Kreditvergabe durch Banken. Mikroökonomische Theorie und gesamtwirtschaftliche Implikationen, Tübingen.
Neuberger, D. (1997), Anteilsbesitz von Banken: Wohlfahrtsverlust oder Wohlfahrtsgewinn?, ifo-Studien, 43, 15-34.
Neuberger, D. (1998), Mikroökonomik der Bank. Eine industrieökonomische Perspektive, München.
Neuberger, D. (1999), Finanzsysteme in Europa: Harmonisieren? Anglifizieren?, Zeitschrift für Wirtschaftspolitik, 48, 11-26.
Neuberger, D. (2000), Kommentar zu: Corporate Governance – Implikationen für die Systemstabilität, in: Conrad, C. A. and M. Stahl, eds., Risikomanagement an internationalen Finanzmärkten, Stuttgart, 293-306.
N.N. (1999a), Banken haben aus der Finanzmarktkrise gelernt, Börsen-Zeitung, September 9th, in: Deutsche Bundesbank, Auszüge aus Presseartikeln, No. 60, Frankfurt/Main, 1-2.
N.N. (1999b), IWF: Vom amerikanischen Aktienmarkt gehen hohe Risiken aus, Frankfurter Allgemeine Zeitung, September 9th, in: Deutsche Bundesbank, Auszüge aus Presseartikeln, No. 60, Frankfurt/Main, 3-4.
Roe, M.J. (1991), A Political Theory of American Corporate Finance, Columbia Law Review, 91, 10-67.
Roe, M.J. (1994), Strong Managers, Weak Owners: The Political Roots of American Corporate Finance, Princeton.
Rybczynski, T.M. (1984), Industrial Finance System in Europe, U.S. and Japan, Journal of Economic Behavior and Organization, 5, 275-286.
Schmid, F.A. (1996), Beteiligungen deutscher Banken und Corporate Performance, Zeitschrift für Wirtschafts- und Sozialwissenschaften, 116, 273-310.
Schmidt, R.H., Hackethal, A. and M. Tyrell (1999), Disintermediation and the Role of Banks in Europe: An International Comparison, Journal of Financial Intermediation, 8, 36-67.
Schröder, U. and A. Schrader (1997), The Changing Role of Banks and Corporate Governance in Germany: Evolution Towards the Market?, Economic Studies Working Paper No. 13, American Institute for Contemporary German Studies, John Hopkins University, Washington D.C.

Schwiete, M. (1998), Finanzsysteme und wirtschaftliche Entwicklung, Abhandlungen zur Nationalökonomie, Bd. 9, Berlin.

Schwiete, M. and J. Weigand (1997), Der Einfluß von Bankbeteiligungen auf das Verschuldungsverhalten deutscher Unternehmen, Kredit und Kapital, 30, 1-34.

Sharpe, S.A. (1990), Asymmetric Information, Bank Lending, and Implicit Contracts: A Stylized Model of Customer Relationships, Journal of Finance, 45, 1069-1087.

Shleifer, A. and R.W. Vishny (1997), A Survey of Corporate Governance, Journal of Finance, 52, 737-783.

Siebert, H. and M.J. Koop (1990), Institutional Competition. A Concept for Europe?, Außenwirtschaft, 45, 439-462.

Stiglitz, J.E. (1985), Credit Markets and the Control of Capital, Journal of Money, Credit, and Banking, 17, 133-152.

Thakor, A. (1996), The Design of Financial Systems: An Overview, Journal of Banking and Finance, 20, 917-948.

Tiniç, S.M. (1995), Derivatives and Stock Market Volatility: Is Additional Government Regulation Necessary?, Journal of Financial Services Research, 9, 351-362.

Weber, A. (1994), Einlagensicherung europaweit, Die Bank, 34, 476-479.

Witherell, W. (1995), Comment, in: Sawamoto, K., Nakajima, Z. and H. Taguchi, eds., Financial Stability in a Changing Environment, London, 103-108.

Zeira, J. (1999), Informational Overshooting, Booms, and Crashes, Journal of Monetary Economics, 43, 237-257.

Zwätz, D. (1999), Der Kongreß bremst die Bankenreform in den USA, Handelsblatt, June 2nd, in: Deutsche Bundesbank, Auszüge

Effects of globalization on national monetary policy[1]

Helmut Wagner

University of Hagen, Postfach 940, D-58084 Hagen, Germany

1 Introduction

Globalization is a widely used term, but is in fact rather vague. It refers to the growing economic interdependence of countries worldwide through the increasing volume and variety of cross-border transactions in goods and services and of international capital flows, and also through the more rapid and widespread diffusion of technology[2].

The main impetus for this globalization process which has been steadily increasing over the past two decades has up to now been based on the increased integration and globalization of the financial markets, favored in particular by the abolition of capital controls and by a drastic decrease of transaction costs thanks to new communication and information technologies[3].

Globalization here is understood as a development which increasingly exposes countries to international competition. This process or competition is regarded as being effective not only in the goods market, but also in the markets for mobile production factors. This exposure to international competition, which manifests itself in the movement of mobile production factors (nowadays in particular of capital) to countries which offer them the highest rate of return, increases a country's costs of maintaining inefficient and overly regulated market structures.

This paper addresses the question: if we assume that this globalization process is continuing[4], what effects would this have on national monetary policy? National monetary policy is usually supposed to be faced with the following *three tasks:*

---

[1] This paper heavily draws on a very recent research study (Wagner (1999b)). Parts of the present paper are taken from this more voluminous study.

[2] See e.g., IMF (1997), p. 45. Economic integration among nations is not a new phenomenon. In many ways it can be regarded as a resumption of the intensive integration which began in the mid-1800s and ended with World War I (for this see ibd, pp. 102 ff; see also O'Rourke/Williamson (1999)).

[3] See e.g. Wagner (1999a,b).

[4] This is only a specific assumption or scenario. History has shown that previous periods of globalization have always been disrupted and reversed by political counter-forces driven by

(1) Providing a "lubricant" for the economy
(2) Stabilizing the economy (in cooperation with other economic policies)
(3) Preventing inflation.

In section 2 we shall only touch on the influence of ongoing globalization on the first two tasks, and then in the following sections will concentrate on the effect on the third task.

2 Consequences of globalization for tasks (1) and (2)

Consequences for task (1): globalization has been accompanied or characterized by massive deregulation and by a process of financial innovation. This has made existing asset markets more liquid. It has also created new opportunities for trading financial market risks. This in turn has enabled investors to achieve a better degree of hedging against these risks[5]. Ongoing globalization in this sense may be interpreted as implying a move towards a more perfect financial market system in which central bank money and its close substitutes lose their unique role as generally accepted means of transactions[6]. This may be discussed within the "New Monetary Economics" (Cowen /Kroszner (1987)), which has pointed out that payment technologies can be conceptualized on the exchange of financial assets other than money and which takes an economy with an unregulated, competitive banking system as its paradigm (Black (1970), Fama (1970), Hall (1983)). The use of base money here shrinks when globalization goes on. However, it may be argued that it is very unlikely that the demand for government-issued money will disappear completely, because governments can and will secure a demand for the money they issue by insisting that all tax payments must be made by using this money[7]. The reason for doing this is discussed in the literature under the term "gains from seigniorage". However, a more important reason may be that governments try to minimize the danger of instability which would arise if there were a multiplicity of privately issued moneys. It is likely that a multiplicity of exchange rates would then also emerge between these privately issued currencies. Even if we assume that eventually only one money would survive as a result of competition between these currencies (Hayek (1977) speaks of a "discovery process"), the question remains about how this competition or discovery process would work in practice. There is reason to believe that this would create instability and inflation in the transition process which damages or even prevents the implemen-

---

particular interests unfavorably affected by the globalization process. See, e.g., O'Rourke/Williamson (1999).

[5] See for this in more detail, e.g., Von Hagen/Fender (1998).

[6] A counter-argument against the above interpretation of the monetary policy consequence of globalization, however, might be that the emphasized financial innovations themselves may generate new uncertainties so that risk may not decline at all (De Grauwe 1998).

[7] Another possible method would be for governments to pay interest on reserves.

tation of such a system[8]. Insofar, it appears unlikely that central bank money will no longer be used. However, the role of central bank money will certainly be reduced when globalization increases.

Consequences for task (2): if the view of the "New Monetary Economics" is realized, central banks will lose their power to influence the real sector. But even under the more conventional view in monetary economics, globalization will reduce the effectiveness of monetary policy. As financial innovations such as derivatives allow banks to react faster to monetary policy shocks and, moreover, allow non-banks to shield themselves against such shocks to a certain extent, the transmission mechanism of monetary impulses to the economy becomes weaker. This can be shown within the traditional IS-LM-paradigm, but may also be analyzed with the credit-market view of monetary policy transmission (Bernanke (1993), Bernanke/Gertler (1995)). This view argues that internal and external finance are imperfect substitutes and that companies rely to some extent on external funding to finance investment projects. Now it can be argued that financial innovations/derivatives increase substitution and that therefore the strength of the monetary transmission mechanism is weakened[9].

Furthermore, it may be stated that in a more complete financial market system (which is a characteristic of ongoing globalization) it is harder for central banks to predict the effect of a given monetary impulse on real output and employment with any reasonable precision. Hence its short-run real effects are more difficult to determine. Against the background of the Brainard (1967) rule, the policy conclusion can then be drawn that central banks should behave in a less discretionary or activist way with regard to task (2).[10]

Finally, we may refer to the argument that expansionary monetary policy will increase wage demands to a greater extent in a more open economy (greater openness to foreign trade is another characteristic of globalization). The reason is that expansionary monetary policy will lead to greater (expected) depreciation of the domestic currency in a more open economy. Therefore, more of a monetary expansion will be reflected in prices and less in output[11]. In other words, the ability of money / monetary policy to affect output is weaker in more open economies. On the other hand, increased financial market integration changes the monetary transmission mechanism by enhancing the role of the exchange rate. This means that domestic interest rates may have to adjust less to attain the monetary policy objective since more adjustment takes place through the exchange rate.[12]

---

[8] See also Issing (1999, p. 13): „we could see the emergence of floating exchange rates between different privately-issued moneys, resulting in an uncertain discovery process without any guarantee of a stable outcome, along with a deterioration in economic communication and co-ordination in the economy overall."

[9] Cf. Issing/Bischofsberger (1996).

[10] Cf. Von Hagen/Fender (1998).

[11] For an empirical substantiation of this hypothesis see, e.g. Karras (1999).

[12] Cf. Citrin/Fischer (1999).

In this paper, we will not work out these two lines of the monetary policy consequences of globalization or financial innovation in more detail, but will concentrate on the consequence of ongoing globalization for *task (3)*.

3 Influence of globalization on preventing inflation

The main question here is whether ongoing globalization would alleviate the task of preventing or fighting inflation for monetary policy.

3.1 Basics/components of inflation

We start from the hypothesis that actual inflation is the function of the socially optimal or desired rate of inflation[13] and an inflation bias, apart from shocks.

The *socially optimal rate of inflation* is often seen as being mainly determined by infrastructural preconditions of the fiscal system in an economy. Inflation may be regarded as part of a nation's tax system. In a world with transaction costs and cost distortions in collecting taxes, inflation becomes part of a second-best tax structure. Rational governments choose the inflation rate that equates the marginal social costs of raising revenues through inflation with those of other discretionary taxes.[14]

In other words, the socially optimal rate of inflation is a function of the costs and benefits of inflation. If the costs of inflation increase and/or its benefits decrease, the optimal (and also the desired?) rate of inflation will decline.

The *inflation bias*, however, is derived from a certain interpretation of the institutional environment in which monetary policy is conducted. An inflation bias is today usually explained in the context of game-theoretic considerations, referred to a view that monetary policy decisions are taken sequentially in a second-best world and therefore a socially desirable monetary policy may suffer from a lack of credibility caused by time inconsistency. The central idea of the time inconsistency theory is as follows: the private agents (knowing the objectives of the policymaker and understanding his/her mode of behavior) are aware of the incentive of the government to deviate/inflate and hence expect that inflation rate which excludes for the government any systematic incentive to deviate from the expected inflation rate. In sum, because of time inconsistency of the (ex ante) optimal, how-

---

[13] Here we ignore that there may be a difference between optimal and desired rate of inflation. There is a difference between optimal and desired rate of inflation insofar as, even with given preferences, the optimal rate of inflation can change if the costs and benefits of inflation change. In principle, however, we can also argue that the desired rate of inflation, i.e. the preferences, may change with changing costs and benefits of inflation, at least in the long term.

[14] This is a main aspect in the public finance literature.

ever not enforceable, monetary policy any implementable credible policy leads to a suboptimal high inflation rate, i.e. an inflation bias.

In the literature one can find mainly three reasons for this credibility-based inflation bias referred to as employment, revenue and balance-of-payments motives (Cukierman (1992)):

Employment motive

This is based on the hypothesis that monetary policy is willing and able to influence the level and variability of employment by means of unanticipated (surprise) inflation. It is supposed that distortions in labor markets induce policy-makers to prefer higher employment than it would be consistent with the natural rate of employment. Because of fixed nominal wage contracts, unanticipated inflation can decrease real wages. This expands output since firms increase labor demand. Therefore, policy-makers can increase output and employment by causing an unexpected increase in inflation, part of which is at the expense of other countries. The temptation of a policy-maker to inflate is, however, tempered by a dislike for inflation (induced mainly by the costs of inflation). The higher the NAIRU (above the socially desired level) and the more significant are nominal rigidities (so that the output gain from an unanticipated monetary expansion is large), the greater is the incentive for the authorities to inflate the economy.[15]

Revenue motive

Monetary expansion may be a means of financing government expenditures. In many countries the government is entitled to borrow directly from the central bank and utilize this privilege to finance part of its budget. Besides this standard public finance aspect, the following argument is important for an inflation bias. In the presence of nominal debt the government has an incentive to generate an unexpected inflation by monetary expansion. Inflation surprises have the consequence that nominal interest rates on government bonds remain unchanged in spite of inflation, and therefore not only the real debt burden declines but also real balances as the basis of seigniorage revenues remain unchanged.

Balance-of-payments motive

Governments may be tempted to use an unexpected devaluation to solve their balance of payments problems. A nominal devaluation is expected to – at least temporarily – lower real wages and boost export supply. This motive is especially strong for countries with insufficient international reserves and limited access to international capital markets unable to borrow their way out of balance of payments difficulties.

---

[15] See the underlying model in more detail in section 4.1 below.

3.2 Effects of globalization on inflation

We shall start with the question of the effect of globalization on the inflation bias motives. We shall argue that globalization reduces the inflation bias by influencing/decreasing its various motives described above. Then we shall treat the effect of globalization on the optimal/desired rate of inflation and point out in particular the increasing international competition for capital.

3.2.1 Effects on the inflation bias

Employment motive

The recent literature has identified openness as one of the countervailing forces that lessen the incentive to inflate. The argument which is originally due to Romer (1993) is that, the more open the economy, the smaller the real benefits of higher output from surprise monetary expansion, and thus the lower the equilibrium rate of inflation. As domestic output increases, the terms of trade worsens: the more open the economy, the larger the fraction of foreign goods in domestic consumption, and the greater the welfare loss from the terms of trade loss. In short, more open economies may be blessed with a lower incentive to inflate.

Revenue motive

The revenue motive, i.e. that the state rids itself of its debts by a temporarily higher rate of inflation, or squeezes its debt burden in the same way, is to be regarded as less expedient in view of open global money and financial markets, at least for developed industrial countries. Because large parts of government debt are continuously being prolonged, a government would in fact in real terms devalue its pending debt load through a surprise inflation, but at the same time it would be forced to provide an additional risk premium for all new debt agreements, and this premium is higher on the open global financial markets. The relief effect would therefore only be of a very short-term nature, and with a more long-term observation the disadvantageous effects on the government's overall debt would probably clearly outweigh this.[16]

Balance-of-payments motive

The more open a currency area is, the greater is the effect of devaluation on domestic price level increases. The price index for imported goods increases through the devaluation, and the more open the economy, the greater the volume of im-

---

[16] The above argument naturally also applies to closed national economies. However, it may be assumed that the risk premium in the situation of open global money and financial markets would be higher, because it can be presumed that international organizations will pay more attention to this.

ported goods in the basket of commodities. From this it may be concluded that the public in an open economy is more sensitive towards expansionary or inflationary monetary policy, and will resist this type of policy at a much earlier stage, because it will tend to see through the connection between inflation and expansionary monetary policy (i.e., the incentives to collect information, to learn, are greater) (cf. Johnson (1972)).

3.2.2 Effects on the optimal rate of inflation[17]

As argued above, the optimal rate of inflation declines if the benefits of inflation decrease and/or its costs increase. We just argued that globalization tends to reduce the inflation bias by inducing a decrease in the inflation motives. That is, the benefits of inflation decrease. On the other hand, we may claim that the costs of inflation increase as well, because globalization exerts a direct threat of losing capital and thus creates a disciplinary mechanism against inflationary policy. This threat results from the decisive aspect of modern globalization, namely the increasing international competition for portfolio capital and mobile production factors. This in turn preconditions an increase in mobility of capital which is a main element of globalization.

The central aspect in the above argument is the following: inflation today functions as an important location factor. That is, relatively high inflation represents a locational disadvantage for a country or region with regard to the attraction of international capital. The main reason for this is that high inflation often correlates with highly variable inflation and international investors tend to view highly variable inflation as a symptom of a government that is functioning badly and is therefore resorting to policies that are detrimental to capital-holders, such as confiscatory taxation (Romer (1996), p. 432). This in turn tends to discourage long-term investment. Hence one can state that ongoing globalization creates increasing costs of inflationary policy for a country or society. Insofar, the attempt to fight inflation is regarded as part of a successful national location policy to a greater extent than some decades ago when globalization or international capital mobility was not as high.

The main reason for the decline in the desired, socially optimal rate of inflation is that a country that commits itself to a lower inflation target may attract additional international capital. The competition for international capital therefore may change optimal monetary (and fiscal) policy towards more price stability (and a

[17] As argued above, there are two effects of an increase in the costs of inflation, caused by globalization, which should be differentiated: one is that, with given preferences, the optimal rate of inflation is increased; on the other hand, a permanent increase in the costs of inflation, caused by globlization, may also change preferences and therefore reduce the *desired* rate of inflation.

more solid budget/fiscal)[18] policy, not least because it increases the costs of short-sighted economic policy. Even if all countries tolerated some unexpected inflation, each country would have an incentive to adopt a rigorous anti-inflationary policy, because it could thereby attract foreign capital and thus eventually raise its living standard. To sum up, a more rigorous anti-inflationary policy is thus borne out by the desire to defend a country's own capital and by the universal attempt to attract capital from abroad.

3.2.3 Reference to recent empirical development?

Up to now, we have only analyzed theoretical relationships. How far the above argumentation can also be used to explain the obvious negative correlation between globalization and inflation during the 1980s and particularly the 1990s (cf. Wagner 1999b), is an open question, as there have not yet been any reliable empirical analyses of this relationship. The decline in inflation over the past two decades may be explained by other developments as well, for instance by the decline in energy prices or by different alteration speeds of employment aims and the so-called "natural" employment rate following supply shocks (cf. Wagner (1999b)). From a theoretical point of view, however, the above argumentation that ongoing globalization may contribute to a drop in inflation by exerting disciplinary mechanisms on inflationary policies and by reducing the benefits from surprise inflation appears to be on solid ground. Insofar it may be stated that ongoing globalization tends to alleviate the task (3) of the national monetary policy of preventing or fighting inflation.

4 Model analysis

In this section we will use a simple mainstream model of monetary policy and inflation to sharpen the logic of the argument in section 3 that globalization may reduce inflation.

[18] The evaluation of fiscal policy by the international financial markets results in location disadvantages for a country with excessive budget deficits. Increasing deficits cause higher interest payments on government debt, with the consequence of further increases in the deficit. In the end (with non-monetization), primary surpluses are required through increasing taxes or reducing government spending. This can lead to companies and labor emigrating because of rationally expected increases in taxation and/or a worsening of the infrastructure services. This itself results in a sinking tax base and the necessity of additional tax increases and reductions in government spending.

4.1 The model

We formulate a mainstream Barro/Gordon (1983)-type model of macroeconomic policy and inflation. Policy is here supposed to minimize the following quadratic loss function:

(1) $$E[L'(\pi,y)] = L = E\{0{,}5[(\pi - \pi^*)^2 + b(y - y^*)^2]\}$$

where π and y denote inflation and employment (or output growth), respectively, π^* and y^* are society's most preferred values for inflation and employment (or output growth), and b is the relative weight on fluctuations in these two variables.

The loss function is minimized under the constraint (4) below which is derived from the modeled behavior of the private sector.

The relevant constraint can be derived from the supply side of the model which assumes that nominal wage-setting aims at implementing an exogenous real wage growth target w_r. Letting π^e denote rationally expected inflation, nominal wage growth w then becomes:

(2) $$w = w_r + \pi^e .$$

Employment (or output growth) is given by:

(3) $$y = a - c(w - \pi) - \varepsilon ,$$

where c is assumed to be equal to 1 (for reasons of simplicity), and where ε is a supply shock (with mean 0 and variance σ_ε^2) and a is a parameter.

By combining (2) with (3), we get an expectations-augmented short-run Phillips curve[19]

(4) $$y = y_n + (\pi - \pi^e) - \varepsilon$$

where $y_n \equiv a - w_r$ can be interpreted as the natural rate of employment (output growth). It is assumed that $y_n < y^*$.

If we add the demand side of our model being represented by

(5) $$\pi = m + v$$

where m is the money growth rate and v is a velocity shock (with mean 0 and variance σ_v^2), and in addition assume rational expectations information so that

$$\pi^e = E(\pi \mid y_n) = E(m \mid y_n)$$

where E is the mathematical expectations operator, we obtain the famous neutrality result:

$$y = y_n + m - E(m \mid y_n) + v - \varepsilon .$$

---

[19] The constraint (4) can also be derived from a model of price-setting firms, or from a Lucas-style "island model".

This neutrality result says that only unanticipated aggregate demand policy affects real variables. Policy, however, can still stabilize employment if it responds to shocks.

Furthermore, the model assumes the following timing of events:

(1) The "institutional design stage": We assume first of all (see below for another institutional design), that the government itself fixes monetary policy and does not delegate this to an autonomous instance.

(2) The private actors develop their inflation expectations with knowledge of the objective function and of the constraints (and on the basis of information on y_n) but without knowledge of shocks v and ε. Private inflation expectations are reflected in nominal wage increases.

(3) Finally, shocks v and ε are observable for the government.

(4) With knowledge of these shocks, the government realizes a defined monetary policy, i.e. it fixes m (which leads to a defined π and y). Given the existence of a binding commitment technology, the ex post optimal policy selected in step (4) can only deviate stochastically from a policy which would be optimal on the basis of information and conditions for action in step (1) (ex-ante optimal policy). However, if there is no such commitment technology, the ex-post optimal policy can also deviate systematically from the ex-ante optimal policy.

Optimal rule

First suppose the policy (rule) is credible and hence enforceable. That is, the policy maker(s) can make a binding commitment to an optimal state-contingent policy rule. The optimal rate of inflation can then be derived as being[20]:

(6) $\pi_O = \pi^* + [b/(1+b)]\,\varepsilon$.

Without a commitment technology, such a policy rule cannot be implemented.

Discretion

The adequate timing assumption here is the following: policy is chosen under "discretion" when the policy instruments are set at stage (4) above, i.e. after inflation expectations have been formed and wages have been set. To be credible, a policy now must simultaneously fulfill two conditions: the policy must be *ex post* optimal (i.e., $dL/d\pi = 0$, given π^e and ε); and expectations must be rational (i.e., $\pi^e = E(\pi \mid y_n)$).

The discretionary inflation rate can be derived as:

(7) $\pi_D = \pi^* + b\,(y^* - y_n) + [b/(1+b)]\,\varepsilon$.

When we compare (6) and (7), we see that there is an inflation bias : $b\,(y^* - y_n)$ with discretionary policy (whereas the employment outcome remains the same as

[20] For the derivation of the equations (6), (7) and (11) see, e.g., Wagner (1998, pp. 138-143).

in the case of the optimal policy rule above, namely $y = y_n - [1/(1+b)]\ \varepsilon$ in both cases). The inflation bias is more pronounced the more valuable is employment on the margin (i.e. the higher is b), and the higher is preferred employment relative to the natural rate (i.e., the higher is y^* relative to y_n). Both factors lead to a greater "temptation" for the policymaker to exploit her short-run ability to raise employment by expansionary policy once wages are fixed.

This inflation bias is due to two key assumptions in our model: (i) the sequential timing of monetary policy decisions, and (ii) $y^* - y_n > 0$, i.e. the assumption that the employment target is higher than the natural rate. This latter assumption reflects a lack of policy instruments and hence that some distortion in the product or labor market keeps employment too low.

4.2 Effects of globalization

In section 3 we interpreted globalization as a technological-institutional process that makes the production of inflation more costly for a society or country. This cost aspect can be modeled in several ways. We shall concentrate here on five possibilities that appear to be the most interesting alternatives. These imply that the cost-increasing effect of globalization can be modeled alternatively as

(1) a lower preferred inflation rate π^*

(2) a higher aversion to inflation, i.e. a lower b

(3) a lower output effect of a surprise inflation, i.e. a lower c (see equation (3) above)

(4) an additional cost factor in the loss function of the central bank or of the government

(5) an additional cost factor in the loss function of the society.

We will see that though the consequences in detail differ, depending on the modeling assumption, they in general are uniform insofar as ongoing globalization decreases inflation.[21]

Case 1) a lower π^*

A lower preferred inflation rate $\pi^{*\prime} < \pi^*$ would decrease the inflation level, but would not change the inflation bias compared to the results in section 4.1.

---

[21] Another possibility of modeling the effect of globalization is the following:
It is often argued that more efficient communication and information technologies in the context of the introduction of financial innovations can lead to greater uncertainties in the transmission process of monetary policy (cf. Taylor (1998)). This can be included in the framework of the model introduced here if we replace equation (5) by the following modified version:
(5a) $\pi = \eta \cdot m + v$ with $E(\eta) = 1$, $\sigma_\eta^2 = \text{const.}$, $\sigma_{v\eta} = \sigma_{\varepsilon\eta} = \sigma_{v\varepsilon} = 0$.
This case is discussed in Wagner (1999b). The result there is similar to that of the other cases, namely that globalization (also in this special interpretation, i.e. an increase in the variance of η) reduces inflation.

(6') $\pi_O^{case\ 1} = \pi^{*\prime} + [b/(1+b)]\ \varepsilon$.

(7') $\pi_D^{case\ 1} = \pi^{*\prime} + b\ (y^* - y_n) + [b/(1+b)]\ \varepsilon$, where $\pi^{*\prime} < \pi^*$.

Case 2) a lower b

Alternatively, we can assume that the cost of inflation caused by globalization, if it is understood and internalized by society, leads to a higher aversion to inflation, i.e. a lower b, let this be b'. This also leads to an inflation reduction by reducing the inflation bias. That is, the equilibrium inflation rate will be

(8) $\pi_D^{case\ 2} = \pi^* + b'(y^* - y_n) + [b'/(1+b')]\ \varepsilon$, where $b' < b$.

Case 3) a lower c

Alternatively, we could interpret the above cost aspect in such a way that it decreases the output effect of a surprise inflation, c. This would mean that the Phillips curve is steeper ($d\pi/dy = 1/c$ increases). This would again reduce the inflation bias:

(9) $\pi_D^{case\ 3} = \pi^* + cb(y^* - y_n) + [cb/(1+c^2b)]\ \varepsilon$, where $c < 1$.

Case 4) an additional cost factor in the loss function of the central bank or of the government

We may assume that the cost aspect enters into the loss function of the central bank or of the government, but not into that of society as a whole. For reasons of simplicity, I assume that the cost factor enters the loss function linearly. The loss function of the central bank (or government) would then change in the following way:

(10) $L_{CB} = E\{0{,}5[(\pi - \pi^*)^2 + b(y - y^*)^2] + f(\pi - \pi^a)\}$

where f(.) expresses the cost of inflation when inflation is higher than the equilibrium world inflation rate π^a.

The social loss function, however, would still be (1).

Globalization here punishes governments or central banks which create inflation above the world inflation level and thus forces or gives them incentives to move towards this level. As one easily can see, this resembles Walsh's performance contract model (1995a).

With (10), which assumes a linear cost on inflation, inflation may be reduced. If the cost f is equal to the inflation bias $b(y^* - y_n)$, we even obtain

(11) $\pi_O = \pi_D^{case\ 4} = \pi^* + [b/(1+b)]\ \varepsilon$,

which is the same as the optimal inflation rate of equation (6). Here the inflation bias is wiped out by the cost threat imposed by globalization.

Case 5) an additional cost factor in the loss function of the society

Alternatively, we can assume that the cost of inflation caused by globalization is understood and internalized by society as a whole and thus leads to a change in the social loss function where the cost factor is added in the same way as in equation (10) above:

$$(12) \qquad L = E\{0{,}5[(\pi - \pi^*)^2 + b(y - y^*)^2] + f(\pi - \pi^a)\}$$

In this case, the solution is quite surprising. The main aspect here is that the optimal rule now is different from the solution in equation (6). The optimal rule now is[22]

$$(13) \qquad \pi_O^{case\ 5} = \pi^* - f + [b/(1+b)]\,\varepsilon$$

The *optimal rule* (optimal here means the best of the alternative rules) consists in undercutting the socially desired rate of inflation because "globalization" rewards this to the extent of $f(\pi - \pi^a)$.[23] The discretionary solution is:[24]

$$(14) \qquad \pi_D^{case\ 5} = \pi^* - f + b(y^* - y_n) + [b/(1+b)]\,\varepsilon$$

The discretionary policy on average leads to a rate of inflation which is above the rule solution. Whether the discretionary inflation is also greater than the socially desired inflation depends among other things on f. If the cost f (accidentally) is equal to the inflation bias $b(y^* - y_n)$, both inflation rates are equal. As in the case of the rule-based policy, inflation is inversely connected to globalization. However, globalization does not reduce the difference from π_D and π_O. This difference still amounts to $b(y^* - y_n)$ and is independent of f.

5 On policy effects

Let us suppose that there is some causal relationship between ongoing globalization and decreasing inflation in the way analyzed in the foregoing sections. What are the consequences which this would have on optimal national monetary policy? We will restrict ourselves in the following to regarding or speculating about three possible lines of consequences:

(1) Would central bank independence become superfluous, or at least less urgent?

---

22 For the derivation see Wagner (1999b).

23 If π^* were equal to π^a, there would also be a general incentive to deviate downwards from the world rate of inflation, i.e. to undercut it. If all states attempted this, there would be a tendency towards deflation. This could possibly be countered by (an appropriate or efficient) economic policy coordination.

24 For the derivation as well as for the interpretation of the result in general see again Wagner (1999b).

(2) Would a greater incentive to coordinate policies (nationally and internationally) arise?

(3) Would recessions become less frequent, less long, less severe?

5.1 Would central bank independence become superfluous?

If globalization leads to a higher aversion to inflation and hence produces for example the inflation rate (8), as argued above as one possible interpretation of the effects of globalization (case 2), one may conclude that globalization creates the same disciplinary effect as central bank independence. Usually central bank independence is interpreted in the following way: society attributes a central banker, who has the same loss function as the society but differs in his personal value of b (has a lower b, let this be b''), with independence. The appointed central banker then sets monetary policy according to her own preferences. This gives the equilibrium outcome:

(8') $\pi_{CBI} = \pi^* + b''(y^* - y_n) + [b''/(1+b'')]\,\varepsilon$.

By comparing (8) and (8') one may, against the background of the alleged costs of central bank independence[25], conclude that central bank independence is then not needed any more, at least not in its function as a shield against the time-inconsistency problem. It appears to become superfluous.

However, this seems to be a wrong interpretation, at least if we stay within the above model world. As long as society has $b' \neq 0$ (i.e., has some aversion against inflation), the optimal b'' (the appointed central banker's personal value of b) will always lie below b'. The solution can still be improved by central bank independence, because the optimal (central banker's) b'' is a function of b'. Globalization

[25] It is often contended that central bank independence increases output or employment volatility: from the above model structure one can derive the following patterns of output or employment $y_D = y_O = y_n - [1/(1+b)]\,\varepsilon$ with discretion and with the optimal state-contingent policy rule, whereas with central bank independence $y_{CBI} = y_n - [1/(1+b'')]\,\varepsilon$. This means that output or employment volatility is greater with central bank independence. This could, however, be reduced by a partial reduction of central bank independence, for instance by implementing an overriding mechanism (cf. Lohmann (1992)). Here, the government appoints a conservative central banker but threatens to terminate his/her contract if deviations from the target inflation become too large. Moreover, central bank independence is found to reduce electorally-induced volatility of output or employment (cf. Alesina/Gatti (1995)); Lippi (1998) provides evidence that could support this proposition. This aspect of a reduction in the political economy cycle may also explain, why the above hypothesis of greater output or employment volatility with central bank independence has not been proved in many empirical studies.

in the sense of a reduction of b' does not therefore replace central bank independence, but increases the degree of optimal inflation aversion of the central banker.[26]

Moreover, one may argue that the institutional competition which was described above as a characteristic of globalization, tends to make institutions such as central bank independence to a "must" for a nation in order to be able to sell bonds on the international financial markets, at least at a "reasonable" price. Central bank independence can be regarded as a kind of institutionalized rating, as a quality label for transparency and financial solidity. This increases the credibility of macroeconomic polices, therefore alleviates capital borrowing on international capital markets and decreases its costs.

In addition, central bank independence should not only be regarded as a strategic shield against an inflation bias. Central bank independence also serves other purposes. What might these purposes be? One example is the avoidance of political business cycles. Furthermore, central banks usually perform a variety of functions (besides those mentioned above), for instance managing the payments system, managing the foreign exchange reserves, promoting the stability of the financial system, by supervising the banks and by serving as lender of last resort. The relevant question which arises here, and which would have to be analyzed in detail, is which of these tasks require central bank independence, or would be better carried out with central bank independence.

5.2 Would a greater incentive to coordinate policies (nationally and internationally) arise?

Let us suppose that ongoing globalization decreases inflation, based on the increase in the costs of inflationary policies caused by globalization described above, and the decrease in benefits that leads to a decrease in inflation motives or incentives for governments. We may then derive from this an incentive for the greater coordination of policies. On the one hand, the increase in the costs of inflationary policies, in particular the worsening of national location conditions through inflationary policy, may induce government (fiscal policy) to resist short-term incentives to push for a more expansionary monetary policy from the central bank, or to counteract its price stabilization policy, in order to finance public goods at lower costs. The main reason is that a worsening of the national location conditions has the consequence that fewer direct foreign investments are attracted and domestic capital flies abroad. This means that government must fear a loss in output, employment and tax income. Hence, government (fiscal policy) will be induced to practice greater coordination with monetary policy in order to control

[26] However, if we depart from the above model and no longer measure central bank independence against b, but against the degree of self-assertion of the central bank, it may in fact be possible to establish the above hypothesis of a decline in the degree of optimum central bank independence with ongoing globalization in the above meaning (8). This is analyzed in Wagner (1999b).

inflation. This in turn may induce central banks rationally to behave less restrictively (or less "strictly cautiously") in their precautionary reactions at the first sight, or on the traditional signals, of inflation, such as increasing levels of industrial capacity utilization.

As inflation expectations are then no longer as high, monetary policy can more easily try to support government or fiscal policy in the fight against other evils such as unemployment. The reason is that the fear of a re-emergence of expansive aims in fiscal policies following a concession by monetary policies would probably then recede, i.e. the credibility of fiscal policies in regarding damping down inflation as a top priority grows with the increasing restrictions created by globalization. However, it must be noted that globalization will not have the same disciplinary effect on fiscal policies/the government in all political regimes. It is to be expected, for example, that the effect will be the greater, the greater the pressure on the government from the social strata which are affected by globalization (cf. Wagner (1999b) for more details).

On the other hand, globalization may give more room to international policy coordination. Implementing international policy coordination is usually criticized or prevented by reference to the expected costs of an international policy coordination set up to combat common recessions, namely the danger of an increase in inflation. These expected costs will probably be reduced by the inflation-suppressing effects of globalization, and international policy coordination may therefore increase.[27]

5.3 Would recessions become less frequent, less long, less severe?

It has been shown that post-war US recessions have mainly been triggered by restrictive monetary policies to control inflation (Romer/Romer (1994)). Such policy-induced recessions which produced substantial output losses to reduce inflation are also regarded as accounting for the continued volatility of the postwar era (Romer (1999)). Because of the fear of increasing inflation (expressed in increasing expectations of inflation), in the past monetary policies have frequently broken off improvements in the economic situation and booms prematurely and initiated economic recessions. On the other hand, the monetary financing or feeding of improvements in the economic situation was frequently protracted for fear of a flare up of (expectations of) inflation, or because of a feeling that the inflation mentality developed in the previous boom was not yet sufficiently broken. These correlations are, it appears, not restricted to the USA. In Germany as well strict anti-inflation (expectations) policies seem to have been common. Now let us suppose that ongoing globalization reduces the danger of inflation and hence these fears of inflation (as we have argued in the foregoing section), then we might expect a re-

---

[27] The „undercutting" result of globalization case 5 in section 4.2 above may also increase the incentive to intensify international policy coordination.

duction in the frequency and severity of recessions (caused by monetary policy)[28]. Since it can be established empirically and explained at least plausibly that recessions are linked with output losses[29] and unemployment, and that the duration and severity of recessions correlate with the duration and extent of unemployment (possibly increased by hysteresis effects), it should be possible to deduce a decline in average unemployment or positive employment effects of globalization.

6 Conclusions

We have argued that globalization will have various effects on national monetary policies. On the one hand, the relevance of outside money will be reduced and, in addition, the effectiveness of monetary policy in stabilizing the economy will decline. On the other hand, however, the monetary policy task of controlling inflation should be alleviated by ongoing globalization. We have concentrated on the latter aspect here in this paper. We started with the hypothesis that ongoing globalization will reduce the trend of inflation. We argued that the benefits of inflation tend to be decreased by globalization. In addition, the costs of inflationary policies increase (triggered above all by the danger of capital flight), thereby developing general disciplinary mechanisms against such policies. Therefore, not only the inflation bias but also the optimal/desired rate of inflation, which are the two main trend components of the rate of inflation, tends to decline.

In this paper we have investigated this effect of an increase in the costs of inflationary policy caused by globalization in a model analysis. We examined several interpretations of this cost effect of globalization, and for each of these cases we were able to substantiate the hypothesis that globalization leads to a decline in inflation.

We then analyzed some of the consequences for stabilization policies of this inflation-suppressing effect of globalization. We found that globalization, through its suppressing effect on inflation, tends to decrease the frequency and severity of recessions, and in addition, to produce an incentive for greater coordination of policies, not only on a national level but also on an international level. There is no indication, however, that central bank independence does in fact become superfluous as a result of the disciplinary mechanism triggered by the increase in the costs of inflation caused by ongoing globalization.

---

[28] The situation in the USA in the last five years, in which the Fed has not initiated a recession out of fear of inflation (as previously) in spite of increasing or sustained overheating trends in the labor market, may serve as a first example here. In other words, recessions are few and less severe if inflation is firmly under control.

[29] Romer (1999, p. 40) emphasizes that „in the absence of monetary policy shocks, industrial production would have risen, rather than fallen“ or fallen by much less as it actually did during US postwar downturns.

References

Alesina, A. and R. Gatti (1995), Independent Central Banks: Low Inflation at No Cost?, American Economic Review 85, 196-200.

Barro, R. J. and D. B. Gordon (1983), Rules, Discretion, and Reputation in a Model of Monetary Policy, Journal of Monetary Economics 12, 101-120.

Bernanke, B.S. (1993), How Important is the Credit Channel in the Transmission of Monetary Policy?: A Comment, Carnegie-Rochester Series on Public Policy, Fall, 47-52.

Bernanke, B.S. and M. Gertler (1995), Inside the Black Box: The Credit Channel of Monetary Policy Transmission, Journal of Economic Perspectives 9, 27-48.

Black, F. (1970), Banking and Interest Rates in a World without Money, Journal of Bank Research, Autumn, 9-20.

Brainard, W.C. (1967), Uncertainty and Effectiveness of Policy, American Economic Review, P.a.P. 57, 411-425.

Citrin, D. and S. Fischer (1999), Meeting the Challenges of Globalization in the Advanced Economies, in: H. Wagner (ed.), Globalization and Unemployment, Berlin, 19-35.

Cowen, T. and R. Kroszner (1987), The Development of the New Monetary Economics, Journal of Political Economy 95, 567-590.

Cukierman, A. (1992), Central Bank Strategy, Credibility and Independence: Theory and Evidence, Cambridge, Mass.

De Grauwe, P. (1998), Comments on the Papers by Salvatore, Hamada, Capie, Fratianni et al., and Von Hagen and Fender, Open Economies Review 9:S1, 532-535.

Fama, E.F. (1980), Banking in the Theory of Finance, Journal of Monetary Economics 6, 39-58.

Hall, R.E. (1983), Optimal Fiduciary Monetary Systems, Journal of Monetary Economics 12, 33-50.

Hayek, F.A. (1977), Entnationalisierung des Geldes, Tübingen.

IMF (1997), World Economic Outlook, (May), Globalization – Opportunities and Challenges, Washington, D.C.

Issing, O. (1999), Hayek – Currency Competition and European Monetary Union, Deutsche Bundesbank / Auszüge aus Presseartikeln 36/1999, 9-17.

Issing, O. and K. Bischofsberger (1996), Derivate und Geldpolitik, in: D. Duwendag (ed.), Finanzmärkte, Finanzinnovationen und Geldpolitik, Berlin, 111-137.

Johnson, H. (1972), cited in: Vaubel, R., Die Politische Ökonomie einer Europäischen Zentralbank. Probleme und Lösungsvorschläge, in: P. Bofinger et al (eds.), Währungsunion oder Währungschaos? Was kommt nach der D-Mark?, Wiesbaden 1993, p. 62.

Karras, G. (1999), Openness and the Effects of Monetary Policy, Journal of International Money and Finance 18, 13-26.

Lippi. F. (1998), On Central Bank Independence and the Stability of Policy Targets, Scandinavian Journal of Economics 100, 495-512.

Lohmann, S. (1992), Optimal Commitment in Monetary Policy: Credibility versus Flexibility, American Economic Review 82, 273-86.

O'Rourke, K. H. and J. G. Williamson (1998), Globalization and History: The Evolution of a 19th Century Atlantic Economy, Cambridge, Mass.

Romer, Ch. (1999), Changes in Business Cycles: Evidence and Explanations, Journal of Economic Perspectives 13 (2), 23-44.

Romer, Ch. and D. Romer (1994), Monetary Policy Matters, Journal of Monetary Economics 34, 75-88.

Romer, D. (1993), Openness and Inflation: Theory and Evidence, Quarterly Journal of Economics 4, 869-903.

Romer, D. (1996), Advanced Macroeconomics, New York.

Taylor, J. B. (1998), Information Technology and Monetary Policy, Institute for Monetary and Economic Studies, Bank of Japan, Monetary and Economic Studies, Dec. 1998, 19-28.

Von Hagen, J. and I. Fender (1998), Central Bank Policy in a More Perfect Financial System, Open Economies Review 9:S1, 493-531.

Wagner, H. (1998), Stabilitätspolitik. Theoretische Grundlagen und institutionelle Alternativen, 5. ed., München.

Wagner, H. (1999a), Einführung in die Weltwirtschaftspolitik, 4. ed., München.

Wagner, H. (1999b), Globalization and Inflation, in: H. Wagner (ed.), Globalization and Unemployment, Berlin, 343-388.

Discussion of Helmut Wagner's "Effects of globalization on national monetary policy"

Wilfried Fuhrmann

University of Potsdam, August-Bebel-Str. 89, D-14482 Potsdam, Germany

The increasingly intense debate on globalization is addressing several aspects of the growing interdependence of countries worldwide. Among some of the most urgent questions are the tasks that national monetary policymaking will take and the role of national monetary authorities in the international monetary system with new global institutions and agreements.

Here, with the only focus on national monetary policy, Helmut Wagner's paper is a fascinating and unusually ambitious one. After distinguishing three tasks with which national monetary policy is supposed to be faced with, these three are preventing inflation, stabilizing the economy and providing a medium of exchange as a kind of lubricant for the economic engine, the paper looks for influences of an ongoing globalization on fighting or preventing inflation.

Literature discusses, at least since Cukierman (1992), the well-known three motives for monetary expansion respectively for the inflationary bias of monetary policy. These three are the employment motive, the revenue respectively seigniorage motive and the balance-of-payments respectively the mercantilistic motive. The most striking résumé, after discussing the effects on all three motives within this classification, is that globalization reduces inflation worldwide. It lowers the inflationary bias as well as the politician's preferred rate of inflation because of increasing costs of inflation due to international capital movements.

And just as this résumé follows from a straight-forward done consideration, the effects of increasing costs of inflation are analysed within a Barro-Gordon-model (1983) of a closed economy. In short, within this design of an economy, effects of an inflation-reduction are shown for changes in behavior, a higher aversion to inflation and a lower price-elasticity of output are assumed. And the effects are shown for changes within the loss functions of the central bank and of the society, thus the preferred rate of inflation is lowered and a linear inflation-rate term as an additional cost factor (Walsh 1995) is added. The derivations itself are published elsewhere (Wagner 1999). Nevertheless, the given results are convincing within the chosen framework.

Though this modelling of a closed economy for analyzing effects of globalization and thus backing up the résumé is impressive, some shortcomings are to be mentioned. Not only financial markets are getting more and more globalized. Expansion and globalization are changing goods- and labour-markets as well, especially the pattern of trade is changing, the international mobility of labour is increasing and multinationals are expanding. These changes address the question, how reliable is a modelling of the effects of globalization on monetary policy within a framework of neutrality respectively with an assumed linearity between growth and employment (Fuhrmann 1998) and with a still given natural rate of employment.

Is globalization not to be understood, first of all, to be a dynamic process, especially a permanent change of the information structure, of trader's market behavior, and of national and international institutions, including the target functions of central banks (Fuhrmann 1995)? For example, the ECBS can be understood as such a consequence. Then globalization stands for an increased fickleness of behavior, including the velocity of money, and a new design of economic policymaking. Thus, not only within the EMU, integration and coordination between fiscal and monetary authorities undergo substantial changes, and, due to the strengthened global institutional competition, the independence of national monetary authories has to be confirmed and enlarged.

The (relative) shock structure of a country is not invariant neither to time nor to the country's degree of internationalization. It goes without saying, there are processes of convergence and demarcation at work simultaneously. The national central bank's optimal governance structure and degree of discretion (flexibility) depend on the economic stage of a country, including its degree of monetization respectively its (relative) transaction costs. These institutions, which are in game- and process-theory normally given with the framework and are characterized as being exogeneous or extremely slow-moving variables, these institutions are becoming more and more endogeneous through globalization. Institutions like an orthodox currency board or a currency board arrangement (Fuhrmann 1999a) or a central bank with discretion, which is politically independent with respect to monetary policy and even to exchange-rate policy (in future), seem to be stage-depending optimal solutions within a dynamic process of an overall institutional change. Thus, I would prefer an open macroeconomic model with the rate of inflation and the exchange-rate as endogenous variables explaining both, the effects of globalization on the real exchange rate and the optimal rule for monetary policy.

Among other variables, expected rates of return, not interest rates, a country's ranking, risks and risk aversion, and the computerized risk-management of globally investing portfolio-funds determine increasingly mobile international capital movements. And further banks mergers will take place – within national boundaries and cross-bordering as well. All these various components of capital flows as well as the changing systematic risk of banking from globalization show monetary policy to have more than those three mentioned tasks. Assuring the quality of the financial intermediaries, of their monies and of the country's international exchanges is the fourth task of monetary policy – though it seems to be the main task for many countries at presence.

New technology reduces transaction costs, changes the whole nature of financial information and increases the competition between national exchanges. We have to look with painstaking care for the so-called inflation of stock-prices and indices, especially concerning their wealth-effects on the economic activity and wealth of a country.

Currency crises are in a globalized world not only a problem of governments. Only to some extend these crises stem from macro-economic sources. Beside those reasons as an unsustainable growth of the national debt burden and the balance-of-trade deficit, which we commonly analyse with models inspired by Krugman (1979) and Obstfeld (1986), we saw new scenarios and forms in recent years. There were microeconomic disturbances within the sector of financial intermediaries setting fire. And nowadays such a fire will be spread out by various contagious and herding effects. We are in need of totally different models of currency crises (Calvo 1998), international banking and exchange-rate dynamics.

Both, the strong international competition for capital, especially for direct investment, which will be intensified with a further deepening of globalization, and the high volatility of capital flows, stress the importance of a severe regulatory and supervisory scheme for banking as well as for the security markets respectively for all financial exchanges.

The institutionalized supervision may be a department within the central bank or an independent board. Principal-agent-problems and constitutional regulatories have to be solved and are to adjust continuously. These optimizations depend mainly on the country's tradition and the way of institutionalization the dominant customer-countries have chosen.

The design of monetary policy, including the governance system, has to be discussed and newly optimized. A new national design and a new internationally co-ordinated architecture of monetary policy seem to be under way. On the whole, the economic answer to globalization seems to be an efficient currency competiton – not via exchange-rate changes and depreciation, but monetary stability and openness. It goes without saying that contrary to this and there is no denying the fact that some politicians do their utmost to establish capital controls and other political measures to be at the control of all international links again.

References

Calvo, G.A. (1998), Varieties of Capital-market Crises, in: Calvo, G.A., M. King (eds), The Debt Burden and its Consequences for Monetary Policy: Proceedings of a conference held by the IEA at the Deutsche Bundesbank, Frankfurt; Basingstoke, pp. 181-202.

Cukierman, A. (1992), Central Bank Strategy, Credibility, and Interdependence: Theory and Evidence; The MIT Press, Cambridge, Mass.

Fuhrmann, W. (1995), Review of A. Cukierman: Central Bank Strategy, in: Journal of Institutional and Theoretical Economics, vol. 151, pp. 399-402.

Fuhrmann, W. (1998), On Currency Boards,in: H. Wagner (ed.), Current Issues in Monetary Economics, Heidelberg, New York, pp. 309-326.

Fuhrmann, W. (1999a), Zur Theorie des Currency Boards, Zeitschrift für Wirtschaftspolitik, 48. Jg., S. 85-104.
Fuhrmann, W. (1999b), Money Supply in a Currency Board Arrangement, in: http://www.makrooekonomie.de
Krugman, P.R. (1979), A Model of Balance-of-Payments Crises, Journal of Money, Credit, and Banking, vol. 11, pp. 311-325.
Obstfeld, M. (1986), Rational and Self-Fulfilling Balance-of-Payments Crises, AER, vol. 76, pp. 72-81.
Vaubel, R. (1990), Currency Competition and Monetary Union, Economic Journal, vol. 100, pp. 936-946.
Wagner, H. (1999), Globalization and Unemployment, Berlin, forthcoming.
Walsh, C. (1995), Optimal Contracts for Independent Central Bankers, AER, vol. 85, pp. 150-167.

Are we facing a stock market bubble?

David I. Fand

The Buchanan Center for Political Economy, George Mason University, Fairfax, VA, U.S.A.[1]

1 Introduction

The explosion of equity prices since 1995 has led some analysts to conclude we are facing an asset bubble in the stock market. In the period February 1995 - July 1997 the Dow-Jones index doubled from 4000 to 8000; in the period November 1995 - May 1999, the Dow doubled from 5000 to 10,000. Overall equity prices in the four years 1995-1998 grew at the amazing and spectacular annual rate of 28%. The stock market returns in the latter half of the 1990s are significantly higher than the average and among the highest ever recorded. (See Table 1 and Table 2)

Moreover, the return on equities in the last two decades – going back to the start of the recovery in 1981 – has been about 19%, compared to the longer term historical average of 10%. (See Charts 1 and 2.)

Admittedly the above average returns in the 1980s may be viewed as a correction to the below average returns in the 1970s. But this does not explain the spectacular 28% annual growth in equity prices in the 1995-1998 period – an average growth rate that is almost 3 times the long term historical average. How do we rationalize this extraordinary performance and the stunningly high returns which are indeed continuing thus far to July 1999? (See Chart 3.)

There are basically two views of this remarkable boom in equities. New Paradigm analysts point to rapid technological advances, globalization and restructuring in recent years. They believe that policy makers have achieved a better understanding and mastery of macroeconomics, and are better able to contain both inflation and the business cycle. Indeed, the New Paradigm analysts conclude that we may now be able to achieve a relatively permanent prosperity. For them, the accelerating stock market boom since 1995 is merely recording, in accounting and financial terms, this dramatic and extraordinary breakthrough in our ability to manage the economy. This is the essence of the New Paradigm view which is

---

[1] I would like to thank Professor James M. Buchanan for many penetrating comments and constructive suggestions. Thanks are also due Professor Bernhard Eckwert for stimulating conversations and probing questions, Dr. Albert M. Wojnilower for insightful analysis and provocative views, David L. Littmann for many helpful discussions, and Jeremy P. Fand for research assistance. The responsibility for any errors is mine alone.

rooted in the idea that we are living in a New Economy. I don't know about Germany and other European countries, but in America there are many people, and especially many in the financial community, who want to believe in the New Paradigm.

A second and more conventional view is that there are some very special factors which led to these remarkably favorable – and unbelievably positive – results starting in 1995, that these factors are not permanent and, more importantly, may readily be reversed.

I do not accept the New Paradigm analysis. But I will attempt to summarize, if not rationalize, what the New Paradigm theorists are saying. They argue first that we are currently experiencing an extraordinary rapid technological advance – a major breakthrough – which is revolutionizing industry and the world economy; and that these technological advances enable us to produce goods with continuously declining costs – a powerful, persistent factor helping us to control and ultimately eliminate inflation. Second is the great pressure on industry to become more efficient by restructuring and downsizing, another factor lowering costs and contributing to this new prosperity. A third factor is globalization. Today the global economy is like one big country, a firm can readily produce and sell its product almost everywhere; and we are, in fact, witnessing an important worldwide trend toward globalization. A fourth factor, emphasized in tne New Paradigm literature, is that labor and management relations are no longer confrontational – the two sides have learned how to live together with many fewer strikes and other costly confrontations. A fifth factor is that we have achieved a greater understanding and mastery of macroeconomics. Finally, and perhaps most important, the Federal Reserve – the central bank – has, it is argued, learned how to control inflation.

While New Paradigm theorists may differ in their emphasis, they typically stress these factors – rapid technological advances, restructuring and downsizing, globalization, non-confrontational labor management relations, superior macroeconomic management, and the relatively successful price level stabilization policies of the central bank to argue that the dramatic and extraordinary acceleration in equity prices in the 1995-1998 period – the 28% annual growth rate – is rational and not a potential cause for concern.[2]

---

[2] An exposition of the New Paradigm and the New Economy view is presented by Steven Weber "The End of the Business Cycle"; *Foreign Affairs*, July-August, 1997, volume 76, no. 4 pp. 65-82. For a critical analysis of the New Paradigm see Paul Krugman "Seeking the Rule of the Waves" *Foreign Affairs*, op cit, pp 136-141 and his "How Fast can the U. S. Economy Grow?" (*Harvard Business Review*, July-August 1997, pp. 123-129) Ugo Sacchetti "Whither the U. S. Economy?" (*Banca Nazionale del Lavoro Quarterly Review* No .208, March 1999, pp 69-94) argues that the trends which have sustained the current boom cannot continue, and are bound to be reversed. He suggests that the U. S. economy may enter a period of significant recession. Chairman Greenspan takes an intermediate position. He states: "The 1990's have witnessed one of the great bull stock markets in American history. Whether that means an unstable bubble has developed in its wake is difficult to assess. A large number of analysts have judged the level of equity prices to be excessive,

2 The new paradigm: A history

There is an interesting historical note on the views espoused in the New Paradigm. If you ask who is the greatest economist that America has produced, most economists agree that it was Irving Fisher. Fisher wrote monumental books – classics – on capital theory, the theory of interest, the purchasing power of money, and introduced distributive lags in his applied research (When Milton Friedman utilized distributive lags in his empirical research, he was building on Irving Fisher.) Fisher wrote a book on the consumption tax, and a classic on the theory of index numbers. In the 1930s Hicks and Allen achieved world wide fame for introducing indifference curve analysis; Fisher's 1896 doctoral dissertation not only used indifference curve analysis but went beyond Hicks and Allen in solving the integrability conditions. I mention all this to show you what an extraordinarily brilliant and remarkably creative individual Fisher was. I should also mention that until recently we measured the GDP deflator with a Laspeyre's Index possessing a well known upward bias. Theorists constructing index numbers always faced the question "Can we produce a price index with the least amount of bias?" Well, it turns out that the closest numerical approximation to the true value is the square root of the product of the Laspeyre Index and the Paasche index. And who first proved that? Irving Fisher, way back in the 1920s when he defined his "Ideal Index". Recently the U. S. government has introduced a chain index in its GDP deflator calculations; this is Fisher's ideal index.[3]

---

even taking into account the rise in 'fair value' resulting from the acceleration of productivity and the associated long-term corporate earnings outlook.". . . . . "But bubbles are generally perceptible only after the fact. To spot a bubble in advance requires a judgement that hundreds of thousands of informed investors have it all wrong. Betting against markets is usually precarious at best." See Alan Greenspan: "Monetary Policy and the Economic Outlook." *Joint Economic Committee*, U. S. Congress, June 17, 1999.

In subsequent testimony he states:"Premptive policy making requires that the Federal Reserve continually monitor economic conditions, update forecasts, and appraise the setting of its policy instrument. Equity prices figure importantly in that forecasting process because they influence aggregate demand. As I testified last month, the central bank cannot effectively directly target stock or other asset prices. Should an asset bubble arise, or even if one is already in train, monetary policy properly calibrated can doubtless mitigate at least part of the impact on the economy. And, obviously, if we could find a way to prevent or delate emerging bubbles, we would be better off. But identifying a bubble in the process of inflating may be among the most formidable challenges confronting a central bank, pitting its own assessment of fundamentals against the combined judgement of millions of investors." Alan Greenspan: *Statement before the Committe on Banking and Financial Services*, U. S. House of Representatives July 22, 1999, p. 13. For a novel interpretation of the New Economy, see J. Bradford DeLong "What 'New' Economy?", *Wilson Quarterly*, Autumn 1998, pp14-26.

[3] Irving Fisher, *The Nature of Capital and Income*. (New York, Macmillan, 1906), ibid. *The Theory of Interest*. (New York, Sentry Press, 1930), ibid. *The Purchasing Power of Money*. (New York, Macmillan, 1931), ibid. *Constructive Income Taxation* (New York, Harper, 1942), ibid *The Making of Index Numbers*. (Boston, Houghton-Miflin, 1927), ibid.

Fisher advised Yale University to invest their endowment in equities. In the 1920s equities were not considered a prudent investment which was typically defined in the minds of most investors as an investment in bonds. Under Fisher's prodding, Yale University put their very considerable endowment into equities and lost much of it in the 1929 crash; many cynics concluded this is what happens when you listen to an economic theorist. So Irving Fisher was often derided by those seeking to highlight and dramatize the irrelevance of economic theory. And I know that when I was a student, Irving Fisher's name was often mentioned disparagingly. When I first read his classic works, it took me a long time to figure it out. Fortunately in recent years we have seen a growing respect and a very considerable increase in Fisher's stature.

Now, why am I relating this? In Fisher's *The Stock Market Crash and After,* published in 1930, each of the factors now cited in the New Paradigm: technology, restructuring, globalization, non-confrontational labor management relations and the central bank's success with price stability – is a chapter in this book.[4,5] Fisher focused on these factors to explain that we had reached a New Era – a permanent plateau of prosperity and why everyone should invest in equities.[6] Theorists of the New Paradigm have not even been able – apparently – to come up with new ideas – they are repeating the hypothesis that goes back to Fisher's 1930 book. I am therefore a little dubious about this New Paradigm.

3 An alternative view – A Keynesian global economy

If one does not accept the New Paradigm how does one explain the boom in equities? In my view the more basic puzzle is why we have so little inflation. We're now in the 9th year of recovery with relatively tame inflation whereas normally inflationary pressures are seen in the third and fourth year of a recovery. The combination of a reasonably strong economy in the 9th year of the recovery with very little inflation is remarkable – it's like seeing a 160 year old individual run a marathon. And one readily appreciates why many observers feel the need for a new theory and are therefore inclined to accept the New Paradigm. The question is how

---

Mathematical Investigations in the Theory of Value and Price. (New Haven, Yale University Press, 1925).

4 Irving Fisher *The Stock Market Crash and After.* (New York, Macmillan, 1930).

5 The factors stressed in the New Paradigm are very similar to those stressed by Fisher. On technology, see Fisher's Chapter 8 on *scientific research and invention*; on globalization and restructuring see Chapter 7 on *the age of merger* and Chapter 9 on *industrial management.* On the non-confrontational labor relations, see Chapter 10 on *labor's cooperative policy*; and on the central bank success with price stability see Chapter 12 *relief in seven years of stable money.*

6 Fisher, in the fall of 1929, stated that "Stock prices have reached what looks like a permanently high plateau." See J. K. Galbraith *The Great Crash* (Boston, Houghton Miflin, 1961), page 75.

can we be in the 9th year of recovery, more than twice the duration of an average recovery, with such low inflation. In fact, for many commodities trading in the global economy, we have thus far been observing a decline in inflation.

In America we construct and calculate the CPI, the PPI and the ECI to obtain a monthly indicator of inflation. The CPI is the consumer price index and the PPI is the wholesale price index. Federal Reserve Chairman Greenspan is personally said to favor the ECI – the Employment Cost Index – which he monitors as perhaps a better gauge of inflation. So right now in America we look at all three indices and all three are behaving reasonably well. However we should also note that these indices are sensitive to prices of commodities and services in the global economy, and to the extent that the European and Asian economies have considerable idle capacity – which depress many prices in the global economy – these three indices may not be telling the whole story.

To be more specific, while inflation as measured by the CPI, the PPI and the ECI have been relatively stable or even declining, some U. S. asset prices are going right through the roof. We have already noted the extraordinary post 1995 boom in equities and we also note a very sharp escalation in real estate prices. Similarly, if we examine the prices of non-tradable goods and services – items that are not sensitive to the global economy – many are also rising rapidly.

It would appear that there is something a little more complicated going on concerning inflation. And although I follow the monetarist framework, I am inclined to believe that America is now living in a *Keynesian* global economy. By that statement I mean the following: There is currently a large quantity of idle capacity in the global economy, because Europe, Japan, Southeast Asia and Latin America (which account for 65% of global output) are all struggling with high unemployment.The *augmented* aggregate supply curve facing America consists of the American aggregate supply augmented by what can be produced in the rest of the world; and, when global idle capacity is substantial – as is currently the case – it adds significantly towards generating an elastic augmented supply for America.

The hypothesis that we live now in a Keynesian global economy carries the implication that the augmented aggregate supply facing America, given the enormous volume of global idle capacity, is almost *infinitely* elastic. As a consequence it follows that an increase in American aggregate demand will lead to an increase in the U. S. trade deficit but not necessarily to any rise in U. S. prices. Indeed, this may be the key to the conundrum of the absence of inflationary pressure, even though we are currently in the ninth year of our recovery.

Consider the current stock market boom: the concern that typically undermines a buoyant equity market is the fear of inflation. When traders begin to see signs of rising inflation they know (1) that the Federal Reserve will act and raise interest rates, (2) that arbitrageurs and speculators will liquidate positions, and (3) that stock prices will decline. One of the keys to the extraordinary boom in U. S. equity prices since 1995 has been – indisputably – the absence of inflation. And the hypothesis I am presenting is that America has escaped and avoided inflation in the 1990s because we are currently confronting a Keynesian global economy; and, more precisely, that the augmented aggregate supply facing America is very elastic.

There is one important proviso. In the 1930s we lived in a Keynesian world that was locally produced. More precisely, disastrously restrictive monetary policies in the U. S. – i. e. a 35% decline in the money stock – caused very high unemployment – exceeding 30% – and resulted in a vast increase in idle capacity. The present Keynesian global economy was not produced in America since we have "full" employment and "shortages" of both labor and capital. It was generated by others such as Chancellor Kohl and the economic officials in Japan. Indeed Chancellor Kohl, through his vigorous, determined and zealous support for the Maastricht agreement and the European Monetary Union has actively supported policies which resulted in a very substantial increase in European idle capacity; in this sense Kohl has contributed significantly, though indirectly, to the extraordinary rise in American equities in the 1990s; similarly, Japanese officials have contributed to our stock market boom by tolerating and accepting a stagnant and depressed recovery for the past nine years.

But, if we live in a Keynesian global economy, then, like the Keynesian world of the 1930s, it is a temporary phenomenon; it is not a permanent feature of the global economy, and we therefore reject the New Paradigm. We view the extraordinary rapid rise in equity prices in recent years as a likely asset bubble, and like all other bubbles, we believe it will burst.

4 Chairman Greenspan's concern about irrational exuberance

As many of you know, Chairman Greenspan has been concerned for some time about the possibility of an asset bubble in the equity market – evidenced publicly in his statement about 'irrational exuberance' in December 1996. Also, at the monthly Open Market Committee meetings in the spring of 1996, the Fed brought in many monetary and financial experts on markets, including specialists on the equity and bond markets, and presented them with the following problem: Does the Central Bank have a right, or duty, to introduce restrictive monetary policies when it sees equity prices rising beyond where they should be – a potential asset bubble – at a time when the other macroeconomic data look reasonable? They actually dealt with that issue. Greenspan has clearly been concerned about the possibility of a stock market bubble since 1996 when Dow Jones was recorded at a little above 6000.[7]

---

[7] "Clearly, sustained low inflation implies less uncertainty about the future, and lower risk premiums imply higher prices of stocks and other earning assets. We can see that in the inverse relationship exhibited by price/earnings ratios and the rate of inflation in the past. But how do we know when irrational exuberance has unduly escalated asset values which then become subject to unexpected and prolonged contractions as they have in Japan over the past decade? And how do we factor that assessment into monetary policy?" See Alan Greenspan "The Challenge of Central Banking in a Democratic Society", December 5, 1996 (Washington, AEI), p. 14.

The kind of evidence often cited to support the hypothesis that we are confronting an asset bubble may be briefly indicated:

1. overvalued share prices (S&P 500 P/E ratios currently over 35) where in the past a ratio of 18-20 was considered high;

2. merger mania;

3 sharply rising real estate prices (both commercial and residential); and

4. an explosion in money growth

The monetary indicator that I think is the most important one is the monetary aggregate M2, and M2 in recent years has grown considerably above the 1% to 5% growth prescribed by the Open Market Committe. Indeed M2 has been growing at almost twice the upper range. Similarly, the recent 1998(4) growth of the M3 monetary aggregate which includes a large array of financial assets and may be a more complete measure of overall liquidity, is the highest in about 20 years. There is considerable evidence that we have enjoyed extremely rapid money growth. Table 3 summarizes the escalation in money growth from 1991. From an average growth of 1.7% in the 1991-1994 period, M2 accelerated steadily to 8.5% in 1998. The growth in M2 in the 1995-1998 is dramatically higher than the 1991-1994 range and similarly for the monetary aggregate M3 which in the fourth quarter of 1998 reached levels not seen in 20 years. (See Chart 4)

Some who question the relevance of monetary growth counter by asking if indeed money growth is so rapid, why is it that we have no inflation? Admittedly, inflation as normally measured by the CPI, the PPI and the ECI clearly has been reasonably well behaved in recent years. But if one examines prices of equities, real estate and non-tradables, there is evidence that the extremely rapid money growth has led to substantial price increases in many markets.

A recent analysis in *The London Economist*, (April 18, 1998) concludes there's an asset bubble in the U. S. equity market and stresses the four factors just summarized. First they cite that stock prices are rising very rapidly, evidenced by the spectacular growth in the S & P 500 since 1995. Second, they focus on the recent merger waves and especially the bank mergers as a typical characteristic of a bubble economy. *The Economist* points out that the four previous big merger waves of this century – in the early 1900s, the 1920s, the 1960s and the 1980s – all coincided with three related characteristics: strong economic growth, rapid credit expansion and a stock market boom. Obviously a stock market boom provides the wherewithal for some companies to buy other companies; and, not surprisingly, the first three merger waves and booms ended in crashes in 1904, 1929 and 1969. The 1980s boom led to a crash in 1987 and the recession of 1990-1991. The *Economist* suggests that the current merger mania is evidence of a stock market boom and also, potentially, of a forthcoming crash.

The third symptom of an asset bubble is the sharp escalation in rents for commercial property. In 1997 commercial rents rose by 20% in one year alone in three major cities: San Francisco, Boston, Dallas. New York bidders offered $180/square foot, twice the price paid 6 month before. *The Economist* concluded that rents and property values are getting out of control.

Less dramatic than the explosion in commercial property rents is the rapid acceleration of house prices. The returns accruing to home owners in the past 60 months are almost on the scale of stock market yields. According to a recent report[8]:

"The typical house in Utah is worth nearly 50% more than it sold for 5 years ago. Michigan, the turn-around phenomenon state of the decade – has seen the value of its average home grow by almost 41% since 1994. Oregon homes have gained about the same – 41.3% Colorado has also sizzled, with average gains in resale value of 39.1% during the last 5 years." This report which tracks "the appreciation rates of millions of individual homes reveals that the average gain nationwide during the past year has been close to 5%. . . or about four times the underlying rate of inflation in the economy overall".

And the fourth reason cited by *The Economist* is the extremely rapid money growth in recent years. The data in Table 3 are from Chairman Greenspan's monetary report to Congress – to the House of Representatives and to the Senate – which he presents twice a year.[9] In this report, he has a chart which indicates that, while the FOMC guidelines for M2 growth are 1% to 5%, it is growing about 9%. Similarly the M3 monetary aggregate is growing at a much faster rate than the FOMC range of 2% to 6%, and, as previously noted, in 1998(4) it was growing at the highest rate in 20 years. There is absolutely no denying that money growth is extremely high.

Admittedly, there is no inflation pressure. But allowing money growth to continue at its recent pace will cause an explosion in prices when the temporary factors that are currently keeping U. S. inflation relatively benign – the extraordinary large volume of idle resources in the global economy and the resulting elastic augmented aggregate supply curve – are no longer operative factors.

5 Chancellor Kohl and Japanese policy officials: Their role in facilitating the American boom

Let us now consider other influences contributing to the extraordinary growth rate of U. S. equities since 1995. Chancellor Kohl, as we indicated earlier, played an important role in igniting this stock market boom, assisted also by Japanese officials and the Japanese banks. First consider Chancellor Kohl's role. His strategic and powerful support for Maastricht and the European Monetary Union (EMU) – which required that members limit fiscal deficits and link their currencies to the mark – resulted in deflationary monetary and fiscal policy in Europe. The Maastricht agreement directly imposed fiscal restraint by limiting their deficits to 3% of

---

[8] See Kenneth R. Harney: "The Nation's Housing". *The Washington Post,* July 13, 1999, pp. G1, G2.

[9] Alan Greenspan "Monetary Policy Report to the Congress Pursuant to the Full Employment and Balanced Growth Act of 1978", February 23, 1999, p. 25. This report by the Fed Chairman, which he delivers twice annually to both the House and the Senate Banking Committees is sometimes referred to as the Humphrey-Hawkins Report.

the GDP and, indirectly, monetary restraint as the other currencies sought to maintain some kind of parity with the mark. The combination of fiscal and monetary restraint led to the underutilization of resouces; the European increase in idle capacity is indicated by the double digit unemployment rates in France, Germany and Italy (relative to the low rates in the U.S. and U.K.).

For the period 1995-1998 the facts may be summarized as follows: While unemployment fell in the post-Maastricht period by 28% in the US, it rose by a staggering 54% in West Germany, by 18% in France and by 13% in Italy. Idle capacity grew rapidly in these European countries following the Maastricht agreement, *pari passu* with the increase in unemployment. Kohl's Maastricht policy generated the idle capacity in Europe which facilitated the extraordinary U. S. stock market boom of 1995-1998.

The evidence shown in Table 4 and Chart 5 may be briefly summarized. The pre-Maastricht (1990) unemployment rates are 6.6% for Germany, 8.9% for France, 11.3% for Italy and 16% for Spain. The post-Maastricht unemployment rate increases in all countries. For the four years 1995-1998 in which U. S. equities reached stratopheric heights, the German unemployment rate is approximately twice the pre-Maastricht rate. Similarly, the unemployment rates rise substantially in France and Spain, with only a modest rise in Italy. The substantial increase in European unemployment and the associated increase in post-Maastricht idle capacity support our hypothesis that, since 1995, the global economy is Keynesian and that the augmented aggregate supply facing America is fairly elastic. Similarly, the decline of manufacturing capacity utilization for Germany, France, Italy and Japan from 1990 to the 1995-1998 period supports the Keynesian global economy hypothesis.

Japan – the second largest economy in the world – has been stagnating with very little growth since 1990 and has a considerable stock of idle capacity. As a consequence, an increase in American aggregate demand can be supplied by the idle capacity in both Europe and Japan. Indeed, the growing volume of imports from Europe and Japan, facilitated by this idle capacity – and measured by the merchandise trade deficit – is a very powerful force which keeps prices relatively stable in the U. S. Ironically, if prices are relatively stable, the Fed cannot easily tighten monetary policy even if money is growing considerably above the FOMC upper band. And, if money growth continues at a high rate it will fuel additional growth in stock prices.[10]

---

[10] Greenspan, in a sense, created this problem when he downplayed the significance of monetary growth rates in his testimony on the 1990-1991 recession. See Section VII, below, on "Greenspan and the Monetarists".
Buchanan and Fand, in discussing Greenspan's testimony during this period, write "One argument offered by Greenspan himself is that the public did not want to hold more M2: thus there was a need to "work down the debt excess", "restructure the balance sheet", "work off the debt overhang" and "work off the excess of the 1980s". But these statements expressed an elementary fallacy. Any nominal target can be achieved by the Fed through central bank operations, especially a target as wide as the low end of the range from 2.5 to 6.5% that was set in 1992.....We may sum up this section by asking defenders of Federal

Japan has another, direct, impact on the U. S. stock boom. Japanese banks have been lending large amounts of money to the U. S. It is estimated that during the 1995-1998 period they were lending at the rate of $25 billion a month – another factor fueling the boom. Japan, with its large stock of idle capacity, can export and satisfy American demand for goods, keeping inflation tame and preventing the Fed from tightening policy. And by lending money at very low interest rates – at less than 1% – the Japanese banks finance the speculators and the arbitrageurs who buy stock with these borrowed funds.

The role of global idle resources in facilitating an asset bubble in America may be gauged by the growing merchandise trade deficit of approximately 4%. This quantity, which excedes a full year's growth of GDP, is what we obtain from the global economy. In addition, the cross elasticity of supply (the percentage change in the quantity of imports to the U. S. relative to the percentage change in U. S. prices) is, I believe, fairly elastic, so it doesn't take much of an increase in the U. S. price to significantly increase imports (especially from countries with considerable idle capacity).

Now, why is a relatively elastic cross elasticity important? Although U. S. unemployment is now down to 4.2%, wage rates are nevertheless stable with only modest acceleration. One naturally wonders why labor costs are so stable? Is it that unions have become less demanding? I think the answer is that the unions know that if they attempt to push up wages, the employer could produce these goods in Europe or Asia. The unions do understand the relevance of an elastic cross elasticity of supply.

6 The handcuffing of the FED: The arbitrageurs liberated

I would like to consider another important factor fueling an asset bubble. The Federal Reserve, and especially Chairman Greenspan, have been concerned about the danger of an asset bubble for more than 2 years. Greenspan knows that high money growth rates can fuel an explosive boom in equities. And in his December 1996 address he has publicly expressed his concern about "irrational exuberance". Why has he allowed money growth to continue at these very high levels?[11] And why is it

---

Reserve monetary policy in 1990-1992 three questions: 1. Could the Fed have produced more M2 in the three years 1990-1992? 2. Would more M2 have increased output, employment and income? 3. Would such increases have been desirable?". James M. Buchanan and David I. Fand: "Monetary Malpractice: Intent, Impotence, or Incompetence?". *Critical Review* volume 6, no. 4, pp 465-466.

See also David I. Fand: "Monetarism and the United States Economy: 1990-1995" in Avi Cohen, Harold Hagemann, and John Smithin (editors); *Money, Financial Institutions and Macroeconomics*, (Boston, Kluwer, 1997). Chapter 12, pp 175-190.

[11] It is interesting to note that after his comments on "irrational exuberance" in December 1996, money growth almost doubled from a 4.6% growth in 1996 to an 8.5% rate in 1998. See Table 3 and Chart 4.

he can't act to restrain this explosion of money? I am referring here to what I call the handcuffing of the Fed.[12]

I define handcuffing as a situation where, in the absence of inflation, the Federal Reserve will not restrain money growth. I believe the handcuffing of the Fed has been an important, indeed critical, facilitator of the boom since 1995.[13]

Suppose you are a Wall Street professional and you have learned that the Federal Reserve will not raise interest rates for the next two or three quarters. What would you do? The market professional has a green light to speculate and to leverage his investments. This is precisely the situation since 1995: (1) the growing idle capacity in Europe, Japan and southeast Asia keeps U. S. inflation benign; and (2) the absence of inflation prevents the Fed from restricting money growth by raising interest rates.[14] More precisely, the idle resources in the global economy and the elastic cross elasticity of supply, absent U. S. inflation, provide a signal for professionals to leverage and speculate.

To recap: What the market professionals fear most (and I use professional to include speculators and arbitrageurs) is that the Fed will raise interest rates forcing them to liquidate a position. But if the Fed appears to be handcuffed – unable to raise rates – the stock market professionals are energized as though they are on an adrenaline high. It really excites them when they know the Fed will not raise rates. That's the best news they can hope for. They are free to borrow, to leverage and to speculate. The handcuffing of the Fed and the liberation of market professionals are, I suggest, the critically important factors in fueling the post 1995 stock market boom.

Those who stress the New Paradign point to rapid technological change, globalization and other factors that, in their view, explain the current boom. There may be some merit in these claims; but, as I have argued in Section II, I doubt that the

---

[12] In response to a question from former Governor Lawrence Lindsay Chairman Greenspan states: "We are constrained by an unwritten set of rules. From where I sit, one of the toughest jobs is to know exactly where we cross the line. We are a central bank in a democratic society that functions under an existing set of laws. We have technical independence in the sense that there is nobody that has the legal capability of rescinding an action we take in the monetary area. But we cannot do things that are totally alien to the conventional wisdom in the professional community. Of course, if we simply look to the conventional wisdom to tell us what to do, we might as well go out of business and have somebody run policy by just conducting a poll." Lawrence B. Lindsey: *Economic Puppetmasters* (Washington, AEI Press, 1999), page 34.

[13] In the interview with Former Governer Lindsey Greenspan also states "There is a fundamental problem with market intervention to prick a bubble. It presumes that you know more than the market. There is also a problem of timing. You might prick it too soon, in which case it comes back, and you may just make it larger the next time. There is also the very interesting question as to whether the central bank is intervening appropriately in the market. This raises some fascinating questions about what our authority is and who makes the judgement that there actually is a bubble." Lindsey, *op. cit*, page 50.

[14] As indicated in the next section, Greenspan's 1990-1991 arguments downplaying the signficance of monetary growth rates further limits the Fed's ability to act. See also Fand and Buchanan, *op cit.*

technological advances and productivity breakthroughs attributed to the current economy are all that different from earlier boom periods such as the 1920's.[15] If there is something uniquely different to the current boom, it is the extent and duration of the handcuffing of the Fed.

7 Greenspan and the monetarists

A second factor that handcuffed the Fed since 1995 is that Greenspan is in a bit of a trap – one that he himself set. He cannot easily or readily raise interest rates even though money growth is excessively high so long as inflation is quiescent. Let me explain. Greenspan is cornered by his 1990-1991 victory over the monetarists. During the recession of 1990-1991, many observers, and especially monetarists, questioned Greenspan since key monetary aggregates, and especially M2, were not growing sufficiently. During the 1990-1991 recession the M2 aggregate grew by only 1% whereas the midpoint of the Federal Open Market Committee (FOMC) recommendation for that period was approximately 2 1/2%. Using that FOMC midpoint, by 1992 "the M2 money stock would have been approximately $200 billion larger and the GDP perhaps $350 billion higher".[16] Many economists questioned why Greenspan was so niggardly in expanding the money supply in 1991 and 1992. And the criticism that money growth in the 1990-1991 recession was much too low came not only from Milton Friedman and other monetarists but also from Paul Samuelson.

Greenspan's defense in the 1990-1991 period when he was very forceful in saying that one cannot gauge the thrust of monetary policy by examining money growth rates created the problem he has faced since 1995. By propounding this view in 1991-1992, testifying in Congress, and arguing against viewing money growth as the proper variable to gauge the thrust of monetary policy, he can not, in the post 1995 boom, easily point to rapid money growth as a basis for Fed restrictive action. So he is in a difficult position.

---

[15] Schumpeter, describing this period as 'the industrial revolution of the twenties' states: "This is what we find. The electrical, chemical, and automobile industries, which together with their subsidiaries and all that directly and indirectly hinges upon them – the motorcar, for instance, is responsible for a great part of the total of postwar construction: roads, garages, gasoline stations, suburban residences – account for 90% of the postwar changes in the industrial organism and for most of the increase in real income." See Joseph A. Schumpeter *Business Cycles* (Abridged, with an introduction by Rendig Fels), (New York, McGraw Hill, 1939). page 305.

[16] "Alan Greenspan's monetary deceleration during and after the 1990-1991 recession was even more stringent and restrictive than the tight money policy that Paul Volcker introduced to reverse double digit inflation in early 1980. The M2 growth rate of 2.8% and 1.9% in 1991 and 1992 fell below even the midpoint of the Fed's target ranges, which were explicitly selected to slow inflation Had the Fed hit the midpoint of its own money targets in 1991-1992, by early 1993 M2 would have been approximately $200 billion larger and the GDP perhaps about $350 billion higher." See Buchanan and Fand, *op cit*, pages 461-462.

The markets and Wall Street can readily point to the lack of inflation, and argue that the Fed has no basis to tighten. They can cite Greenspan's 1990-1991 testimony concerning the inappropriateness of focusing on money growth to gauge the thrust of monetary policy, especially when prices are stable. They will also point out that we now have a low 4.2% unemployment rate, that many former welfare clients have finally found jobs, and that if he tightens these former welfare recipients may lose their jobs. Greenspan will be charged with racism – they will not only call him a bad central banker, they will also charge him with other transgressions. So his basis for action has been taken away. Greenspan was too successful in fighting the monetarists in 1991. He downplayed the significance of high monetary growth – the one argument that he could have used in the 1995-1999 period.. I conclude that Greenspan's 1990-1991 victory over the monetarists is limiting his current policy options.

Greenspan's June 1999 testimony at the JEC suggests that he may now feel that he could raise interest rates and limit money growth even though current inflation is still relatively benign.[17]

8 Was the FED handcuffed in the 1980's?

One final point. Some readers may find it hard to accept that the central bank cannot act even though it may want to. Some may also question the notion that if market professionals believe that the Fed is handcuffed they will increase their speculative demand for credit. Let me therefore cite a prior example. In the 1984-1985 period there was growing concern in the United States that the dollar was too strong. The dollar was approaching 300 yen then (it's about 120 currently) and it was about 4 DM. The American automobile industry was worried that a strong dollar would help the Japanese make more powerful inroads in the domestic automobile market. In addition many U.S. export industries were hurt because a strong dollar made it difficult for them to sell to foreign markets. Both the export industries and the import competing industries were demanding remedial action from James Baker who was then the Secretary of the Treasury, the finance minister. In most countries the finance minister is responsible for foreign economic policy – and in the U. S. that is the domain of the Secretary of the Treasury; the exchange

[17] Greenspan in his testimony states: "While bubbles that burst are scarcely benign, the consequences need not be catastrophic for the economy. . . . .The bursting of the Japanese bubble a decade ago did not lead immediately to sharp contractions in output or a significant rise in unemployment. Arguably, it was the subsequent failure to address the damage to the financial system in a timely manner that caused Japan's current economic problems. Likewise, while the stock market crash of 1929 was destabilizing, most analysts attribute the Great Depression to ensuing failures of policy. And certainly the crash of October 1987 left little lasting imprint on the American economy." Alan Greenspan: Joint Economic Committee testimony, June 17, 1999, *op cit*.

rate is therefore under his province. But if the Treasury Secretary seeks to control, or peg, the exchange rate, he is effectively immobilizing monetary policy.[18]

The Chairman of the Fed then was Paul Volcker who was considered to be a very strong chairman. The situation in 1985 was that Secretary Baker said the dollar was too high and this had obvious implications for monetary policy. The professionals on Wall Street understood that constitutionally the exchange rate and foreign economic policy were under the jurisdiction of the Secretary of the Treasury. The market professionals came to believe that Volcker would not conduct monetary policy in a manner that would raise the exchange rate. They believed that Volcker was, in effect, handcuffed – that he would be reluctant to raise rates and risk a further rise in the dollar. If Volcker, an appointed but unelected official, would raise interest rates and further strengthen the dollar, he would be acting against the Secretary of the Treasury. It is a very difficult issue. Volcker didn't tighten policy and the market may have believed that Volcker was handcuffed. The market built up over a two year period, and it finally ended in the crash of 1987. But from 1985 to that fateful day in October 1987 the market was booming. And it was booming for precisely the reason that market professionals thought that Volcker was handcuffed.

Because Secretary Baker was strongly opposed to any appreciation of the dollar, many Wall Street professionals borrowed and speculated. They assumed, I think correctly, that Volcker would not take any action to further cause the dollar to rise, and especially since he knew, and understood, that Baker was under enormous pressure from protectionists in Congress. I conclude that once the market professionals consider that the Federal Reserve is handcuffed, they are liberated.. I believe this has been true in the last few years and that we are, in fact, in an asset bubble. Whether Greenspan is ready now (July, 1999) to take the handcuffs off, as suggested in recent JEC testimony, remains to be seen.

9 Conclusion

In this paper we argue that the extraordinary boom in the U. S. equity market results from a number of special factors and we reject the New Paradigm and the

[18] Volcker, in his analysis of this period, writes as follows: "Baker explained to me his idea of a G-5 meeting to coordinate intervention to reduce the value of the dollar. He also said he was aware the whole thing would be undercut if monetary policy were tightened, and he did not want to proceed against that possibility. i replied, as any Fed Chairman should, that I was not in a position to give anyone committments about monetary policy over any substantial period of time. Nonetheless, I was personally convinced that, quite independent of any policy he might adopt towards the dollar, there was not a serious risk that monetary policy would need to be tightened during the next few weeks or months. I pointed out that the economy was slowing and inflation was declining to the lowest level in years. We discussed his plans for joint intervention, and he said he might as well go ahead with them." Paul A. Volcker and Toyoo Gyohten: *Changing Fortunes* (New York, Times Books, 1992) p 243.

notion of a New Economy. The special factors facilitating this extraordinary boom in which P/E ratios have reached an all time high in excess of 35 are summarized below.

First we note the large volume of idle resources in 65% of the Global Economy – in Europe, Japan, Asia and Latin America. Second, the global idle resources and unused capacity ensure that America faces an elastic aggregate supply that can be readily augmented by the global idle resources. Third, the resulting elastic augmented aggregate supply guarantees that inflation rates in the U. S. are fairly tame. Fourth, the absence of inflation in the U. S. tends to handcuff the Fed since Chairman Greenspan finds it difficult, in light of his prior public position, to restrict the accelerating growth of the money supply in the absence of inflation. Fifth, the perception that the Fed is handcuffed liberates the market professionals to borrow and leverage their portfolio positions, knowing that the Fed is handcuffed.

We suggest that this mechanism explains the relative absence of inflation in the U. S. in the face of a recovery in its ninth year, extremely high monetary growth rates, an extraordinary boom in equities and real estate, and the highest P/E ratios in recorded history.

The boom in America is directly related to high unemployment rates and low capacity utilization rates in Europe, Japan, Asia and Latin America. The post-1995 U. S. boom is dependent on the idle resources in post-Maastricht Europe, on the stagnant Japanese economy of the 1990s and on the considerable idle capacity in Asia and Latin America. In short, America's spectacular boom – its ability to grow for over nine years without inflation – is dependent on the very substantial volume of idle resources in the global economy – on the fact that we are currently living in a global economy that is *Keynesian.*

Greenspan's June 1999 and July 1999 testimony to Congress may indicate that he is now ready to raise interest rates and limit money growth – take the handcuffs off – even though inflation is still relatively benign.

We do not deny that there have been spectacular breakthroughs in computer technology and advances in telecommunications with corresponding increases in productivity in the 1990s. But as our citation from Schumpeter suggests, similar claims were made for the motor car in the 1920s. Indeed Schumpeter describes this period as the "industrial revolution of the twenties".

But if the secret of our post-1995 boom is that we are living in a Keynesian global economy, then, like the Keynesian world of the 1930s, it is a temporary phenomenon and not a permanent feature. We therefore reject the New Paradigm;

and we conclude that the extraordinary rise in equities since 1995 is a likely asset bubble.[19]

References

Cameron, Rondo, Crisp, Olga, Patrick, Hugh T. and Tilly, Richard (1967), Banking in the Early Stages of Industrialisation, New York: Oxford University Press.

Buchanan, James M. and David I. Fand, "Monetary Malpractice: Intent, Impotence, or Incompetence?" Critical Review volume 6, no. 4.

DeLong, J. Bradford, "What 'New' Economy?" Wilson Quarterly, Autumn 1998.

Fand, David I., "Monetarism and the United States Economy: 1990-1995", in Avi Cohen, Harold Hagemann, and John Smithin (editors); Money, Financial Institutions and Macroeconomics, Boston, Kluwer, 1997.

Fisher, Irving, Constructive Income Taxation, New York, Harper, 1942.

Fisher, Irving, Mathematical Investigations in the Theory of Value and Price, New Haven, Yale University Press, 1925.

Fisher, Irving, The Making of Index Numbers, Boston, Houghton-Miflin, 1927.

Fisher, Irving, The Nature of Capital and Income, New York, Macmillan, 1906.

Fisher, Irving, The Purchasing Power of Money, New York, Macmillan, 1931.

Fisher, Irving, The Stock Market Crash and After, New York, Macmillan, 1930.

Fisher, Irving, The Theory of Interest, New York, Sentry Press, 1930.

Galbraith, J. K., The Great Crash, Boston, Houghton Miflin, 1961.

Greenspan, Alan, "Monetary Policy and the Economic Outlook", Joint Economic Committee, U. S. Congress, June 17, 1999.

Greenspan, Alan, "Monetary Policy Report to the Congress Pursuant to the Full Employment and Balanced Growth Act of 1978", February 23, 1999.

Greenspan, Alan, "The Challenge of Central Banking in a Democratic Society", December 5, 1996, Washington, AEI.

Greenspan, Alan, Statement before the Committe on Banking and Financial Services, U. S. House of Representatives July 22, 1999.

Harney, Kenneth R., The Nation's Housing, The Washington Post, July 13, 1999.

Krugman, Paul, "How Fast can the U. S. Economy Grow?" Harvard Business Review, July-August 1997.

Krugman, Paul, "Seeking the Rule of the Waves" Foreign Affairs, July-August 1997, volume 76, no. 4.

---

[19] Former Federal Reserve Governor Lawrence Lindsey, who discussed these issues in an interview with Chairman Greenspan, writes "We have one other very important consideration. The bigger the bubble in asset prices, the more dependent the economy is on the wealth-generated spending caused by the bubble. The economy will get a dose of "the higher they rise, the harder they fall".

Greenspan acknowledges as much "Of course there are dangers and to be sure, we don't want to get ourselves hung up on a very expensive bubble" Greenspan is well aware that this is the dilemma he faces: "If you had a gold standard there wouldn't be the choice. No matter what we do, we're creating potential trouble. Absent the gold standard, open market policy should endeavor to create monetary conditions in the least worst manner?" So Greenspan sits on the horns of a dilemma. On the one hand, if he tightens monetary policy he risks disturbing both the political concensus that supports the Fed's independence and the economic conditions that underpin having society making the most of a supply shock. On the other hand, if Greenspan does not act to tighten policy, the bubble simply gets bigger and bigger, until the Fed has no choice." Lindsey: *op cit.*, p. 52.

Lindsey, Lawrence B., Economic Puppetmasters, Washington, AEI Press, 1999.
Sacchetti, Ugo, "Whither the U. S. Economy?" Banca Nazionale del Lavoro Quarterly Review, no. 208, March 1999.
Schumpeter, Joseph A., Business Cycles (Abridged, with an introduction by Rendig Fels), New York, McGraw Hill, 1939.
Volcker, Paul A. and Toyoo Gyohten, Changing Fortunes, New York, Times Books, 1992.
Weber, Steven, "The End of the Business Cycle" Foreign Affairs, July-August, 1997, volume 76, no. 4.

Appendix: Tables and charts

Table 1 1000 Point Milestones in the Dow Jones Index

Date	Market Close
November 1972	1000
January 1987	2000
April 1991	3000
February 1995	4000
November 1995	5000
October 1996	6000
February 1997	7000
July 1997	8000
April 1998	9000
March 1999	10,000
May 1999	11,000

Table 2 Dow-Jones and S & P 500 at Year End:1980-1999

Year	Dow-Jones	S & P 500
1980	963.99	134.03
1981	875.00	126.60
1982	1046.54	141.77
1983	1258.64	165.47
1984	1211.57	162.47
1985	1546.67	202.99
1986	1895.95	251.17
1987	1938.83	223.92
1988	2168.57	277.69
1989	2753.20	348.55
1990	2633.66	329.07
1991	3168.80	379.10
1992	3301.12	432.06
1993	3754.09	466.43
1994	3834.44	453.11
1995	5117.12	620.18
1996	6448.27	739.60
1997	7908.25	983.79
1998	9181.43	1176.74
1999 (7/1/99)	11,145.00	1388.12

Table 3 Growth of M2 and M3 (in Percent): 1991-1998

	M2	M3
1991-1994*	1.7	1.1
1995	3.9	6.1
1996	4.6	6.8
1997	5.8	8.8
1998	8.5	11.0

*the average of the values for these years

Table 4 European Unemployment 1989-1999 (Percent at Year End)

	Germany	France	Italy	Spain
1989	7.6	9.0	12.0	16.5
1990	6.6	8.9	11.3	16.0
1991	6.3	9.9	11.0	17.1
1992	8.9	10.9	9.6	20.4
1993	10.6	12.4	11.1	24.0
1994	10.2	11.9	11.9	23.5
1995	11.0	11.7	12.1	22.6
1996	12.0	12.5	12.2	21.7
1997	13.0	12.3	12.4	20.1
1998	11.9	11.5	12.6	18.0
1999*	11.7	11.4	12.1	17.3

- 1999 data for end of May

Chart 1

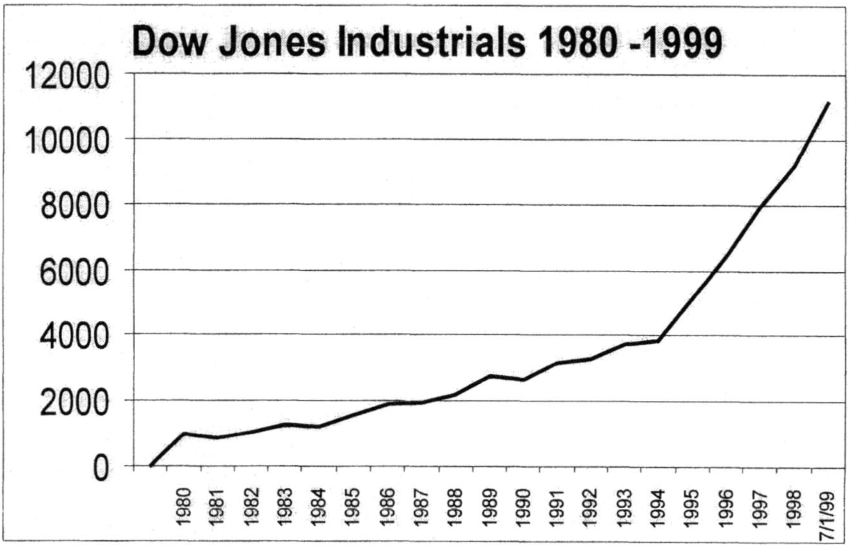

Chart 2

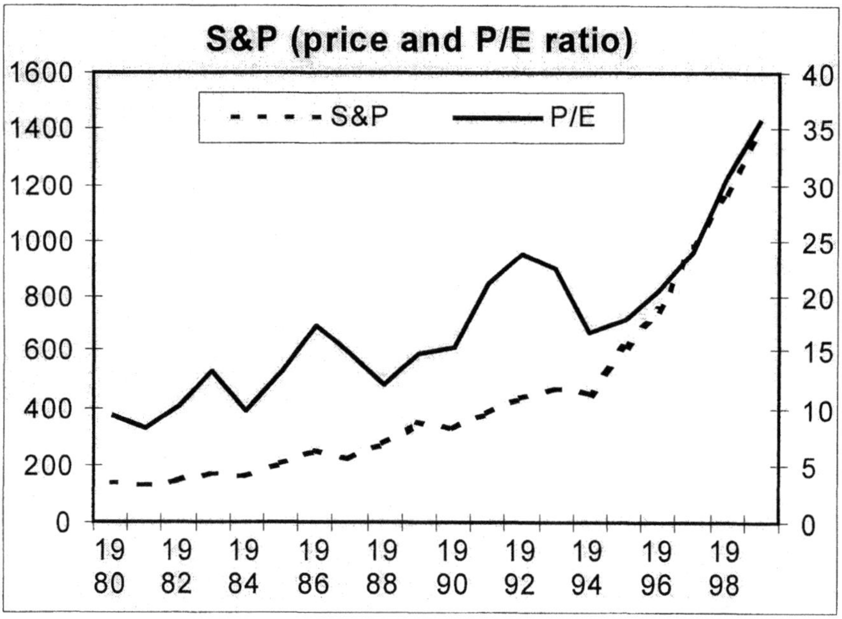

Chart 3

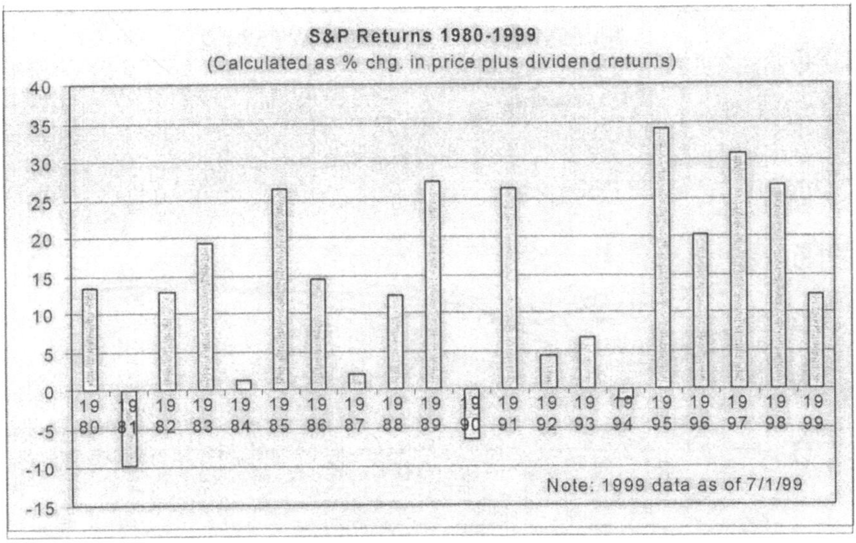

Chart 4

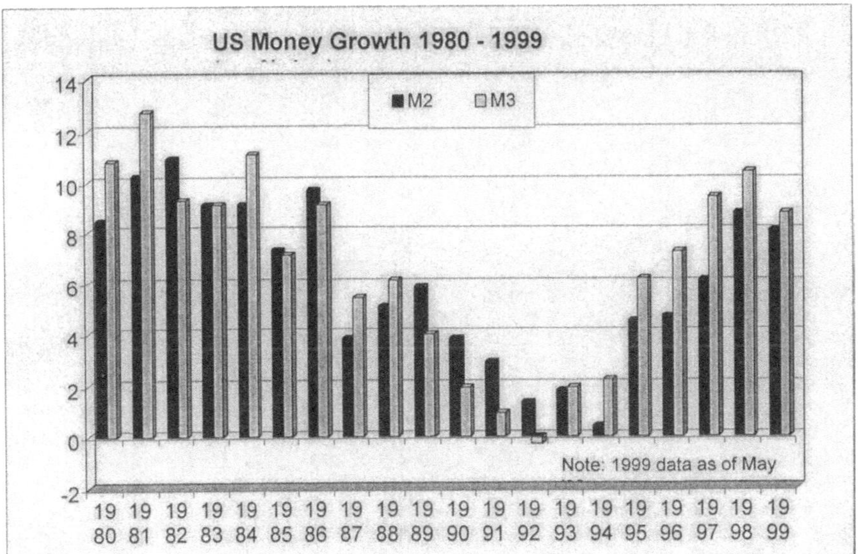

Chart 5

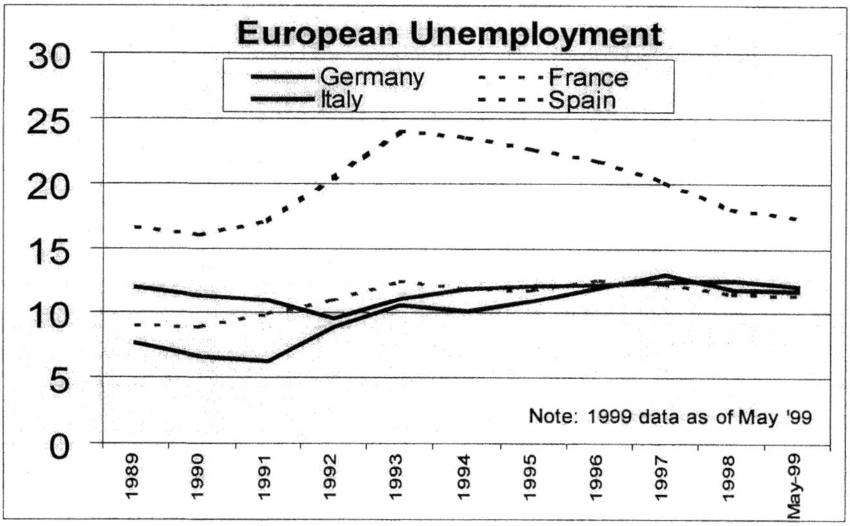
European Unemployment
30
25
20
15
10
5
0
Germany
Italy
France
Spain
Note: 1999 data as of May '99
1989
1990
1991
1992
1993
1994
1995
1996
1997
1998
May-99

Discussion of David I. Fand's "Are we facing a stock market bubble?"

Hans Wiesmeth

Dresden University of Technology, D-01062 Dresden, Germany

1 Introduction

Substantial idle capacities in Europe, Japan, Southeast Asia and Latin America add significantly towards generating an elastic augmented supply for America. As a consequence of this hypothesis of a Keynesian global economy, an increase in American aggregate demand will lead to an increase in the U.S. trade deficit but not necessarily to any rise in U.S. prices as measured by the CPI, the PPI or the ECI. There is, however, strong evidence that the extremely rapid money growth has led to substantial increases in the prices of equities, real estate and non-tradables. But the absence of inflation in the U.S. tends to handcuff the Fed since the chairman finds it difficult to restrict the accelerating growth of money supply in this rather extraordinary situation. Consequently, market professionals are liberated to borrow and leverage their portfolio positions, and equity prices continue to rise.

This is, in short, the main line of arguments applied by David I. Fand (1999) to explain the absence of inflation in the U.S. on the one hand and the explosion of asset prices on the other, even though the U.S. economy is already in its ninth year of recovery.

The central idea of a Keynesian global economy is interesting in itself and certainly contributes towards an explanation of this surprisingly long-lasting boom on the stock markets in the U.S. Meanwhile the Fed has raised interest rates as a reaction on the development on the labour markets and in view of the strong monetary growth. The higher interest rates as well as the continuing „tightening bias" emphasized by the FOMC, has led to a slight decrease in equity prices without, however, ending in a dramatic burst of the stock market bubble, at least for the moment.

Thus, although the Fed seems to be less „handcuffed" as before, the concept of a Keynesian global economy is still attractive. It deserves some comments, which perhaps allow a more thorough understanding of the current economic situation primarily in Europe, Japan, and the U.S. The hypothesis of a Keynesian global economy is certainly more convincing than the views of the New Paradigm analysts, who point to rapid technological changes, globalization and restructuring in recent years as the origin of this remarkable boom in equities.

2 The Keynesian global economy

The model of David I. Fand (1999) is based on the hypothesis of a „Keynesian global economy", emerging from the large idle capacities in the global economy outside America. As a consequence, the aggregate supply curve facing the U.S. from the rest of the world is assumed to be almost infinitely elastic. Thus, the aggregate supply curve for Europe, Japan, Southeast Asia and Latin America should be perfectly elastic, too. In conclusion, there should be a Keynesian unemployment in all or most of these parts of the world. Some empirical facts, however, do not fully support this theoretical consequence.

- If there was a typical Keynesian situation for Europe, then there should be one for Germany as well. Indeed, Fand (1999) emphasizes the role Chancellor Kohl played „in igniting the stock market boom". Idle capacities characterize vast parts of the German economy and, in particular, unemployment of labour has been in the two digit area almost always since the last five or six years. A similar development characterizes the economic situation in other member states of the European Union.

There is, however, no doubt that many economists hold institutional inflexibilities on the labour market and wage rigidities responsible for this persistent unemployment rather than the fiscal restraints associated with the Maastricht agreement. Therefore, many economists deny the possibility of a typical Keynesian unemployment for Germany. In fact, right now the German government is eager to cut public spending with the goal to reduce the public deficit. This is certainly not the textbook method to handle a Keynesian unemployment. Similar observations hold both for Japan and for Southeast Asia.

- There was, over the last few years, no extraordinary increase in German exports. In fact, German exports declined from the last quarter of 1998 to the first quarter of 1999. Only since the last few months, German exports seem to rise at a faster pace. In August 1999 German exports into the member states of the European Union were 15 % above the exports in August 1998, whereas exports into other countries were 0.9 % below those a year ago. Again, a similar development is true for most parts of Europe, for Southeast Asia in general, and Japan in particular. Thus, there is no clear evidence that the American trade deficit is linked to exceptionally soaring export markets in the rest of the world. In particular, Japanese exports have been down over the last few years due to the financial crisis in East and Southeast Asia.

As a consequence, it is not really clear, whether the economic situation in Europe and in other parts of the world contributed substantially towards a perfectly elastic aggregate supply curve in America. At least the degree of this effect is probably less than it had to be in order to generate the situation described above.

The growing unemployment in Germany and elsewhere in Europe in the post-Maastricht period supports this view.

Hence, there is a need for a slightly different, more precise explanation of the recent economic development in order to accommodate these observations.

A promising alternative approach makes use of on an idea, proposed by Donald R. Davis (1998). In his paper Davis develops a „global" approach in a general equilibrium context with free trade, which allows for a simultaneous determination of factor prices in the two countries „America" and „Europe". Institutional differences in factor markets can then be incorporated into the analysis and their consequences thoroughly investigated. Davis considers institutional characteristics of national labour markets and starts out with flexible wages in America and, for simplicity, fixed wages in Europe. The model, of Heckscher-Ohlin-type, then yields interesting and even surprising results, relevant for the problem at hand.

- If the fixed minimum wage rate in Europe is above the equilibrium wage rate, then unemployment results in autarky. However, if America and Europe are assumed to be comparable in economic size and structure, unemployment in Europe will typically increase with free trade. Flexible wages in America prevent unemployment there, whereas European workers have to bear the burden of high unemployment to maintain not only their own high wage but that in America as well.
- Free trade with Europe will carry over the high European wage rates to America, if factor prize equalization holds.[1] Moreover, modest shifts in import demand from the U.S. will not affect relative prices of the traded commodities. Free trade thus links the goods prices, whereas the extent of trade between America and Europe is not that important.

What can we learn from this alternative approach for the hypothesis of a Keynesian global economy? Well, Davis' model is based on minimum wages in Europe. The justification for this assumption is that the stronger European unions make wage rates in Europe more rigid in comparison to those in America. Assume that unions respond to a decreasing unemployment, resulting from an increase in public spending or any other expansionary fiscal measures, with higher wage rates. Then the economic situation is, as mentioned above, not of a typical Keynesian unemployment, at least not, if the governments are aware of these interdependencies.[2]

But exactly this seems to be the case in Germany and elsewhere in Europe. As a result, governments in the European Union and also in Japan are hesitating to ini-

[1] Factor price equalization in the strict sense of the Heckscher-Ohlin model is certainly not necessary to obtain the required results. Wage rates in America should, however, be linked to those in Europe.

[2] This is, of course, a highly simplified presentation of the actual situation. In reality the arguments applied on both sides of the labour markets are much more sophisticated and refer to aspects of international competitiveness as well as to distributional justice and consequences for the purchasing power.

tiate expansionary fiscal policies in the current economic situation. There are, however, continuing efforts to reduce institutional rigidities on the labour markets and wage rigidities in these countries. Thus, Davis' approach seems to model relevant institutional characteristics of European and American labour markets. More importantly, however, this approach allows an explanation of the fact that, over the last few years, there has been no significant upward pressure on the wages, neither in Europe nor in Japan. We therefore arrive at a Keynesian situation in Europe and in Japan, which, however, cannot be dealt with in the „classical" Keynesian way.

Moreover, Davis' results show that institutional characteristics of purely local labour markets can be „transferred" via free trade in commodities to the other countries. The necessary link to the global markets is provided by factor price equalization and the goods prices. If there are no other global developments affecting e.g. the exchange rates, then the „stable" situation on the European and Japanese labour and commodity markets, characterized by the absence of inflation, transfers itself to the American labour and commodity markets. The extent of the trade between America and Europe and Japan is not that important. Important is only the fact that there is the possibility of free trade.

3 Conclusion

David I. Fand (1999) presents an interesting explanation for the current development on equity markets in the U.S. His model is based on the hypothesis of a Keynesian global economy. Some clarifying comments help to make this hypothesis compatible with empirical facts. A closer look at the actual economic situation in most parts of Europe and in Japan reveals indeed a Keynesian situation, to which governments do not and cannot react in the standard textbook manner.

The model of Douglas R. Davis (1998) demonstrates that rigid wages in Europe and other parts of the world may be „transferred" to America by free trade. The extent of the international trade is less important than the fact that there is the possibility of trade. Together with the absence of effects influencing the exchange rates, price stability in Europe is also „exported" to America.

The rest of Fand's story remains the same, although the handcuffs keeping the Fed away from discrete monetary policies are meanwhile taken off.

References

Davis, D.R. (1998), „Does European Unemployment Prop Up American Wages? National Labor Markets and Global Trade", American Economic Review, Vol. 88, No. 3, p. 78-494.

Fand, D.I. (1999), „Are we Facing a Stock Market Bubble?", Discussion Paper, George Mason University.

What explains the Asian balance of payments crisis? – A simple third-generation approach

Michael Frenkel

WHU Koblenz, Otto-Beisheim-Hochschule, Burgplatz 2, D-56179 Vallendar, Germany

1 Introduction

In 1997, the previously existing enthusiasm of investors for Asia was dramatically shaken by the occurrence and persistence of currency and banking crises. The series of crises initially started with speculative attacks on the Thai baht which, in July 1997, forced the authorities to abandon the fixed exchange rate system versus the US dollar. The crisis soon spread to other countries of the region and seriously afflicted South Korea, Indonesia, the Philippines, and Malaysia, too. Only days after the speculative attack on the Thai baht occurred, speculative attacks forced both the Philippine and the Indonesian central bank to give up the fixed parity against the US dollar and introduce a float. The values of the Malaysian ringgit and the Korean won also fell sharply in international markets. In addition, the banking crises forced the authorities in Thailand and Indonesia to close a number of financial institutions. Other countries like Hong Kong, Singapore, Vietnam, Taiwan, and China were indirectly affected because they suffered a significant deterioration of their competitiveness against the more seriously hit countries whose currencies depreciated.

In basically the whole region, the crises included sizable declines in equity prices and a series of closures of financial institutions. Although governments introduced policy packages, which were partly developed in coordination with the IMF, they had to realize that investors' confidence was difficult to restore. The continuing speculative attacks on the currencies of the most seriously affected countries led to a general revision of economic prospects in Asia and an increased awareness of the vulnerability of many emerging economies to seemingly unforeseeable shocks.

Both banking crises and currency crises are not new phenomena but have emanated in other parts of the world before. More recent examples are provided by the crises in the European Monetary System in 1992 and 1993, and by the crises in Latin America following the Mexican crisis in 1994. The Asian crisis was not the last crisis either as the Russian crisis in 1998 and the Brazilian crisis in 1999 demonstrated. However, the earlier crises already inspired a wide research on the explanation of the reasons and the timing of speculative attacks as well as on the development of an early warning system for such crises.

The Asian crisis triggered a debate about which type of model best explains the empirical evidence of the countries in this region prior to and during the crisis. This paper reviews different approaches and presents an alternative model for the Asian balance of payments crisis. The rest of the paper is structured as follows: Section 2 reviews the contribution of the first-generation models and the second-generation models for the explanation of balance of payment crises. Section 3 examines how well these models explain the East Asian crises. Section 4 highlights important features of the East Asian crises. Section 5 presents a simple new model of balance of payments crisis. Section 6 investigates the dynamics of key economic variables in the new approach and compares the results with the East Asian developments around the crises. A summary and several conclusions are given in section 7.

2 Explanation of currency crises by first-generation models and second-generation models

Among the formal analyses of exchange market and banking crises, two approaches have dominated the academic discussion. They are referred to as first-generation and second-generation models.[1] Given their dominance in the literature the question arises whether they are able to explain developments in Asia.

First-generation models are based on the seminal paper of Krugman (1979) and the extension of the approach by Flood and Garber (1984). The framework of these papers develops ideas initially put forward by Hotelling (1931) in the context of government buffer stocks of commodities and by Salant and Henderson (1978) in the context of gold stocks. Krugman's approach sees an inconsistency between a fixed exchange rate and expansionary fiscal policy financed by an increase in money supply at the origin of the balance of payments crisis. Money-financed and persistent fiscal deficits thus lead higher absorption relative to production and a deterioration of the current account. The resulting balance of payments deficit steadily decreases the foreign exchange reserves of the central bank. Once reserves reach a critical threshold, a balance of payments crisis develops during which private agents attack the remaining reserves. When the reserves are exhausted, the central bank is forced to abandon the fixed exchange rate and to adopt a floating rate. If the central bank wants to re-peg the exchange rate later, it first has to accumulate foreign exchange reserves in order to defend the new peg.

The basic framework of Krugman (1979) as well as of Flood and Garber (1984) has been extended by a number of papers which modified several simplifying assumptions of the first models. These extensions include analyses which deal with

[1] The distinction between "first-generation models" and "second-generation models" was first used by Eichengreen et al. (1996).

alternative post-collapse regimes, imperfect asset substitutability, real sector effects, uncertainty about the minimum reserve level, and the question of the appropriate policy response.[2]

There are at least two important conclusions to be drawn from first-generation models. First, the models show that continuing policy inconsistencies together with complete anticipation of the policy effects by rational agents can lead to abrupt changes in the foreign exchange reserves and trigger a crisis which quickly leads to the breakdown of the exchange rate system. In addition, the collapse of the system occurs before the minimum reserve level is reached. However, no major changes in fundamentals occur immediately before the crisis. Second, first-generation models suggest that macroeconomic fundamentals determine the crises. According to this class of models, a currency crisis is preceded by steadily declining reserves, rapid increase in domestic credit, relatively high fiscal deficits, a real appreciation of the currency, and a deterioration of trade and the current account.

Second-generation models of balance of payments crises are more complex. Obstfeld (1994, 1996), Ozkan and Sutherland (1995), and Masson (1995) focus on optimizing governments which choose whether or not to stick to a fixed exchange rate or switch to a float. While the first policy offers credibility in the long run, the latter policy provides more flexibility with respect to achieving certain policy objectives. In this case, a switch to a float arises if a speculative attack on the domestic currency occurs and market participants believe that the peg can ultimately not be defended. Then, the central bank finds it too costly to stick to a fixed exchange rate regime given that it would require, for example, a drastic loss of reserves and high interest rates, which exert negative real effects on growth and an additional burden on the budget in case of high government debt. Since the government chooses to opt out of the fixed exchange regime, these approaches are sometimes referred to as escape clause models. Under the circumstances described, a speculative attack can be triggered either by an abrupt worsening of expectations or by self-fulfilling speculation. If successful, the attack leads to a sudden change in fundamentals.[3] Since agents do not know the preferences of the central bank or, more generally, the government, they may test the peg leading to reoccurring attacks. The fundamentals crucial for the success of a speculative attack are the macroeconomic variables that influence the temptation of the government to escape the peg. Some of the models as the ones put forward by Ozkan and Sutherland (1995) and Masson (1995) emphasize adverse economic develop-

---

[2] For a review of the first-generation models of balance of payments crises see Agénor et al. (1992) and the comprehensive survey of Flood and Marion (1998).

[3] Several studies show that changes in expectations played a crucial role in the development of balance of payments crises. For example, Calvo and Mendoza (1995) and Cole and Kehoe (1996) show that the response of private agents' expectations to the increase in the governments's short-term debt contributed to the Mexican crisis in 1994.

ments as the reason of the attack, while others emphasize self-fulfilling prophesies as a possible cause (see, for example, Obstfeld 1994, 1996).

Another feature of second-generation models is the existence of multiple equilibria. The latter exist if, for example, one equilibrium of the system is consistent with current fundamentals and another equilibrium resulting from a different set of fundamentals expected to prevail after a successful attack is incompatible with a fixed exchange rate regime. Therefore, the developments of fundamentals depend on whether the market expects the government to prefer a float if the currency is attacked or defend the peg. If agents expect the attack to be successful they anticipate the development of fundamentals of the alternative equilibrium and thereby induce the crisis. The first model in this direction was developed by Obstfeld (1986). A significant characteristic of this approach and the models based on these arguments is that no clear correlation between the development of fundamentals and a balance of payments crisis shows up in the data.

The important lesson of the second-generation models is that fundamentals which appear to be consistent with a fixed exchange rate may not be sufficient to avoid speculative attacks. An additional requirement is that the central bank has enough credibility for agents to exclude the possibility of success for any attack on the exchange regime.

Despite the large number of papers on variations of first-generation and second-generation models, there can be doubts as to how much they can really explain the dramatic crisis in East Asia in 1997.[4] Therefore, the next section examines whether the arguments of the models surveyed above are consistent with the stylized facts of the most seriously hit countries in the East Asian crisis.

3 How well do traditional models explain the stylized facts of the East Asian crisis?

In particular first-generation models suggest that macroeconomic fundamentals indicate the occurrence of a currency crisis or at least the possibility that such crises could arise. We focus here on the five seriously afflicted countries in East Asia, i.e., Thailand, Indonesia, the Philippines, Malaysia, and Korea. Although we only examine the stylized facts, we show that this allows us to draw some general answers to the question of this section.

[4] A number of papers study the empirical evidence on the models reviewed in this section for currency crises before the East Asian crisis. The general impression is that the evidence on the determinants of speculative attacks as suggested by these models is mixed. Sachs et al. (1996) and Eichengreen et al. (1996) present comprehensive empirical studies. Eichengreen et al. (1996) also provide a survey on the empirical work on speculative attacks and contagion.

Figure 1 Gross foreign exchange reserves in selected Asian economies
(in billions of US$)

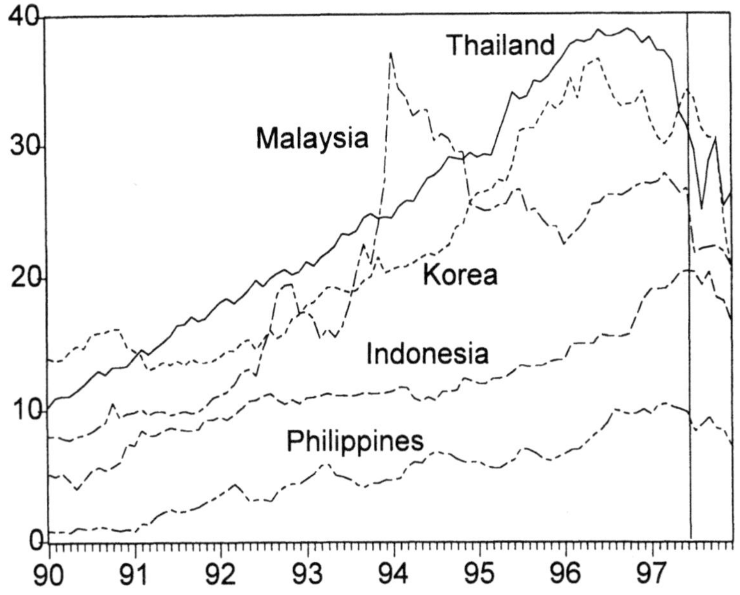

The vertical line shows the beginning of the currency crisis in Thailand.
Source: International Monetary Fund (1999).

None of these five countries exhibited declining reserves of the central bank before the crisis. Figure 1 shows the development of gross reserves of these countries expressed in US dollars for the period 1993-1997. In all of the five countries, there was a general increasing trend. This trend was rather steady in Indonesia and the Philippines, although their level was relatively small. A continuous increase in reserves occurred also in Thailand before end-1996 and in Korea before early 1996. Malaysia's reserves were more fluctuating over the period but were more than 60 percent higher at the time of the beginning of the crisis in Thailand compared to early 1993. In Figure 1, the vertical line shows the beginning of the speculative attack on the Thai baht in July 1997. Thus, reserve developments did not indicate the occurrence of a crisis.

Excessively expansionary monetary policy was not pursued in the East Asian economies, either. To examine the stance of the monetary policy we plot the ratio of money and reserves in Figure 2.

Figure 2 Ratio of money to reserves in selected Asian economies

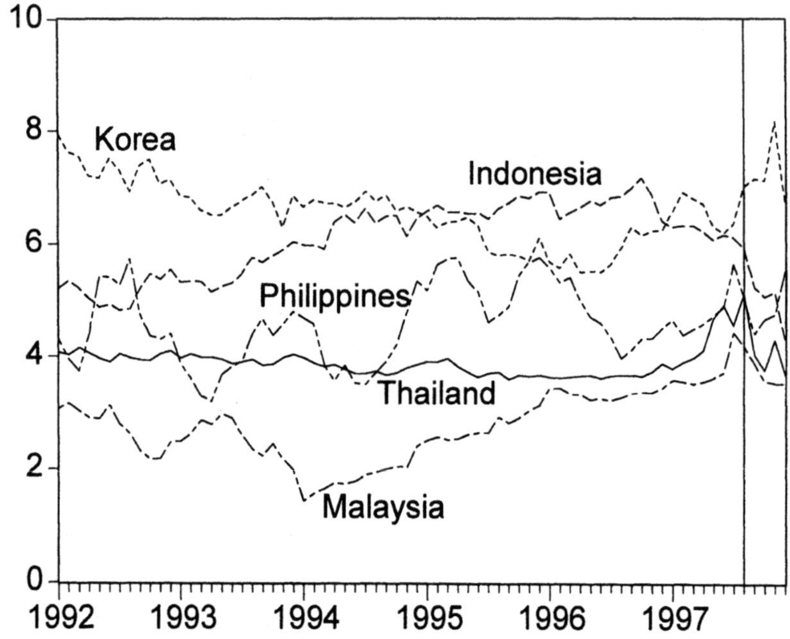

The vertical line shows the beginning of the currency crisis in Thailand.
Source: International Monetary Fund (1999).

In a fixed exchange rate system, overly expansionary monetary policy, which is brought about by an increase in domestic credit, can be expected to lead to an increase in money relative to reserves. The data for all five crises economies in East Asia do not indicate such a policy stance. On the contrary, while this ratio virtually remained unchanged in Thailand in several years preceding the crisis, it even declined in Korea. This can explain why inflation was quite low and stable in these countries during the period examined here. Thus, we conclude that monetary policy did not appear to be in conflict with the exchange rate system in any of the five countries.

The five Asian economies examined here experienced also strong and sustained growth over the four years before 1997. As shown in the first part of Table 1, real GDP grew by on average eight percent in Indonesia, Korea, Malaysia, and Thailand, while it averaged about five percent in the Philippines. As a result, there was also no substantial unemployment immediately before the crises. This suggests that GDP growth did not signal any arising balance of payments crisis. The decline in growth shown for 1997 already reflects the effect of the crisis on economic activity.

The middle of Table 1 shows that fiscal balances expressed as a ratio of GDP did not show high deficits during the years before the crisis. In Indonesia, Malaysia, and Thailand the general government finances had even been in surplus for several years. Thus, fiscal policy was also not incompatible with the exchange rate system.

Table 1 Real GDP and current account of selected Asian economies

	1993	1994	1995	1996	1997
			Growth of Real GDP in %		
Indonesia	7.3	7.5	8.2	8.0	5.0
Korea	5.8	8.6	8.9	7.1	6.0
Malaysia	8.3	9.2	9.5	8.6	7.0
Philippines	2.1	4.4	4.8	5.7	4.3
Thailand	8.5	8.9	8.7	6.4	0.6
			Government Budget Balance in % of GDP		
Indonesia	-0.7	-	0.8	1.4	2.0
Korea	-1.0	1.0	-	-	-
Malaysia	-2.6	2.5	3.8	4.2	1.6
Philippines	-1.6	-1.6	-1.4	-0.4	-0.9
Thailand	2.1	2.0	2.6	1.6	-0.4
			Current Account in % of GDP		
Indonesia	-1.5	-1.7	-3.3	-3.3	-2.9
Korea	0.1	-1.2	-2.0	-4.9	-2.9
Malaysia	-4.8	-7.8	-10.0	-4.9	-5.8
Philippines	-5.5	-4.5	-4.4	-4.7	-4.5
Thailand	-5.0	-5.6	-8.0	-7.9	-3.9

Source: International Monetary Fund (1999).

First-generation models imply that the current account can be expected to worsen before the crisis, reflecting the excessively expansionary monetary and/or fiscal policy. The data on the current account balance as a percentage of GDP (lower section of Table 1) indicates that there was some deterioration of the current account in all five countries and the current account deficit was also quite sizable by international comparison. However, in 1996, the year preceding the crisis, the current account ratio declined in Malaysia and stayed nearly unchanged in Indonesia, the Philippines, and Thailand. In Korea, where a significant increase in the current account deficit occurred in 1996, the new level was only as high as in Malaysia and the Philippines.

Figure 3 Development of real exchange rates of selected Asian economies (1990=100)

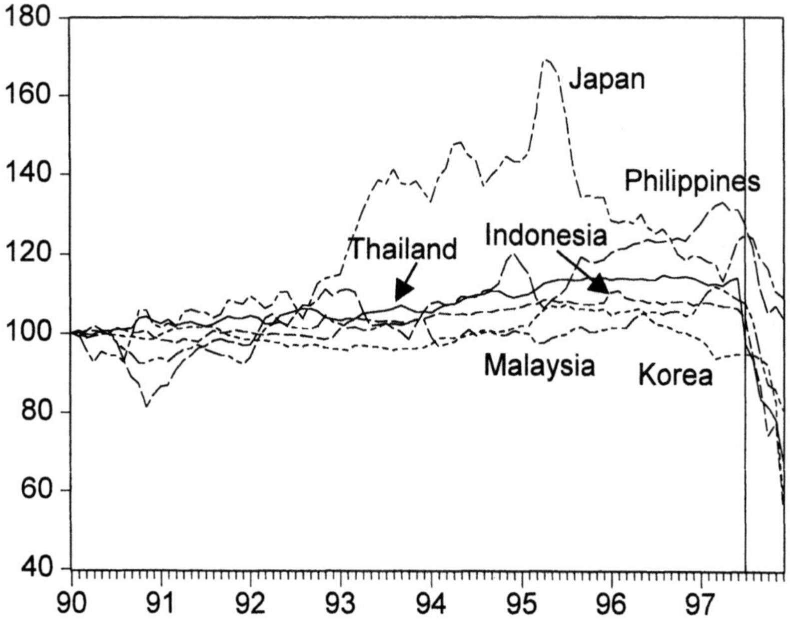

* A reduction indicates a depreciation; the vertical line shows the beginning of the currency crisis in Thailand. For Malaysia, Japan, and the Philippines the lines show the real effective exchange rate. For Korea, Thailand, and Indonesia no data on real effective exchange rates were available; therefore, the lines show real bilateral exchange rate versus US$.
Source: International Monetary Fund (1999)

First-generation models also imply that a real appreciation could precede speculative attacks on currencies. A real appreciation implies a loss of competitiveness which, in turn, leads to a deterioration of the current account and a decline in reserves so that the risk of a speculative attack rises. Figure 3 shows the real effective exchange rate of Malaysia, the Philippines, and Japan as well as the bilateral real exchange rate versus the dollar of the currencies of Thailand, Indonesia, and Korea. The vertical line indicates again the beginning of the crisis in Thailand.

Figure 3 indicates that the Philippines experienced some real appreciation during the two years before the East Asian crisis, while the currencies of the other four afflicted countries show relatively flat curves. However, there is a caveat, at least for the time series of the Thai baht, the Korean won, and the Indonesian rupiah. As they only exhibit the bilateral real exchange rate versus the dollar, their curves do not show that, by pegging to the dollar, the real exchange rate versus a strong competitor like Japan may have changed. For this reason, Figure 3 also illustrates real exchange rate developments for the Japanese yen. Since the yen depreciated since early 1995, the East Asian countries, while pegging to the US dollar, which appreciated against major currencies between 1995 and 1997, experienced some real appreciation against the Japanese yen.

In sum, in early 1997 the fundamentals stressed by the first-generation models of balance of payments crises hardly indicated the possibility of a near crisis. There were basically no indications of a policy conflict, which is at the heart of the first-generation models. Only the current account deterioration was in line with this class of models. However, as explained above, the development of the current account was far from being an alarm signal for a crisis of the kind these countries experienced later.

With respect to second-generation models, the causes are more difficult to see in the data because, for example, a change in expectations cannot be observed directly. However, with respect to the incentives of the government to opt out of a peg, it can be stated that there were no signs of such a consideration. Possible candidates for macroeconomic variables that could indicate the degree of temptation of the government to opt out and pursue more expansionary policies thereafter are the public debt level, the debt service on the government debt, and the unemployment rate. Neither the public debt and the debt burden on it nor the unemployment rate were at a level at which such an assumption could have been warranted.

We conclude that traditional models of balance of payments crises contribute relatively little to the explanation of why the crisis in East Asia occurred. After the beginning of the crisis, some observers of East Asia stated that the current account deficits, together with a relatively rigid peg to the US dollar in face of a considerable depreciation of the Japanese yen, were the causes of the crisis. However, our discussion suggests that it is difficult to believe that this can indeed fully explain the East Asian crisis. The developments of the main macroeconomic fundamentals were, in principle, not at odds with the fixed exchange rate regime. Therefore, given the fact that these models served quite well in explaining other currency crises, at least part of the reasons for the East Asian crisis was apparently very different from the standard crisis story.

4 The fundamentally different causes of the East Asian balance of payments crises

To derive a more comprehensive explanation for the East Asian crisis it is necessary to look beyond the traditional macroeconomic fundamentals. This involves a closer investigation of international capital flows and their usages. During the period between 1993 and mid-1997, a main characteristic of all afflicted East Asian economies was the high and increasing net private capital inflow from foreign banks to domestic financial intermediaries. These capital flows were largely of short-term nature. Table 2 includes data on net private capital flows into Thailand, the Philippines, Indonesia, Malaysia, and South Korea. The data are shown as a percentage of GDP in order to take into account the size of the economies. During at least the three years preceding the crisis, there was a growing capital inflow into these economies reaching a level of about five to ten percent of GDP in 1996. As capital flew primarily to financial institutions in East Asia, liabilities of the banking system of these economies increased steadily over the 1990s.

As a result of high and continuing net capital inflows, liabilities of financial institutions of the East Asian countries vis-à-vis foreign banks increased significantly in the mid 1990s. As Figure 4 shows, the increase was particularly pronounced during the immediate period before the crisis occurred. The capital inflow to East Asian countries was supported by a liberalization of domestic financial markets over the years. However, the liberalization was not accompanied by an appropriate regulatory systems for banking. In addition, a large share of the high capital inflows had maturities below one year. This share reached more than 60 percent in 1996.

What caused the high capital inflows into the East Asian economies? One reason was a relatively attractive interest rate level compared to, for example, the markets for dollar and yen assets. Another reason was the belief of international lenders that the peg to the US dollar in most of these countries would continue and no exchange rate risk would exist. Such expectations were supported by the governments' assurance that the peg would not be changed. An additional reason can be seen in the low risk associated with lending to East Asian countries. This was the result of a number of statements of central banks and governments which implicitly suggested that financial institutions were not only sound but they could also rely on the support by the government if necessary. Such implicit guarantees drove a wedge between private and social costs of bank loans and gave rise to a moral hazard problem. Risky lending with chances of a high return were preferred over cautious projects, because an implicit insurance generates the assumption on the part of the lender that the downside risk was basically the same for all loans.

A consequence of the high short-term external financing was a maturity and currency mismatch of assets and liabilities. This made the economies particularly vulnerable to an abrupt reversal of capital flows and, thus, to currency crises.

The use of the funds borrowed in international market played a major role in the development of the crisis. The regulatory weakness of the financial system led to a situation in which lending institutions did not base their decisions on how the proceeds of the loans were used. Together with implicit government guarantees and the moral hazard problem, this resulted in incentives for over-investment in risky assets and induced price bubbles in asset markets. Thus, the capital inflow was used to a large extent to finance investments in real estate and in equity shares. Such investments were facilitated by liberalization measures which were put in place during the 1990s in several East Asian countries and which also included the reduction of restrictions on lending to real estate. As a consequence, asset prices rose dramatically in the years preceding the crises. The unprecedented equity and real estate boom in all afflicted economies were fueled by an expectation of continued export boom and growth.

Table 2 Net private capital inflows of selected Asian economies (in % of GDP)[1]

	1991	1992	1993	1994	1995	1996	1997
Indonesia	4.6	2.5	3.1	3.9	6.2	6.3	1.6
Korea	2.2	2.4	1.6	3.1	3.9	4.9	2.8
Malaysia	11.2	15.1	17.4	1.5	8.8	9.6	4.7
Philippines	1.6	2.0	2.6	5.0	4.6	9.8	0.5
Thailand	10.7	8.7	8.4	8.6	12.7	9.3	-10.9

[1] Net capital inflows comprise net direct investments, net portfolio investment and other long-term and short-term net investments.
Source: International Monetary Fund (1997).

Figure 4 Liabilities vis-a-vis foreign banks (in billions of US$)

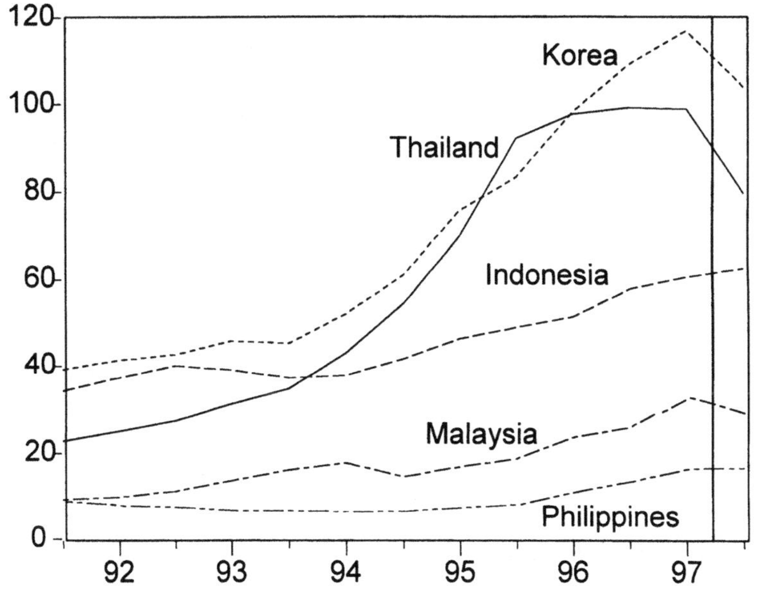

Source: Bank for International Settlement, International Banking and Financial Market Developments, various issues.

The microeconomic structures made these economies particularly vulnerable to currency crises. A small change in expectations with the consequence of a swing in capital flows would have been able to put the fixed exchange rate system under heavy pressure. This was ultimately the case, when there were the first indications of a slowdown in exports and growth. The reasons for the slowdown in exports included the recessions in Japan and Europe in the mid-1990s and the appreciation of the dollar to which the East Asian countries pegged their currencies. When expectations about future export and growth performance changed, international investors reconsidered their exposure. As a consequence, they sharply increased the risk premia on East Asian investment and started to pull their funds out of the region. This ultimately triggered the banking and currency crises and led to the bursting of the price bubbles of real and financial assets. For the five economies studied here, the swing in capital movements amounted to more than US$100 billion or about 10 percent of GDP in 1997.

In sum, the main problems of the seriously affected East Asian economies included insufficient financial regulation of the banking system and implicit government guarantees for financial institutions, the combination of which induced a maturity mismatch of assets and liabilities. These problems did not occur because the governments of the East Asian countries interfered too much, but because they did not do enough. The elimination of financial market restrictions was not supported by an appropriate regulatory framework. As Sachs et al. (1996) point out, the weaknesses of the banking system typically do not surface until massive capital outflows occur. The awareness of similar structural problems in other East Asian countries caused a spreading of the crisis from Thailand to other countries of the region. The turmoil alerted market participants that the connections between individual markets had become more complex.

The combination of balance of payments crises and banking crises is not a new phenomenon. It has already been observed for several Latin American countries. For example, Kaminsky et al. (1998) find in their study of 20 countries in Asia, Europe, Latin America, and the Middle East that banking crises often precede currency crisis but that the reverse sequence hardly ever occurs. The reasons of the crisis in East Asia as outlined in this section also suggest that the banking crisis was at the origin of the currency crisis. Krugman (1998) even argued that the currency crisis was merely a symptom of the banking crisis. In the following section we present a model of balance of payments crises which takes into account crucial features of the described capital flows to East Asia.

5 A simple model of a new type of balance of payments crisis

The turmoil in East Asia induced a rethinking about the models of balance of payments crises and has led to a new type of approach which emphasizes the role of government guarantees in the evolution of a crisis. This approach is referred to as the third-generation model of balance of payments crises. Dooley (1997) uses insurance arguments and without using a formal model argues that government guarantees lead to a period of capital inflows is followed by a speculative attack on the reserves of the central bank. However, Dooley's core argument was completely informal. Krugman (1998) uses a similar argument and models implicit government guarantees leading to moral hazard problems and, thereby, to over-investment. In his model of so-called "Pangloss over-investment", a self-fulfilling financial crisis occurs, in which the drop of asset prices leads to the insolvency of banks and thereby further asset price plunges. The banking crisis is then followed by a currency crisis. Irwin and Vines (1999) develop a model in which guarantees induce higher capital accumulation and growth, but also multiple short-run equilibria with the result that a balance of payments crisis is possible. In this section, we start from Dooley's arguments and develop a formal model with implicit government guarantees on international capital flows. In this simple third-generation model of balance of payments crises sizable capital inflows precede the crisis although private agents fully anticipate the breakdown of the fixed exchange rate system.

We focus on a small open economy and assume that there are no restrictions on international trade and capital flows. The domestic economy and the rest of the world produce the same composite good. In addition, in order to focus on capital flows, we assume full price flexibility in the goods and the labor market resulting in permanent full employment. The domestic economy also has a fixed exchange rate vis-à-vis the rest of the world. The formal model consists of seven equations:

$$M_t / P_t = \alpha Y_t - \beta i_t; \qquad \alpha, \beta > 0 \tag{1}$$

$$\mathrm{M_t} = \mathrm{D_t} + \mathrm{R_t^g} \tag{2}$$

$$\dot{D}_t = \mu D_t; \qquad \mu \geq 0 \tag{3}$$

$$\mathrm{P_t} = \mathrm{s_t} \tag{4}$$

$$\dot{L}_t = \eta_t (z_t)\, L_t \tag{5}$$

$$F_t = \tau L_t; \qquad \tau \geq 0 \tag{6}$$

$$i_t = i_t^* + E_t(\dot{s}/s) + \rho_t + z_t; \qquad \rho \geq 0 \tag{7}$$

All values are in domestic currency. Equation (1) represents a traditional money market equilibrium condition. Here, M, P, Y, and i denote nominal money supply, the price level, income, and the interest rate, respectively. Real money demand increases with income and declines with the interest rate with α and ß representing the reaction coefficients. Equation (2) is the definition of the nominal money supply, which comprises the domestic credit D and reserves R. For the subsequent analysis, we distinguish between gross and net official international reserves.

Gross reserves are denoted by the superscript "g" to the variable R and represent the assets of the central bank in foreign exchange. Subtracting from the central bank's foreign exchange assets the foreign exchange liabilities yields net reserves of the central bank. Equation (3) describes the development of domestic credit - with μ denoting the growth rate.

Equation (4) is the purchasing power parity. Normalizing the foreign price level to unity, the domestic price level is equal to the spot exchange rate s. Equation (5) shows the developments of capital imports of foreign investors and thus the foreign liabilities of the domestic economy denoted by L. The growth rate of capital inflows from abroad is 0 and depends on the additional yield z offered to foreign investors given exchange rate expectations and risk considerations. For simplicity, we assume that the yield advantage of domestic assets for foreign investors is exogenous. To treat the additional yield as an endogenous variable would be more satisfying in a model, but would not have significant implications for the qualitative results of the model. The higher the additional yield of domestic assets compared to foreign assets is, the higher is the increase in capital imports. Treating capital adjustment in terms of flows implies the assumption of adjustment lags in international portfolios. In addition, additional savings could be the basis of capital flows. An additional simplification is the assumption that capital inflows result in no immediate reserve changes. This implies that the central bank does not intervene but capital flows offset current account deficits.

Equation (6) shows the amount of foreign exchange reserves F which represents the collateral for implicit guarantees of the central bank for capital inflows. Implicit guarantees could be signaled, for example, by official statements that the banking system is solid and will be supported by the authorities should any crisis emerge. How clearly a government expresses this support and, thereby, the guarantees, can differ widely. In the case of Korea, most observers felt that the government was very vocal about the intention to help banks if they encountered serious financial difficulties. This suggests that investors could rely more or less on some bail out. We assume in our model that markets assume a guarantee ratio of τ so that portfolio decisions are not based on full guarantees. However, guarantees are credible only if the central bank has reserves to back them up. This signals to international investors the ability of the authorities to pay for the liabilities of domestic financial institutions with foreign exchange. Note that implicit guarantees can be assumed to be a function of the supervision of financial markets. It can be expected that τ is higher in financial markets with weak regulation.

The model is closed by the modified interest rate parity condition (7). The domestic interest rate exceeds the foreign yield i^* by the sum of the expected exchange rate change, the risk premium Δ, and the additional yield component z.

To derive an expression for the evolution of gross foreign exchange reserves of the central bank, we use equations (4) and (7) in equation (1) and get

$$\frac{M_t}{s_t} = \alpha Y_t - \beta i^* - \beta E_t(\dot{s}/s) - \beta \rho_t - \beta z_t .$$

Setting $dY_t - ßi^* = \delta$ reduces the previous expression to

$$\frac{M_t}{s_t} = \delta - \beta E_t(\dot{s}/s) - \beta\rho_t - \beta z_t. \tag{8}$$

This shows that the real money supply accommodates each change in the money demand. Ultimately, this is achieved by exchange rate flexibility. Replacing the definition of money supply in equation (2) by equation (8) yields the following expression for the level of gross reserves

$$R_t^g = s\delta - s\beta E_t(\dot{s}/s) - s\beta\rho_t - s\beta z_t - D_t. \tag{9}$$

Assuming a credible exchange rate fix, we use $E_t(\dot{s}/s)=0$ in equation (9) and get

$$R_t^g = \bar{s}\delta - \bar{s}\beta\rho_t - \bar{s}\beta z_t - D_t. \tag{10}$$

The dynamic version of equation (10) gives the development of gross reserves over time as

$$\dot{R}_t^g = -\dot{D}_t - \bar{s}\beta[\dot{\rho}_t + \dot{z}_t]$$

Assuming that the risk premium and the additional yield component of domestic assets do not change as long as the exchange rate is fixed $(\dot{\rho}_t = \dot{z}_t = 0)$ this expressions simplifies to

$$\dot{R}_t^g = -\dot{D}_t = -\mu D_t. \tag{11}$$

This shows that gross reserves, given a certain level of risk premium, decline as money supply grows due to an increase in domestic credit.

We now turn to possible obligations of the central bank or the government resulting from implicit guarantees for capital inflows. Combining equations (5) and (6) shows how the amount of foreign exchange reserves that serve as collateral for the implicit guarantees depend on capital inflows:

$$\dot{F}_t = \tau\dot{L}_t = \tau\eta L_t \tag{12}$$

Since we assume that $\dot{z}_t = 0$, we have dropped the time index of η.

Participants in the foreign exchange market know that the central bank can only stabilize the exchange rate through interventions as long as it has reserves. However, implicit guarantees reduce the degrees of freedom of the central bank since part of the reserves may have to be used to bail out domestic financial institutions for their international liabilities. Therefore, it is useful to derive an expression for the amount of foreign exchange reserves that is available for foreign exchange market interventions even if a banking crisis occurs during which all guarantees would have to be paid. We refer to this remaining level of reserves as the net reserves of the central bank (R^n), which are, thus, defined as

$$R_t^n = R_t^g - F_t.$$

The development of net reserves can be derived from combining equations (11) and (12) which yields

$$\dot{R}_t^n = -\mu D_t - \tau\eta L_t.$$

Denoting initial values of domestic credit and capital inflows by D_0 and L_0, respectively, equation (13) can be written as

$$\dot{R}_t^n = -\mu D_0 e^{\mu t} - \tau\eta L_0 e^{\eta t}. \tag{13}$$

Thus, the higher the rate of domestic credit expansion and the higher the growth rate of capital inflows are, the faster the decrease in net reserves is. Both factors ultimately cause that foreign exchange reserves are exhausted either through interventions or through their serving as collateral for implicit guarantees. Comparing equations (13) and (11) indicates that the decline in net reserves is faster than the decline in gross reserves, since the latter is only affected by the rate of domestic credit expansion.

When rational investors realize the continuing decline in foreign exchange reserves they will anticipate that the fixed exchange rate system cannot be sustained indefinitely. They will therefore expect that a balance of payments crisis will occur and that the central bank will have to give up the peg. They will therefore try to exchange their domestic assets into foreign assets before the central bank is forced to abandon the fixed exchange rate system and introduce a floating exchange rate system. If their attempt of selling off all domestic assets for foreign assets also induces a crisis in the financial system as has often been observed in cases of balance of payments crises investors will also claim the guarantees of the government or the central bank.

When will the fixed exchange rate system collapse? More specifically, what will be the level of foreign exchange reserves at the time of the collapse? Even if investors anticipate that, once the peg has collapsed and a float has been is introduced, the government cannot anymore issue implicit guarantees they incur from an expected continuation of domestic credit expansion that the domestic currency will continuously depreciate under the float. This alone already indicates that, on the basis of uncovered interest parity, domestic interest rates will be higher under the float than under the peg. Therefore money demand will be lower after the collapse of the peg than before. The only way to reduce money holdings for the private sector as a whole is to sell domestic currency to the central bank in exchange for foreign currency. When the level of reserves declines below the level of the money demand changes, the private sector cannot change its money holdings as planned. Thus, just when reserves reach the level of money demand changes, a run on the remaining foreign exchange reserve of the central bank occurs during which reserves are completed depletely. For simplicity, we assume that the speculative attack is accompanied by a financial crisis during which all guarantees are claimed.

To derive the exact level of reserves at the time of the speculative attack, we start by denoting with subscript T- the time immediately before the speculative attack and with subscript T+ the time immediately after the attack. Taking into account money demand from equation (1), the level of net reserves at the beginning of the balance of payments crisis is

$$R^n_{T-} = \alpha Y_{T-} - \beta i_{T-} - (\alpha Y_{T+} - \beta i_{T+}).$$

This implies that the speculative attack can occur despite a considerable level of gross reserves. Of course, after the crisis, both gross and net reserves are zero ($R^g_{T+}=R^n_{T+}=0$). Assuming that the foreign interest rate remains unchanged and taking into account that the risk premium (ρ) and the additional yield component of domestic assets (z) can change at the time of the collapse of the peg, the level of reserves immediately before the speculative attack can be expressed using equation (7) as

$$R^n_T = \beta[E_t(\dot{s}/s) + \dot{\rho}_T + \dot{z}_T]. \tag{14}$$

Hence, the change in net reserves caused by the speculative attack is a positive function of the expected rate of depreciation after the crisis and the change in the risk premium and the additional yield component. The expected depreciation is driven by the increase in domestic credit. With a worsening of the financial situation of the government, recourse to monetary financing may increase. Higher uncertainty about future developments and the necessary policy response may also induce an increase in the risk premium.

To determine the time at which reserves reach the level shown in equation (14), we start from a level of net reserves R_0^n at t=0 which is some time before the balance of payments crisis. Taking into account the development of net reserves as described by equation (14) and the fact that the drop in money demand at the time of the speculative attack equals the remaining net reserves, we get

$$\beta\left[E_T(\dot{s}/s)^+ + \dot{\rho}_T + \dot{z}_T\right] = R^n_0 - \int_0^T (\mu D_t + \tau\eta L_t)\,dt.$$

This yields

$$T = \frac{R^n_0 - \beta(E_T(\dot{s}/s) + \dot{\rho}_T + \dot{z}_T)}{\mu D_0 + \tau\eta L_0}$$

Hence, the lower the initial level of reserves and the higher the values of η and μ and of the induced changes in the expected exchange rate, ρ, and z, the earlier will be the run on the reserves of the central bank.

Figure 5 Time path of key economic variables of the model

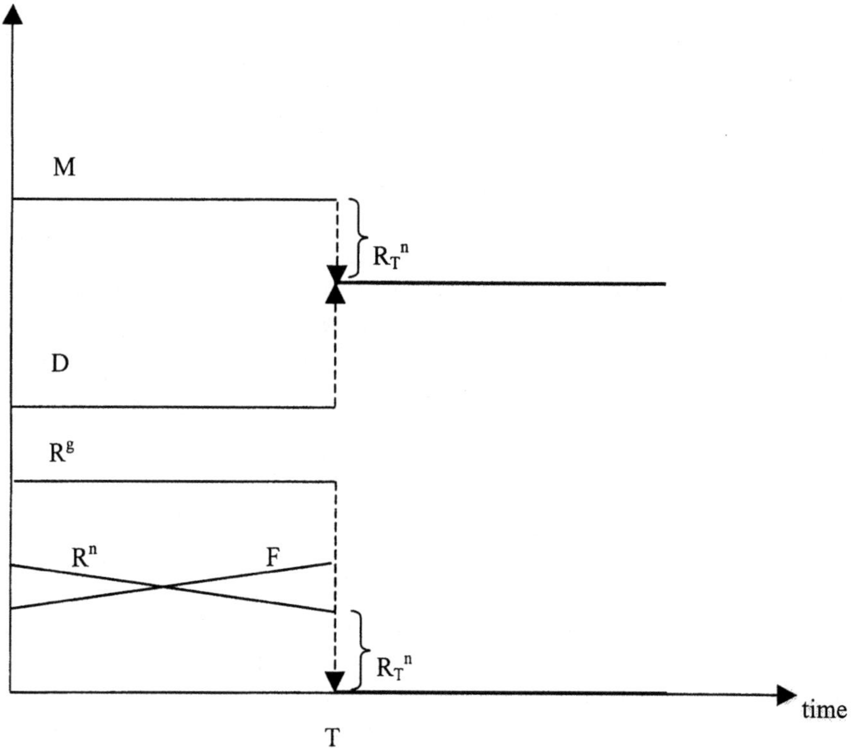

Figure 5 illustrates the time paths of the main variables of the model. In order to focus on the new feature of this balance of payments model and, hence, on the effects of implicit guarantees, we use the simplifying assumption that the rate of domestic credit expansion is zero. In this case, credit expansion does not represent a cause of the balance of payments crisis and the development to a crisis is exclusively induced by the guarantees on capital inflows. Then, before the attack occurs, i.e., for $t<T$, domestic credit, money supply, and gross reserves are constant. However, as capital imports occur and as they lead to implicit guarantees, net foreign exchange reserves decline. This represents an unsustainable situation. Once net reserves reach the level of the drop in money demand accompanying the crisis, the speculative attack occurs and completely exhausts net reserves. Assuming that, simultaneously, guarantees force the central bank to use the corresponding amount of reserves, gross reserves also decline to zero. At the same time, money supply drops to the new level of money demand.

The developments described in Figure 5 exhibit considerable similarities with the stylized facts of the East Asian crisis. As emphasized earlier, the Asian balance of payments crises were not triggered by too high a rate of monetary expansion as in a first-generation type of balance of payments crisis. There was no significant decline in gross reserves either. However, consistent with the model presented here, massive capital inflows could be observed as shown in section 4. In addition, statements of the authorities in virtually all of the East Asian countries that were affected by a balance of payments crisis could have been interpreted as implicit guarantees, especially for international investors.

6 Summary and conclusions

The model developed in this paper focuses on the effects which implicit guarantees on international capital inflows may have on the evolution of a balance of payments crisis. At the origin of the sequence, the government offers free insurance on a set of liabilities issued by residents (mainly financial institutions) for certain maturities. A period of capital inflows is followed by a balance of payments crisis. This helps to explain the East Asian crisis without having to take recourse to irrational panic behavior. The guarantees lead to a yield differential and increase the attractiveness of the investments to foreign investors. When the level of reserves exactly matches the contingent insurance liabilities of the government or the central bank, risk considerations induce the yield to decline below market rates. As a consequence, international private agents sell their insured assets to the government or central bank and, thereby exhaust the remaining reserves of the central bank. The resulting balance of payments crisis is fully anticipated just as in the traditional first-generation models of balance of payments crises. The crisis forces the central bank to abandon the fixed exchange rate and to, at least temporarily, introduce a float.

Paradoxically, the significant capital inflows, which may initially be interpreted as a sign of good economic performance, represent, in this model, the basis for the development towards a balance of payments crisis and, ultimately, the breakdown of the fixed exchange rate system. Implicit guarantees associated with capital inflows do not immediately affect gross reserves but indirectly use them up. This is the case because market participants realize that the central bank's only resources that can be used to fulfill the guarantees are its foreign exchange reserves. The model shows that it can be perfectly rational for investors to buy assets in a country despite the expectation of an upcoming balance of payments crisis. In addition, it can be consistent with optimizing behavior that net capital inflows continue until the balance of payments crisis occurs. Once the crisis begins, international capital flows turn around and massive net capital outflows start. In this model the balance of payments crisis is accompanied by a financial crisis. The latter is triggered, for example, by investors trying to sell their predominantly short-term assets which causes a liquidity problem for financial institutions which engage in maturity transformation. The central bank quickly loses its reserves both because of the decline in money demand and because of the obligations resulting from the previously issued implicit guarantees. Once, reserves are drawn down, the central bank is forced to give up the peg and introduce a floating exchange rate regime.

Several features of the model pointed out above are consistent with the developments prior to and during the East Asian crises in 1997. First, unlike in first-generation models of the balance of payments model literature, development in monetary aggregates do not signal the evolution of a crisis. Nevertheless, with capital inflows and corresponding government guaranties for investors, the crisis is inevitable. Second, a crisis can emerge without prior fiscal deficits. Third and also different from first-generation models of balance of payments crises, the evolution of gross reserves in East Asia did not indicate the arising crisis. More generally, the balance of payments crisis as explained in this new approach is independent of the type of fundamentals that are crucial in the first-generation models of balance of payments crises. Fourth, capital inflows in East Asia continued until fairly shortly before the beginning of the crisis. Fifth, the currency market crisis in the most seriously affected East Asian countries was accompanied by a banking crisis.

There are several policy implications resulting from the model. One of them is the advise not to attract foreign capital (especially not short-term capital flows) through government guaranties. In contrast, the government should leave the risk to private investors. This leads to the best incentive structure in a market economy. Of course, a condition for an efficient allocation of resources is that private investors can evaluate the risk of assets which, in turn, requires appropriate supervision of financial institutions. Another conclusion of the model is that private capital inflows should be closely monitored. The higher these inflows are, the more they can contribute to the currency crisis.

Although the model presented in this paper can explain important aspects of the balance of payments crisis in East Asia, it is still very simple and can, therefore, be criticized easily. First, the model abstracts from the real effects of the distortions caused by the use of the capital inflows. Second, the model does not take into account uncertainty of investors regarding the level of foreign exchange reserves of the central bank or the credibility of the guarantees. Third, there is also no explicit modeling of the financial sector so that the emergence of the banking crisis cannot be explained within the model. Fourth, guarantees could also be applied to assets held by domestic residents. Therefore, it is a simplification to assume that they are associated with international capital inflows, only. However, the model can explain some of the crucial features of the recent banking and currency crisis in East Asia. In addition, it demonstrates that the profile of capital flows as observed in Asia can be fully consistent with rational behavior.

References

Agénor, P.-R., Bhandari, J. S., and Flood, R. P. (1992), Speculative Attacks and Models of Balance of Payments Crises, IMF Staff Papers, Vol. 39, S. 357-394.

Bank for International Settlement, International Banking and Financial Market Developments.

Calvo, G., and Mendoza, E. (1995); Mexico's Balance-of Payments Crisis: A Chronicle of a Death Foretold, Journal of International Economics, Vol. 41, 235-264.

Cole, H., and Kehoe, P. (1996), A Self-Fulfilling Model of Mexico's 1994-1995 Debt Crisis, Journal of International Economics, Vol. 41, 309-330.

Dooley, M. (1997), A Model of Crises in Emerging Markets, NBER Working Paper No. 6300, Cambridge, Mass.

Eichengreen, B., Rose, A., and Wyplosz, C. (1996), Speculative Attacks on Pegged Exchange Rates: An Empirical Exploration with Special Reference to the European Monetary System, in: Canzoneri; M., Ethier, W., and Grilli, V. (eds.), The New Transatlantic Economy, Cambridge and New York.

Flood, R. P., and Garber, P. (1984), Collapsing Exchange-Rate Regimes: Some Linear Examples, Journal of International Economics, Vol. 17, 1-13.

Flood, R. P., and Marion, N. P. (1998), Perspectives on the Recent Currency Crisis Literature, IMF Working Paper WP/98/130, Washington.

Hotelling, H. (1931), The Economics of Exhaustable Resources, Journal of Political Economy, Vol. 39, 127-175.

International Monetary Fund (1997), World Economic and Financial Surveys, December, Washington.

International Monetary Fund (1999), International Financial Statistics, Washington.

Irwin, G., and Vines, D. (1999), A Krugmen-Dooley-Sachs Third Generation Model of the Asian Financial Crisis, CEPR Discussion Paper No. 2149.

Kaminski, G., Lizondo, S., and Reinhard, C.M. (1998), Leading Indicators of Currency Crises, Staff Papers, International Monetary Fund, Vol. 45, 1-48.

Krugman, P. (1979), A Model of Balance-of-Payments Crises, Journal of Money, Credit and Banking, Vol. 11, 311-325.

Krugman, P. (1998), What happened to Asia? http://web.mit.edu/krugman/www/DISINTER.html

Masson, P. (1995), Gaining and Losing ERM Credibility: The Case of the United Kingdom, The Economic Journal, Vol. 105, 571-582.

Obstfeld, M. (1986), Rational and Self-Fulfilling Balance of Payments Crises, American Economic Review, Vol. 76, 72-81.

Obstfeld, M. (1994), The Logic of Currency Crises, Cashier Economiques et Monetaires, Bank of France, Vol. 43, 189-213.

Obstfeld, M. (1996), Models of Currency Crises with Self-Fulfilling Features, European Economic Review, Vol 40, 1037-1047.

Ozkan, F. G., and Sutherland, A. (1995), Policy Measures to Avoid a Currency Crisis, The Economic Journal, Vol. 105, 510-519.

Sachs, J. Tornell, A., and Velasco, A. (1996), Financial Crises in Emerging Markets: The Lessons from 1995, Brooking Papers on Economic Activity, No. 16, 147-215.

Salant, S., and Henderson, D. (1978), Market Anticipation of Government Policy and the Price of Gold, Journal of Political Economy, Vol. 86, 627-648.

Causes and consequences of the Asian economic crisis

Timothy M. Devinney

Australian Graduate School of Management, University of New South Wales,
Sydney, Australia 2052

This article does not offer a complete answer to the question of what causes the collapse of the spectacular growth seen in the developing economies of Asia. Rather, it aims to identify the lessons that business people and policy-makers should draw from the available evidence about economic development and the antecedents of, and consequent events surrounding, the economic crisis that rocked the leading economies of Asia in the late 1990s.

Before we begin, it is important to note that Asia is discussed in some circles as if it is a homogeneous economic, political and social entity for which a single set of rules apply and within which a singular set of events has occurred. Nothing can be further from the truth. Asia represents 24 countries, ranging in population size from 300,000 (Brunei) to 1.2 Billion (China) and accounting for 60 per cent of the world's people. On the income scale, it contains some of the world's poorest people (per capita GDP in Nepal is US$200) to some of its most affluent (per capita GDP in Japan is US$39,640). Even on the growth tables we see enormous variance. Historic growth in oil rich Brunei has been stagnant at less than 1 per cent while growth in China tops 12 per cent for the decade. Hence, simple conclusions about any aspect of economic development and change in Asia must be viewed with suspicion.

In many respects, the events of the last half decade (and the growth that preceded the recent economic downturn) have been an unfortunate confluence of predictable and random events. In the sections that follow we outline some approaches to the theory of economic development, discuss some of the more compelling evidence that this implies about the Asian economic crisis and close with what these conclusions imply for the future development of the developed and developing Asian economies.

1 Theories of economic development and advantage

1.1 Neoclassical theory and its endogenous offspring

Traditionally, economists have followed the approach of Swan and Solow,[1] which is based on traditional microeconomic notions of production functions and declining marginal rates of productivity. According to this approach (in its simplest form), growth is a function of four factors: the level of capital stock; the level of labour input; the productivity of capital; and the productivity of labour. Differences in growth are explained by reference to differences in the quantity and the quality of inputs. Natural limits to growth are set by the upper limits to productivity and inputs.

In one of the simplest expositions of the implications of this theory,[2] Paul Krugman argues that Asian growth is almost entirely driven by inputs and is not sustainable over the long run without a fundamental alteration in the nature of the usage of inputs. The essence of his argument, as applied to Singapore, is represented by the data in Table 1.

According to Krugman, Singapore's growth was driven by the improving utilisation of capacity: the rise in employed share of the population, the rise in savings and hence investment, and the increase in the quality of the labour input. But future growth is limited because (i) there is no longer any excess labour capacity (a fact reflected by increasing labour rates); (ii) there is almost no room for increasing the education level of Singaporeans (99 per cent of those under 40 years of age have a high-school degree); and (iii) savings rates of 40 per cent are almost impossible to sustain in the long run as a society ages and increases consumption.

But traditional growth theory, including Krugman's example as it relates to Singapore, fails to explain how and why rapid growth began when it did. Advocates of the 'factor accumulation model' attribute much of recent Asian growth to an exogenous shock in the form of the Plaza Accord of 1985, which increased the level of Japanese foreign direct investment in the area. Yet, although the rapid rise of the yen following this agreement by the major trading nations provides some explanation for spurt of development in the emerging economies of China, Thailand, Malaysia and Indonesia, it does little to explain the pre-1985 growth of Korea, Hong Kong, Singapore and Taiwan.

---

1 See Solow (1970) and Swan (1956).

2 See Krugman (1994a) in *Foreign Affairs* (March/April) and responses and rejoinder in the July/August issue of the same year. Further discussion of this and similar ideas can be found in Krugman (1994b) and Krugman (1996).

Table 1 Factor inputs and growth in Singapore

	1966	1990
Annual percentage growth of per capita GDP, 1966-90	8.5	
Employed percentage share of population	27	51
Education	At least 50% had no formal education	66% had at least 12 years of schooling
Investment	11% of GDP in savings	40% of GDP in savings

Source: Krugman (1994b).

Modern variants of the theory have attempted to take into account factors other than 'pure' inputs as the causes of growth. What has come to be called 'endogenous' growth theory[3] postulates that growth arises from random and purposeful developments or innovations within the economy. At one level, the theory simply accounts for the growth in technical and labour productivity that in earlier models had been assumed to be diminishing with factor accumulation or subject to random jumps. At a more sophisticated level, the theory attempts to account for purposeful and natural evolutionary changes in factor productivity.[4]

1.2 Michael Porter's competitive advantage theory (the 'diamond')

Building on his highly successful articulation of the value chain and competitive advantage, Porter argues that growth arises from the interaction of the four fundamental forces presented in Figure 1. Economic development is driven by the underlying sources of competitive advantage that emanate from these areas. In addition, as the economy evolves from being factor-driven to investment-driven and to innovation-driven, the sources of advantage change.

According to Porter, early factor-driven growth arises from the circumstances in which a firm finds itself: countries like the United States and Australia, which are rich in natural resources, develop industries based on these endowments, whereas countries like Korea, Singapore and Japan, which are poor in natural resources, develop industries based on human capital. The second stage of growth occurs

[3] See Romer (1990); Krugman (1990); Shleifer (1986); Murphy et al. (1993).
[4] See, for example, Barro (1991).

when resource expansion reaches its limits and investment is necessary to increase the productivity of existing factors of production. This is essentially a building stage of development, which most countries appear able to reach. Stage three requires real changes in the nature of development: innovation in management and technology, and sophistication of demand, replace investment and factor endowments as the future source of growth. Finally, some countries fail to sustain themselves in the innovation stage and enter the wealth stage, living off endowed and accumulated capital, thereby eroding their sources of advantage. Among Asian countries, Burma, Vietnam, China and India are in the first stage of development; Taiwan, Korea and Singapore have reached the investment stage; and Japan is at the innovation stage.

Figure 1 Porter's 'diamond' approach to growth

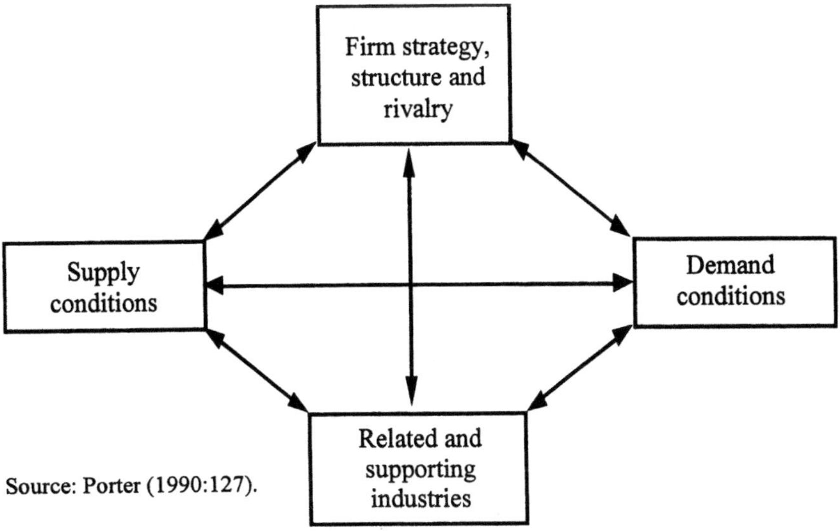

Source: Porter (1990:127).

Porter's theory is certainly not rigorous and is unlikely to be falsifiable. However, it is something of a natural extension of traditional growth theory (in spite of its criticism by economists). First, it relies quite heavily on the notion of factor endowments as a source of trade and growth. Second, it focuses on the role that internal demand conditions play in setting the organisational and political agenda associated with the development of a commercial sector. Third, it highlights the importance of industry clusters and the role that externalities play in the development of an industry knowledge base. Macroeconomists had, for too long, been ignoring the importance of microeconomic industry structure, intra-country competition and role of the firm in affecting economic growth. Fourth, it allows us to begin talking about the role that innovation plays in driving growth. Traditional theory had, until recently, left the story off at investment.

In some sense, Porter's theory picks up from Schumpeter's (1939) notion of innovation as the real source of growth in an economy and merges it with his own blend of industrial organisation (which followed from Chandler's [1962; 1990] ideas about industry and corporate evolution). Nor is it far from recent developments in endogenous growth theory discussed above. But, despite its immense appeal, its perhaps fatal weakness is that it is primarily a theory based on evidence gathered from developed economies (even though it has been applied to developing countries). Moreover, it is less a theory of economic growth than of how economies develop firms that can compete globally—for which task it is a reasonable theory.

1.3 The neo-institutional economics perspective

A third theory of growth stems from the neo-institutional economics (NIE) literature associated with Douglass North (1990) and Mancur Olson (1996). The NIE perspective holds that political and economic institutions, rather than factor endowments, are the fundamental determinants of growth. These institutions define the opportunity set and incentive structures at work in an economy. The most important institutions are those of private property, the rule of law and freedom of exchange (free trade). The right institutional framework allows economic actors to best capture the gains from trade. The wrong framework will encourage rent-seeking, speculation and other welfare-reducing activities.

For example, Olson (1996) notes that there is very little difference between the two Koreas in terms of their respective natural endowments, cultural traits or historical circumstances. The only plausible explanation of the vast difference between their incomes is their different political and economic institutions. More generally, Olson argues that this explains why differences in incomes between nations are so much greater than the differences between regions within countries: the nation-state, for better or worse, is that fundamental unit of institutional difference.

According to Olson, neither the old nor the new growth theories can explain why only a subset of low-income countries experience faster growth than both the developed countries and the other low-income countries. The explanation for this is that 'any poorer countries that adopt relatively good economic policies and institutions enjoy rapid catch-up growth: since they are far short of their potential (as Krugman argues), their per capita incomes can increase … by narrowing the huge gap between their actual and potential income. Countries with the highest per capita incomes do not have the same opportunity' (Olson, 1996:20).

The evidence in support of the NIE view is considerable. For example, Sachs and Warner (1995) find that economic growth in the newly industrialised economies is explained very well by economic openness, which is essentially an institutional variable. The fundamental lesson from the NIE literature, Olson argues, is that 'the best thing a society can do to increase its prosperity is to wise up' (1996:21). Growth is available to any society that is willing to adopt liberal social, economic and political institutions. What the NIE literature has failed to address adequately to date is the fact that growth rates vary considerably over time but the institutional structures of many countries do not.[5] We will address this issue shortly.

1.4 The World Bank's eclectic theory

The last theory is essentially an amalgamation of traditional and newer theories used by the World Bank in *The Asian Miracle: Economic Growth and Public Policy* (1993). The Bank concentrates in four areas: policy choices, competitive discipline, growth functions and outcomes. Its approach has become the standard explanation of the source of sustained growth in East Asia, and the basis of its guidance to other developing nations.

The World Bank's view of growth is related quite strongly to its agenda and mode of operation. Because the Bank deals with governments, it is hardly surprising that the theory puts emphasis on the role that the government plays in (i) setting up the economic environment; (ii) selectively intervening; (iii) establishing an appropriate bureaucratic infrastructure; and (iv) ensuring balanced distribution of economic rewards. It prescribes 'pragmatic conservatism' on the part of governments.

The World Bank's results from examining the economies of Taiwan, Korea, Japan, Indonesia, Hong Kong, Singapore, Malaysia and Thailand can explain about one-third of economic growth using primary and secondary education, investment, and population growth alone. Adding the relative position of these economies *vis-à-vis* the US allows the Bank to claim that its model accounts for two-thirds of the growth in these economies. This result, among others, led the Bank to conclude that growth policy was best aimed at ensuring quality resource inputs, particularly in the case of labour.

The World Bank's analysis stops short of explaining the next source of growth for these economies. This is where Porter's approach and endogenous growth theory have some relevance. Indeed, we understand more about growth in rapidly developing economies (since our simple models seem to work better) than we do about the developed economies, where the natural limits of factor productivity have been reached. Future surges in growth become dependent not on the quantity of inputs but on their quality and how they are arranged. Explaining and predicting these facets of growth have proven to be difficult.

---

[5] See Easterly et al. (1993).

2 Economic development and advantage: Evidence and rules

2.1 The role of input factors

The primary conclusion that arises from our discussion is that inputs play an important role in driving growth. The World Bank's findings are supported by Young (1994, 1995), who argues that the growth of Asian newly industrialising countries (NICs) is explained by labour-force participation rates, sectoral transfers into manufacturing, and investment, rather than by productivity increases that would be considered out of the ordinary.

But how can such rapid increases in the cost of labour in NICs be sustainable in economic systems for which there is supposedly little or no technical progress? It is equally difficult to explain the differences in total factor productivity between countries where the expenditure on R&D ranges from virtually nothing (Philippines and Thailand) to almost 2 per cent of GDP (Japan and Korea) and where the relationship between that investment and total factor productivity is weak at best. However, Young (1994, 1995) and Krugman (1994a,b) argue that, in most cases, growth and development is, more often than not, driven by more and better inputs rather than fewer inputs used in an extraordinary fashion. This is certainly one possibility. The important general point is that to understand growth it is necessary to look at the distribution and quantity of factor inputs first.

The quality of input also appears to be important. Barro's (1991) study of 98 countries over 1960–85 found that quality of labour inputs, defined in terms of primary and secondary school enrolments and student-teacher ratios, is critical to growth. Coe and Helpman (1995) and Devinney (1996) find that innovation is a strong determinant of growth. Murphy et al. (1991), however, show that the rent-seeking activities of law students are negatively related to growth.[6] Their further finding that the importance of education lies in where it is concentrated has drawn attention on the distribution and arrangements of inputs. Sachs and Warner (1997) show further that even quality can have its disadvantages: beyond some point the consumption side of human capital development (measured as life expectancy, literacy and schooling) comes to dominate the investment side, as the society has too many old poets and not enough young engineers.

2.2 The importance of economic openness

Virtually every developing country makes approval of foreign direct investment conditional on export generation. However, the evidence suggests a strong relationship between economic growth and the share of GDP represented by both exports and imports. A recent table in *Far Eastern Economic Review* (10 October

---

[6] They found that a 10 per cent increase in engineering graduates leads to a 0.5 per cent increase in growth while a 10 per cent increase in law graduates leads to 0.3 per cent decrease in growth.

1996) shows that the world's top exporters are also the world's top importers, implying that growth depends on openness. Export-driven growth is important, but the benefits of openness lie not in trade as such but in the discipline and open institutional structures that accompany it. But, with some minor exceptions (such as Luxembourg, Bahrain, Hong Kong and Singapore), most nations are predominantly closed since they naturally trade most with their closest neighbours. Hence the extremely strong positive relationship that is found between the size of a country, the number of bordering countries, and its openness to trade (Dowrick, 1994).

In general, the economic openness of the average economy increased by 28 per cent between 1960–65 and 1985–92. The openness measure of Korea, Japan, Indonesia, the Philippines, Malaysia and Thailand increased from 35 per cent in 1960–65 to 70 per cent in 1985–92. However, during that same period the measure for all other countries increased from 53 per cent to 68 per cent. The ranking of countries did not greatly change over time: a country that was relatively closed in 1965 was likely to be relatively closed in 1992.[7]

2.3 The role of institutions

The role of government and the value of democratic institutions have received much attention in recent years. The World Bank notes that intervention sometimes seems to work; but it remains non-committal on the role of industrial policy. Other commentators, most notably Lester Thurow (1992, 1996) and Tyson (1993), advocate Japanese-style industrial policy as a source of growth. The evidence is mixed. Government involvement in the economy (as measured by its share of GDP) is indeed negatively related to growth but the variance is so large as to make any substantial conclusion moot.[8] Indeed, those countries with the lowest growth rates are more, not less, likely to have low government shares of GDP.

However, the Heritage Foundation's index of economic freedom (Johnson & Sheehy, 1995)[9] suggests that the link between economic freedom and economic growth is quite positive. This result is supported by Mauro's (1995) detailed study of the relationship between corruption and growth, which found that about 20 per cent of growth was explained by the presence or absence of corruption.[10] For example, based on his evidence, if India could reduce its corruption level to that of

---

[7] Data from Penn World Tables at http://datacentre.epas.utoronto.ca:5680/pwt/pwt.html.

[8] Every study we have seen has shown a partial correlation coefficient between growth and government expenditure. The magnitude and significance of the coefficients are strongly effected by the structure of the models employed.

[9] The index includes measures of tax burden, trade policy, government consumption, monetary policy, foreign investment rules, banking rules, wages and price restrictions, property rights protection, regulation and the existence of a black market. Easton & Walker (1997) provide detail on the relationship between this measure and growth.

[10] Mauro's index does not include assassinations, coups, government spending and general political instability, all of which are clearly related to corruption.

Italy its investment is estimated to increase by 4.87 per cent of GDP and its growth by 0.5 per cent a year.

2.4 What really matters?

Development economists seem frustratingly unable fully to capture the complexity of the phenomena they wish to characterise. Growth may be dependent on the quality of factor inputs or economic institutions; but what are the appropriate measures? In a paper humorously titled 'I Just Ran Two Million Regressions', Sala-I-Martin (1997) examines the relationship between growth and nine sets of variables based on regions, politics, religion, market distortions and performance, investment, industry production, economic openness, economic organisation, and whether or not the country was a former Spanish colony. From all this it can be concluded that Protestant/Catholic, closed, socialist ex-Spanish colonies located close to the equator that are relatively resource-rich but are suffering from revolutions and wars and must deal with a black market premium on their currency will have poorer growth than countries not possessing these characteristics.

Faced with these difficulties, simple rules should dominate until such time as better information allows more complex rules to be formulated. Our prior discussion suggests that all the research to date supports three almost common-sense rules: factor accumulation is good; open economic systems and institutions are good; and persistence in these two rules is critical.

3 The economic crisis and its aftermath

Using the before mentioned rules as a basis, we can narrow down the issues associated with the Asian economic crisis into two areas: (1) the extent to which the nature of factor inputs changed and (2) the character and quality of the institutional structures. These are inter-related issues but for the sake of discussion we will keep them separate.

3.1 The Asian economic crisis as factor input realignment

As noted in our review of growth theory, most people accept the arguments of Young and Krugman at face value but insist that more is involved in determining when a country will experience economic growth. However, the events of recent years have strengthened the hand of the neoclassicists. Rather than discuss the issues in minute detail, we can examine the issue quite simply by looking at the events leading up to the crisis and some basic economic logic.

When the crisis broke in 1997, the countries affected first (and ultimately the worst) were Thailand, Malaysia, Indonesia and Korea. The subsequent follow-on effects for places such as Singapore, Hong Kong and Taiwan were difficult but, as time has shown, the impact was less critical and less fundamental. The early discussion in the business press concentrated on the crisis as one started by 'currency speculators' and almost exclusively talked about a currency crisis. In retrospect this was a mistake, but it is easy to see how such as byline would play to the public when countries' currencies where falling by 10, 20 and 30 per cent in a single day.[11]

In examining the numbers up to the beginning of the crisis we find an interesting anomaly. All these countries—Thailand, Malaysia, Indonesia and Korea—were running current account deficits. In the case of Thailand (the supposed ground-zero of the crisis), this number was almost 10 per cent of GDP! With the exception of Korea, which was a foreign investor, all these countries had experienced several years of robust inward foreign investment.[12] Similarly all these countries had relatively low levels of foreign exchange liquidity as a percent of their international (normally dollar denominated debt) liabilities. For example, US dollar denominated debt in Thailand, Malaysia, Indonesia, Korea and the Philippines[13] went from around US$20 billion in 1994 to over US$50 billion in 1996, with external dollar denominated debt and equity of almost US$100 billion. What is most interesting is that during this same period, the amount of foreign equity increased, and the value of the currencies of the main Asian countries was either stable or appreciating.

An astute reader will see where this is going. The countries most affected by the crisis had companies with rising asset values supported by rising currencies, which allowed it to borrow on its asset base. These currencies were being supported by two forces, foreign direct investment and portfolio investment by foreign companies and funds managers—both of which created a demand for local currency. For example between 1994 and 1996 FDI investment grew slightly in the five affected countries but portfolio investment and bank debt more than doubled from the 1994 base.[14] What began occurring in 1996 was a reversal of this phenomenon, particularly with respect to FDI. However, the governments and the monetary authorities of Indonesia, Thailand and Malaysia had strong incentives to keep their currencies strong; or, perhaps more importantly, stable at some level that unfortunately proved to be too high. Over time, these policies led to a substantial gap between the nominal and real value of assets that was not sustainable.[15] Caught in the bind

[11] From January 1997 to January 1998, the Indonesian Rupiahe lost almost 80 per cent of its value, the Thai Baht nearly 70 per cent, the Korean Won nearly 60 per cent and the Malaysian Ringgit around 40 per cent.

[12] In many respects, the FDI, current account balance and liquidity structure of these countries were eerily similar to those of the Mexican earlier in the decade.

[13] These are what the IMF refers to as the 'five affected countries'.

[14] In 1994 these countries had FDI inflows of US$6.5 billion, portfolio investment of US$8 billion and bank debt of US$18 billion. In 1995, these numbers were US$8.7 billion, US$17 billion and 36.9 billion, respectively. The amounts for 1996 where similar.

[15] Between January 1995 and January 1997 the Thai Baht remained around THB25 to the US dollar; the Indonesia Rupiah rose from 2,194 to 2,362 to the dollar; the Ringgit stayed around 2.5 to the dollar; and the Korean Won depreciated slightly from 789 to 858 to the dollar.

of dollar denominated liabilities and declining local currency denominated assets, the crisis quickly spread as inter-related companies found it difficult to avoid radical asset revaluation.

All the countries of Asia were affected by the events of 1997. However, Hong Kong stands out as a strange exception in the way in which these events flowed through the economy. As the only economy with a fixed exchange rate regime, Hong Kong quickly became subject to speculative attack by currency traders. In the end, Hong Kong emerged with its currency intact but with sections of its economy battered and the government owning a substantial portion of the equity in Hong Kong blue-chip companies. The experience of Hong Kong shows how the revaluation of assets was the core of the crisis. In Singapore, the currency declined and some Singaporean companies lost market value based on the nature of their activities in the region (Singaporean companies are not large sources of FDI and Singapore has a larger manufacturing base than Hong Kong). However, wages and property markets where affected only moderately. In Hong Kong, the brunt of the impact was on the labour and property sectors. Unemployment rose (but only modestly), wages and bonuses were slashed, and property prices and rents collapsed (approximately 30 to 40 per cent).

3.2 The role of institutions

The political, social and business institutions of the majority of Asian countries could not be though of as either economically or political open. Not withstanding the recent tribulations of Anwar Ibrahim in Malaysia or the upheavals in Indonesia or the difficulties facing Hong Kong's legal establishment,[16] quasi-objective measures of political and economic freedom, such as the Heritage Foundation's measure mentioned earlier, put the vast majority of Asian countries in a middling or poor category. The reality is that the countries most affected by the changing economic winds discussed in the prior section were those with the most fragile political and business structures. Indonesia is the most extreme example of poor institutional structures and will serve as the basis of our discussion.

The situation presented by Indonesia is encapsulated in a very simple way in Figure 2. If we use Frye and Shliefer's (1996) terminology, Indonesia was (and perhaps still is) a classic example of a 'grabbing hand' structure. The government is above the law and uses its power to extract rents. For example, it was expected that businesses contribute to high profile 'charities' that were overseen by mem-

[16] Anwar was the chosen successor of Malaysia Prime Minister Mahathir Mohamad, who has been jailed and tried on what most consider trumped up sodomy and corruption charges. Indonesia's problems are more obvious and it is currently suffering from domestic violence in the capital, Jakarta, focussing on the recent election, and concerns about secession movements buoyed on by the successful independence movement in East Timor. Hong Kong's legal independence is being eroded by the move of the government of Tung Chee Hwa to appeal a Court decision on Immigration to the government in Beijing, which subsequently over-ruled the judicial decision.

bers of former-President Suharto's family. What became of most of this money is anyone's guess. The legal structure is ineffective and a 'mafia'—in this case the Suharto clan and the military—replaces the state as the enforcer of 'law'. The regulatory structure is predatory and corrupt. Although the situation seen in Indonesia is extreme, it is representative of structures that operate somewhat more benignly throughout Asia. For example, recent events in Malaysia show how the government has used the national petroleum company, Petronas, to bailout troubled companies, including one owned by the Prime Minister's son. Since the crisis hit, Petronas has invested almost 16 billion Ringgit, mostly in businesses unrelated to it fundamental skill in petroleum extraction and refining. Once the cash rich diamond in the Malaysian crown, Petronas now has a debt to equity ratio of more than 100 per cent. The *Far Eastern Economic Review* recently referred to Petronas as 'auxiliary to the national treasury'.[17]

Figure 2 The Indonesian situation

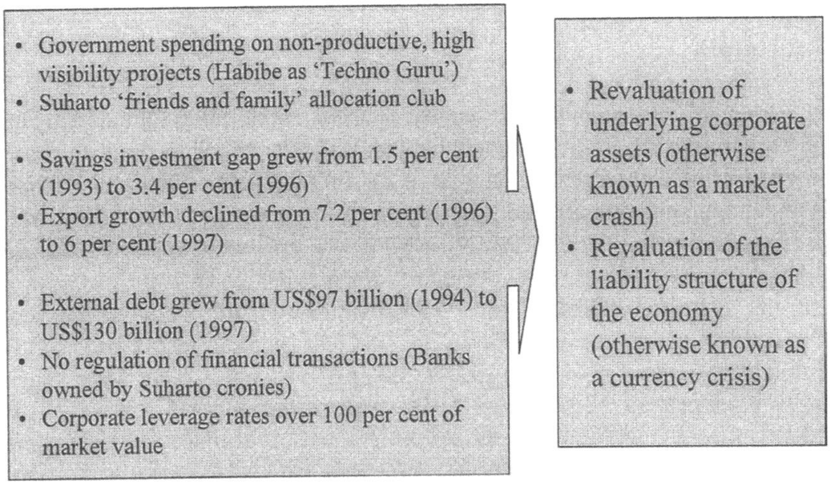

Perhaps even more critical to the evolution of the crisis than the poor macro institutional structures existing in Asia is the fact that the business structures in most Asian countries are quite immature and inflexible in responding to the sort of changes that arose in 1997. The style of capitalism operating in Asia is normally though to be different in form and substance from more traditional 'Anglo-Saxon' capitalism most obviously represented by American corporations. Unlike Anglo-Saxon capitalism, Asian capitalism is more relational, being based upon expansive networks of family, ethnic and regional ties that replace the contractual arrangements dominant in developed economies. The traditional nature of Asian capital-

[17] See the 17 August 1999 edition of the *Far Eastern Economic Review* with the cover story, *Saving Malaysia Inc: Petronas goes to the rescue of weak companies—again.*

ism, with its emphasis on frugality, authoritarianism and simple top-down management structures was well suited to the needs and demands of developing societies, particularly those with a weak tradition of societal transparency, most clearly seen in a lack of rule of law, and thin capital markets with a dubious relationship between investment in a company and the ability to exercise any degree of ownership. However, in the face of radical change, these conservative structures prove woefully inadequate in responding innovatively and quickly.

The role of business institutions shows up most obviously in the ability of Hong Kong and Singapore to weather the economic crisis better than countries with less well-developed business structures where the basis of advantage is simply comparative. The strength of many Hong Kong and Singaporean firms has been their openness to outsiders at the very senior levels of management and on their boards and the application of sound organisational and management principles in their day-to-day operations. There is little doubt that the institutional strength and business acumen were critical in helping them be prepared for and to weather the economic changes that arose unpredictably.

4 Conclusion

Much is said and written about the role that financial markets played in causing the Asian economic crisis. There is little doubt that with better banking, regulatory and financial structures in place that countries such as Malaysia, the Philippines, Thailand, Indonesia and Korea would have weathered the storm differently. However, this sort of discussion begs the point of whether the crisis was primarily financial or primarily institutional. If it was primarily financial, then the sort of regulatory reform that is being demanded from groups such as the IMF may go a long way toward addressing the problems. However, if the problem was (and perhaps still is) institutional, and institutional in a fundamental business way—rather than a regulatory way—then such approaches will fail to address the root problems.

In Korea, we see evidence that the problem is more fundamental and culturally engrained in the nature of Asian business practices. Now that the worst days seem to be over and growth is returning to Korea, traditional political and business routines are stifling true reform. Similarly, the doldrums facing Japan appear to reflect an endemic cultural psychology rather than anything that can be solved with neo-Keynesian tinkering. Japan, it seems, is too rich and too politically grid locked to do anything but muddle through. In Malaysia, Prime Minister Mahathir has weathered the crisis and solidified power, all while bucking the IMF trend toward greater transparency (again witness the use of Petronas). However, latent political resentment is a wild card that will most likely be manifested only when the inevitable leadership transition occurs. Indonesia descends further into chaos, while in the Philippines it is business as usual, in a Philippine's sort of way. Only in Thailand has reform had an effect both at the macro governmental level and the micro business level.

It is typical of macro economists to look on crises of this sort as purely macro institutional. Examination of the web sites devoted to the crisis, including that of the IMF, once is amazed at how little space is taken by discussions of non-governmental institutional structures. There is the occasional paper or discussion about 'crony capitalism' but little discussion about the morphology of those businesses that do not rely on political influence but suffer from the same managerial problems that plague business in the region. It is only when these issues are addressed at the level of importance of the macro institutional structures that capture the attention of the IMF that the developing countries of Asia will be able to better insulate themselves from a repeat of the events of 1997.

References

Barro, R. (1991), 'Economic Growth in a Cross Section of Countries', Quarterly Journal of Economics 106: 407–44.
Chandler, A. (1962), Strategy and Structure, MIT Press, Cambridge, Mass.
—— & H. Takashi (1990), Scale and Scope: Dynamics of Industrial Capitalism, Belknap Press, Cambridge, Mass.
Coe, D. & R. Helpman (1995), 'International R&D Spillovers', European Economic Review 39: 859–87.
Colvin, J., T. Devinney & S. Kirchner (1997), 'As Law and Regulation Grows, So Economic Development Slows', Business Review Weekly, 17 February: 57–8.
Devinney, T. (1996), Characterising International Patent Behaviour, University of New South Wales, Sydney (unpublished working paper).
Dowrick, S. (1994), 'Openness and Growth', pp. 9-41 in P. Lowe & J. Dwyer (eds), International Integration of the Australian Economy, Reserve Bank of Australia, Sydney:
Easterly, W., M. Kremer, L. Prichett & L. Summers (1993), 'Good Policy or Good Luck? Country Growth Performance and Temporary Shocks', Journal of Monetary Economics 32: 459–83.
Easton, S. & M. Walker (1997), 'Income Growth and Economic Freedom', American Economic Review 87: 328–32.
T. Frye & A. Shliefer (1996), 'The Invisible Hand and the Grabbing Hand', Unpublished Working Paper. Cambridge MA: NBER.
Johnson, B. & T. Sheehy (1995), The Index of Economic Freedom, Heritage Foundation, Washington DC.
Krugman, P. (1990), Rethinking International Trade, MIT Press, Cambridge, Mass.
—— (1994a), 'Competitiveness: A Dangerous Obsession', Foreign Affairs 73(2): 28-44.
—— (1994b), The Myth of Asia's Miracle, Foreign Affairs 73(6): 62–78.
—— (1996), Pop Internationalism, MIT Press, Cambridge, Mass.
Mauro, P. (1995), 'Corruption and Growth', Quarterly Journal of Economics 110: 681–712.
Murphy, K.., A. Shleifer & R. Vishny (1991), 'The Allocation of Talent: Implications for Growth', Quarterly Journal of Economics 106: 503–30.
—— (1993), 'Why Is Rent Seeking So Costly to Growth?", American Economic Review 83: 409–14.
North, D. (1990), Institutions, Institutional Change, and Economic Performance, Cambridge University Press, New York.
Olson, M. (1996), 'Big Bills Left on the Sidewalk: Why Some Nations are Rich and Others Poor', Journal of Economic Perspectives 10: 3–24.
Porter, M. (1990), The Competitive Advantage of Nations, Free Press, New York.

Romer, P. (1990), 'Endogenous Technical Change', Journal of Political Economy 98(October) (part 2): s71–102.

Sachs, J. & A. Warner (1995), 'Economic Reform and the Process of Global Integration', Brookings Papers on Economic Activity, Macroeconomics 1: 1–118.

—— (1997), 'Fundamental Sources of Long-Run Growth', American Economic Review 87: 184–8.

Sala-I-Martin, X. (1997), 'I Just Ran Two Million Regressions', American Economic Review 87: 178–83.

Schumpeter, J. (1939),Theory of Economic Development, Harvard University Press, Cambridge, Mass.

Shleifer, A. (1986), 'Implementation Cycles', Journal of Political Economy 94: 1163–90.

Solow, R. (1970), Growth Theory: An Exposition, Clarendon Press, Oxford.

Swan, T. (1956), 'Economic Growth and Capital Accumulation', Economic Record 32: 334–61.

Thurow, L. (1992), Head to Head, William Morrow, New York.

—— (1996), The Future of Capitalism, William Morrow, New York

Tyson, L. (1993), Who's Bashing Whom?, Institute for International Economics, Washington DC.

World Bank (1993),The East Asian Miracle: Economic Growth and Public Policy, Oxford University Press, New York.

Young, A. (1994), 'Lessons from East Asian NICs', European Economic Review 38: 964–73.

—— (1995), 'The Tyranny of Numbers: Confronting the Statistical Realities of the East Asian Growth Experience', Quarterly Journal of Economics 110: 641–80.

Functions of economic policy in promoting the efficiency of thc international financial system

Wolfgang Filc

Trier University, Universitätsring 15, D-54286 Trier, Germany

1 The role of financial markets in ensuring stable macroeconomic development

Efficient financial markets are an essential requirement for a high level of employment, for adequate economic growth, for price stability. This is undisputed. What is disputed is whether the market system satisfies this requirement automatically and free of charge. Yes it does, say fellow economists arguing solely on the basis of neoclassical equilibrium theory, firmly entrenched behind their dogma of constantly infallible price signals from unregulated markets given the rational forming of expectations by economic agents. Others contest such automatism. For if the expectations of economic agents are heterogeneous, if the forming pattern changes, if elements of adaptive or extrapolative forming are occasionally identified, expectations will sometimes be determined by a single dominant issue rather than by all the information relevant to evaluation; information will be ignored; information uncertainties will increase to an extent where information fails to trigger appropriate transactions; the markets in a macroeconomic system will be linked at least intermittently by quantitative restrictions instead of by allocation-optimising relative price shifts, hence placing exclusively private-interest optimisation endeavours into a risky and thus not precisely known conjunction with results that are not fully informative; all this will trigger sequences of prices and yields in financial markets resulting in misdirected macroeconomic trends.

We must then say goodbye to the idea that financial markets steered solely by private striving to optimise potential yields will consistently produce results that are also efficient in macroeconomic terms. There is no longer any justification for the reliance on consistently correct price signals, given unrestricted price formation, that has hitherto been the basis for deregulation on financial markets if the financial markets fail to process information efficiently. Configurations of interest rates, exchange rates and pay rates that are necessary to achieve non-inflationary growth at a high level of employment can be established only by chance if economic policy accepts price movements in financial markets even when such acceptance sows the seeds of undesirable macroeconomic trends. If distortions in financial markets are also attributable to threatened changes in assets values having been caused by forgoing economic policy measures with the aim of checking interest and exchange rate fluctuations as well as to the reduction of institutional provisions, then these causes must be targeted in order to limit misdirected financial market trends. Only then will financial markets be able to fulfil their intended function, namely that of internationally reconciling planned investments with planned savings, guiding capital to the places where it will contribute most effectively to non-inflationary growth and maximising world-wide prosperity. The international financial system should advance rather than impede the international division of labour oriented to economic fundamentals.

Interest and exchange rate movements should reflect and not determine international factor allocation. Greater stability in financial markets and international capital movements presupposes steady price developments in foreign exchange markets geared to monetary and real economic fundamentals. If exchange rate volatility increases and exchange rate trends depart from fundamental factors, the foreign exchange market can become the source of misdirected macroeconomic trends, can trigger external and internal imbalances, can contribute to recession and unemployment of boom and inflation and in the final analysis can severely damage a country's financial system.

A retrospective look at the financial market crisis of countries in south-east Asia since 1997 can show what effects massive exchange rate shifts between the currencies of major industrial economies can have on the stability of a country's financial system (cf. Eichengreen 1999). The financial crisis was preceded by a substantial move into deficit in the current accounts of these countries since 1993, financed by dollar loans from commercial banks, principally those in industrial economies. But the financial market crisis was triggered by the abrupt appreciation of the U.S. dollar (cf. UNCTAD 1998, 58).

To give an example: In mid-1995 a Korean exporter supplying goods to Germany in the value of DM 20,000 realised a yield of $ 14,400. Two years later this export yield had declined to $ 11,100 for the sole reason that the dollar had appreciated against the D-mark. Korea's foreign debt turned into a debt overload. Thus the ability of a country to service a foreign debt denominated in dollars is determined less by the rate of exchange between the dollar and its own currency than by the rate of exchange between the dollar and the currencies in which that country realises export yields.

The intention is neither to disregard nor to play down the economic policy errors and omissions on the part of Korea and other tiger economies in the run-up to the financial market crisis. But it must be acknowledged that there can be no stability in global financial and foreign exchange markets unless monetary relations between the major currency areas of the world are placed on a more stable footing. Hence responsibility for global economic development calls for a cooperative approach by the major currency areas. The leading industrial nations must not shirk from their common global responsibility. Misdirected trends in foreign exchange markets spread to other financial market segments; they acquire international impact, triggering inflation, deflation or recession with rising unemployment, and that on a global scale.

2 Requirements for financial market stability

2.1 Microeconomic requirements

The recent financial market crises have dramatically underscored the potential threat from instability in national financial markets and international financial relations. Financial market crises lead to sudden impoverishment of broad sectors of the population and undermine the political and social foundations in the countries concerned. Moreover, market globalisation means that regional financial market crises develop world-wide impact.

Thus a central task is to identify and to eliminate structural weaknesses in national financial markets and international financial relations. In particular, the aim must be to adapt the institutional framework to conditions in globalised financial markets. Reform efforts are at present concentrated in the following areas:

- Improving the transparency of national economic and monetary policy, of the policy of international organisations (in particular of the IMF and World Bank) and of the activities of the private sector (corporate governance, accounting).
- Intensifying the supervision of financial markets at national and international level: building up reliable supervisory structures for the national financial markets in emerging and transition economies and closer cooperation between national and international supervisory authorities.
- Continuing the liberalisation of capital movements hand in hand with the creation of stable national financial sectors and the concomitant supervisory structures.
- Improving crisis management, among others by involving the private sector at an early stage.
- Strengthening the role of the financial institutions: ensuring that they work together effectively and that they are capable of taking action, inter alia by providing them with adequate funding.
- Institutional reforms to strengthen the international financial institutions, in particular in view of their role as global fora for discussion.

It should be noted that until recently many of these reforms were still being rejected as representative of outmoded ways of thinking because trust was placed in principle in the efficiency of market allocation. It has now been generally accepted that there is no automatic guarantee of liberalisation having an impact conducive to stable economic growth.

The need for reform along these lines is uncontested. Progress has been made in these fields in the past few years, and further measures are soon to be implemented. But it has also become apparent in the course of past years that such structural reforms are not sufficient to ensure the stability of financial markets. Microeconomic reforms are not capable in themselves of eliminating systemic risks that are generated and nourished by strongly and indeterminably volatile interest and exchange rates. Therefore the indispensable structural reforms of the financial architecture must be backed up by a stable macroeconomic framework adapted to the liberal environment of international economic relations. This is doubtless the point that marks the parting of the ways.

2.2 Macroeconomic requirements

One view is that economic activity and growth are a reaction to real exogenous shocks reflected both in price and yield changes in financial markets and in non-monetary adjustments. There is no scope for policy measures. If all financial market prices and yields are fully flexible and correctly reflect all relevant determinants currently obtaining and expected to obtain in the future, there can be no misdirected trends in the financial markets on the one hand, and on the other financial relationships cannot give rise to any effects resulting in misdirected macroeconomic developments.

The conclusion drawn from this is that efficient results cannot be improved by economic policy measures, financial markets should be left to themselves and regimentation should be eliminated, because only then will the prosperity-optimising allocative function of the financial markets take full effect. Thus far the one way of looking at the issue.

Another view refers to the growing inherent dynamism of the financial markets, to the decoupling of the financial from the non-monetary sector, to price trends in financial markets that cannot be explained on the basis of generally accepted economic theory. Hence it is assumed that financial markets are susceptible to speculative excesses and by extension to price and yield movements causing economic distortion – current account imbalances, recessions with rising unemployment, cyclical booms accompanied by inflationary growth.

A high degree of uncertainty in assessing the movement of prices and returns in capital asset markets increases the risk of economic activity. As a rule, economic agents are averse to risk. The higher the risks, the lower the economic activity, the more marked the endeavours to identify means of hedging against those risks. Risk premiums charged for the provision of hedging instruments are reflected in higher market prices. It goes without saying that investors in securities with no hedge against declining-value risk, other than in fixed-interest securities, will of course ensure that they are remunerated for bearing the risk by a higher return. This is the other view.

Both interpretations are founded on what are, in themselves, consistent concepts drawing non-contradictory conclusions from given data. But this alone is not sufficient to serve as orientation for an economic policy solution. It must always be asked whether theoretical concepts are capable of reflecting reality. The evidence is disillusioning, as far as the reliance on consistently correct price signals from deregulated financial markets with fully flexible price formation is concerned.

For decades, the point of reference in the study of financial investment had been the capital market model, stipulating that investors build efficient portfolios on the opportunity line. This provides diversification benefits and reduces the relevant risk. Of the aggregate risk, only the systematic risk component plays a part after diversification. Accordingly, systematic risks are the central factors accounting for observed divergences in returns from different securities. In theory, high-risk securities compensate investors by affording higher risk premiums on the risk-free component; low-risk securities compensate only with small premiums. These interactions were held to be assured.

The empirical evidence looks different. Fama/French found in 1992 that in the normal case the risk parameters, however they were measured, displayed no statistically significant interaction with differences in returns. With this, the entire concept collapses. It was further found that in exceptional instances there is a statistically significant risk-return link, though in a direction contrary to that postulated in the theory: high-risk instruments have a small return (growth stocks), while low-risk instruments have a high return (value stocks). It may be concluded from this that no instrument is on the securities market line. This implies that several central assumptions of the capital market model must be invalid (cf. Haugen 1995; Cochrane 1999). Experts in financial investment are therefore agreed that the crucial assumption of the information-efficiency of securities markets must be relinquished (cf. Haugen 1996).

Empirical studies on the efficiency of the dollar exchange market in Germany point in the same direction (cf. Filc 1997, Frömmel/Menkhoff 1999). The results clash with the supposition of constantly rational forming of expectations on the part of economic agents as the keystone in the concept of information-efficient markets.

All this gives reason to refrain from regarding as set in stone, as it were, the permanent efficiency of deregulated, speculative competitive-bidding markets, such as foreign exchange and bond markets. But if there is justifiable reason to doubt the information efficiency of financial markets, even greater reserve should be entertained with regard to the contribution that price formation in financial markets governed solely by private-interest optimisation endeavours can make towards promoting employment and economic growth with stable prices.

In non-informative efficient markets there are multitudes of asymmetrical situations blocking profitable transactions. Institutional designs are needed if partial or total market failure in securities transactions is to be avoided. The purpose of such designs is to bridge information asymmetries. However, inefficiency requires design considerations not only for securities but for organisations and for the institutional embedding of trading in financial markets as well. This also holds in particular for foreign exchange markets as interface between monetary and non-monetary sectors and for the linkage between economic and currency areas.

In the sixties and early seventies the risks of financial asset change were slight, to the extent that they were expressed as imponderabilities in interest and exchange rate movements, because they were limited by institutional arrangements and economic policy measures, namely by fixed exchange rates and by monetary policies geared to stabilising interest rate movements. One consequence of this was that international capital movements were geared mainly to international interest differentials, which themselves were principally the reflection of differing cyclical trends. This is the macroeconomic framework within which individual financial investment institutions operate. Stable and predictable macroeconomic conditions lessen the hazards of taking up a specific risk position in the financial markets (cf. Hellwig 1998). This framework has been absent since the breakdown of the Bretton Woods system. The belief that in a flexible exchange rate regime markets would by themselves always return to rates that were in equilibrium and hence stable has proved illusory. Although flexible exchange rates can penalise unsound economic policy measures, there were repeated instances of misdirected trends in foreign exchange markets when there was a lack of clearly-defined guiding principles, when information asymmetries increased, when there was growing difficulty in drawing explicit conclusions from a mass of information. This is where macroeconomic design of the international financial architecture comes into play.

Thus structural or microeconomic reforms alone are not enough to ensure stability in the financial markets and the international financial system. In particular, these microeconomic reforms are not a suitable means of eliminating or at least reducing systemic risks. A dependable, global macroeconomic framework is needed. The question is how to shape institutions and the macroeconomic policy mix in order to take account of the globalisation of markets and the resulting challenges.

Bank risks that spread to a banking system have both microeconomic causes and a macroeconomic dimension. Banking system crises are a manifestation of the past two decades. Up to the mid-seventies bank collapses occurred only as very isolated events. There were no instances at all of bank crises affecting entire banking systems. This phase of stability in banking systems is the outcome of a special historical constellation of stable macroeconomic conditions underlying the financial sector (cf. Hellwig 1998). This includes exchange rates that can be approximately assessed as being geared to economic fundamentals. If these are lacking, misdirected trends in foreign exchange markets will trigger similar trends in other financial market segments, causing distortions throughout the economy. With the advance of globalisation, the impact may be felt world-wide.

3 The contribution of the international monetary system to a stable international financial architecture

3.1 The role of exchange rates for aggregate economic stability

Exchange rate changes in response to economic policy measures that are not agreed between the countries in question and result in very unbalanced economic development constitute the free formation of prices as a consistent market reaction. But experience also reveals as misleading the belief that foreign exchange markets will constantly and as it were automatically lead to stable exchange rate patterns in line with fundamental factors. Given a high degree of uncertainty about the future course of the economy there have time and again been instances of erratic fluctuations or lengthy misalignment of exchange rates, especially when individual market participants made use of differing information or when information gave rise to ill-defined conclusions for price formation. Hence the possibility of exchange rates in future repeatedly following the principle of self-justifying expectations cannot be ruled out. This will result in misdirected trends affecting the economy as a whole, with other financial market sectors being drawn into the wake of the foreign exchange markets.

Therefore interest rates in a specific country may rocket or plunge dramatically in contrast to aggregate economic requirements and against the monetary policy course, given a fortuitous, damaging constellation of exchange rates, exchange rate expectations, international interest rate differentials and quickly reversible changes in the assessment of the risk of exchange rate shifts. Hence it is an extremely risky undertaking in all circumstances to leave prices and returns in the financial markets in the hands of an "autopilot" designed to steer the world economy with complete reliability into the future. This holds true for interest movements as well, because central banks exert a fundamental influence on the entire range of interest in monetary markets by setting interest rates for the central bank money supply (cf. Filc 1998 b, 110 ff.). Scarcely any need to take action is perceived as far as price movements in foreign exchange markets are concerned, presumably because it is realised that monetary policy solo flights are destined to fail.

The major industrial economies, however, must not shirk their joint responsibility to adopt countermeasures in response to perceptible, severely misdirected trends in foreign exchange markets both in their own best interests and as a requirement of global economic stability. This is at the core of a system of "managed exchange rate flexibility" that has been under discussion in several countries, Germany among them, for some time now. Both financial and foreign exchange markets are to be put to the service of achieving sustained economic growth at a high level of employment. And this objective cannot be attained without close international cooperation between the shapers of stabilisation policy, hence also monetary policy.

3.2 The system of "managed exchange rate flexibility"

3.2.1 For reference: Cyclically neutral exchange rate movements not affecting capital transactions

Where countries have approximately equal levels of economic growth, exchange rate trends should be geared to international inflation differentials which in turn reflect the interest rate differentials between currency areas. Real exchange rates will then be constant, nominal exchange rate movements will offset differences in the yield from financial assets and exchange rate movements in the foreign exchange markets will be cyclically neutral (in relation to current transactions with other countries, to economic growth, employment and the rate of inflation) and will not affect capital transactions. In this case, price movements are systematically geared to underlying fundamentals without generating exchange rate risks. Exchange rate shifts then reflect the optimum international allocation of goods and capital.

Accordingly, exchange rate trends decoupled from international inflation and interest differentials will become a disruptive factor for progress towards macroeconomic objectives in individual countries and for the world economy. They generate tension that can subsequently lead to abrupt price adjustments in foreign exchange markets and overshooting exchange rates. Welfare losses are the outcome.

Trends in the European Monetary System (EMS) up to the currency crisis in the summer of 1992 may be cited as an example. The last preceding general realignment of central rates in the EMS had been made in early 1987. The impact of the single European market and plans for the completion of European monetary union caused the spread of an exchange rate illusion. It was thought that transition to a common European currency could be effected at the prevailing central rates despite the fact that price and cost trends still differed substantially as between the countries at the centre of the EMS, which had long enjoyed virtual price stability, and those on the periphery. In the course of time, an appreciable real depreciation of the D-mark developed within the EMS matching a real appreciation of the currencies of other countries, for instance Italy, Spain and the United Kingdom. International current transactions displayed a text-book response: record surpluses in Germany's foreign trade, especially with European Union countries, increasing current account deficits and appreciable loss of growth in those countries opposing the realignment of central rates despite diminishing ability to compete on prices.

In the summer of 1992 the exchange rate illusion faded away. This was followed by a series of central rate realignments in the EMS and by the withdrawal of the lira and the pound sterling from the exchange rate mechanism, preceded initially by severe and overshooting devaluations of both currencies. The necessary adaptation of the exchange rate structure of European currencies was quickly followed by adjustments in the countries' external positions, with the current account of Italy moving from a deficit of 2.5 % of GDP in 1992 to a surplus of 0.9 % in 1993 and that of Great Britain from a deficit of 1.7 % in 1992 to a surplus of 0.3 % in 1994. This example shows that with an approximately equal level of economic growth, exchange rates should follow a trend set by international price and cost differentials. In this case, real exchange rates will be virtually constant, international current transactions will be determined by the underlying economic fundamentals and exchange rates and their movements will have no effect on the ability of businesses in different countries to compete at international level.

In a rather longer-term perspective, exchange rate movements must also be approximately in line with international interest rate differentials. Given the globalisation of international financial relations and the almost complete liberalisation of capital transactions, substantial divergences in yields from similar financial assets of different countries with equal debtor ratings cannot be permanently upheld. If capital is perfectly mobile, international interest rate differentials are fully offset by matching shifts in exchange rate expectations, which determine exchange rate movements. In such case it is immaterial whether financial assets are purchased in a high-interest or low-interest country because the expected rates of yield adjusted to take account of exchange rate movements are the same. Time-limited deviations from this norm can occur only in the case of an exchange rate illusion, i.e. the conviction that given exchange rates will be maintained. Once the exchange rate illusion vanishes, the subsequent exchange rate adjustments will be all the more drastic.

There are examples of this as well. Since the early nineties it was possible on purchasing South Korean financial assets and taking account of shifts in the exchange rate of the won against the dollar to achieve yields far in excess of those obtainable from investment in other national markets. In this way it was possible for the rapidly growing current deficits to be financed without the need for devaluation of the won. This illusion vanished on reorientation of expectations as to exchange rate movements, leading to a drastic and overshooting devaluation of the won. High interest rates to finance a rising current account deficit, as in the case of South Korea, are an acceptable means only when they go hand in hand with appropriate, credible domestic measures to reduce internal and/or external imbalances. If these measures are lacking, the exchange rate illusion will sooner or later be dispelled by a sober evaluation of facts and turbulence on foreign exchange and financial markets will be the result (Furmann/Stiglitz 1998, 72 ff.). Developments in Brazil from 1998 on provide a further example of these interrelationships.

Thus in a somewhat longer-term perspective and given approximate cyclical consistency, exchange rate trends should follow the course set by international price increase differentials as also reflected by international exchange rate differentials.

3.2.2 The machinery of the system

This calls for a suitable institutional design. It should aim to prevent excessive volatility and different forms of exchange rate misalignment. There are two starting-points. Firstly, consideration should be given to the possible effects of central bank interest policy measures on exchange rate movements. There is a need for international discussion here. Secondly, operators in foreign exchange markets should be afforded guidance on the price trends in foreign exchange markets that are in line with the aggregate economic environment in the major currency areas. This could be undertaken by the finance ministers and central bank governors of G 7 countries, possibly with support from international institutions such as the IMF. This body should collect, evaluate and publicly interpret information relevant to exchange rates, in other words it should assume the role of an information broker. Thus the Financial Stability Forum launched in February 1999 at the meeting of finance ministers and central bank governors of G 7 countries, the function of which is to monitor the microstructure of international financial relations, should be backed up by a macrostructure forum.

In the event of abrupt changes in nominal or real exchange rates, this body should publicly comment on the course taken by exchange rates and, where necessary, explain what form the possible economic policy response could take. If there is a lack of clearly-defined pointers for the formation of market expectations, guidelines must be set to ensure that expectations remain stable. In particular, where the available information is indefinite, credible statements by an international body of high repute can provide essential guidance in shaping exchange rate expectations and stabilising foreign exchange markets. Moreover, it is important for this body to be assigned decision-taking powers on economic policy, as debate and the exchange of views cannot by themselves resolve any problems (cf. Eatwell/Taylor 1999).

On this basis the system could be designed as follows:

- The current market rates of the currencies in the system should be taken as a starting-point in the initial phase. Upper and lower reference values are to be established around these rates which, while leaving adequate scope for the necessary alterations to exchange rates, would also trigger timely consultations between the participating countries.
- Moreover, reference values for real rates of exchange should be determined. The method of computing real exchange rate changes remains to be discussed. While different procedures of deflating exchange rates produce matching trend results (revaluation or devaluation in real terms), they also produce differing values (cf. Deutsche Bundesbank 1998).
- The reference values for nominal and real exchange rates must be made public.
- The reference values should be reviewed at regular intervals, say every six months.
- When the lower or upper reference values are reached, compulsory consultations should lead the central banks and finance ministries of the participating countries, possibly with the involvement of international institutions, to a joint interpretation of exchange rate trends and if necessary to a joint strategy aiming to stabilise exchange rates. The interpretation and any economic policy measures regarded as practicable must be made public in order to provide guidance for and to steer the expectations of market participants.

One objection to this concept arises from the target zone debate of the mid-eighties. At that time, Williamson (1983) proceeded from the assumption that it was possible to define fundamental equilibrium exchange rates. The problem is that equilibria or disturbances of equilibria in monetary markets or in the foreign exchange market attain a comprehensible dimension only if their impact on other markets, above all product markets, on output and employment is taken into consideration.

The problem of defining equilibrium exchange rates, a problem admitting of no satisfactory solution, also arose in connection with the EMS. For this reason, the preceding day's rates were used when the EMS was put into effect, rather than equilibrium exchange rates determined on the basis of model calculations, because those rates were perceived as appropriate by the governments and monetary authorities of the participating countries. Thus the determination of reference rates in the foreign exchange market should be geared to a common perception of their appropriateness rather than to conceivable equilibrium exchange rates.

The procedure is similar to that by which central banks set money supply targets. When they went over to announcing such targets, central banks did not attempt first of all to determine the "equilibrium money supply" but defined an "appropriate" money supply that was then rolled forward using data on expected aggregate economic development for the period under review. "Soft" limits for monetary expansion were set around the central figure in the form of upper and lower limits to the envisaged money supply growth. It is not evident why the central bank procedure of setting money supply targets with the aim of stabilising financial systems has so often proved successful in the past, while a comparable procedure for determining practicable reference values for exchange rates is destined to fail.

3.2.3 Economic policy measures

Hence the most important element in a system of "managed exchange rate flexibility" is a compulsory consultation process between central banks and finance ministers of the G 7 countries. Other than with fixed exchange rate or target zone systems there are no strictly defined and binding economic policy measures to be taken in response to specific developments in foreign exchange markets. But in the event of acute volatility in foreign exchange markets and marked divergence from the entry rates the system should require readiness on the part of the world's major industrial economies to study the causes in detail and to submit a joint interpretation of the trends.

If the outcome of such analysis and interpretation is that current developments are justified on account of changes in the underlying fundamentals, for example currency appreciation in the wake of vigorous economic growth, this should be noted in the comments. Moreover, reference values could be adapted to take account of exchange rate trends.

But if the body of central bank governors and finance ministers reaches the conclusion that there are clear signs of currency misalignment in the foreign exchange markets, further steps will need to be taken in the monetary cooperation process.

- In some instances it may be sufficient to issue credible statements in order to talk down economically unwarranted trends in foreign exchange markets. This will be the case where the information provided exerts selective influence on the expectations of market participants.
- In addition, it should be examined whether economic policy measures are considered appropriate to stabilise exchange rates without triggering other target infractions, and if so, what measures these should be (cf. Filc 1998a, p. 35 ff.).
- In exceptional circumstances, the necessary measures should include, as ultima ratio, concerted interventions by central banks in foreign exchange markets, provided this does not jeopardise price stability. Both sterilised and non-sterilised interventions can give important signals influencing expectations of exchange rate changes, and by extension exchange rates themselves, whereas

market interventions through the portfolio channel are likely to be of less significance for exchange rates.

Market globalisation as now established is to be reinforced and secured by international non-market institutions, hence by an adequate institutional design at international level. It may be debatable whether the proposed approach is sufficient to achieve the desired results. But it does point in the right direction, namely to reinforce the necessary structural and thus microeconomically-oriented reforms of the international financial architecture with a macroeconomic stabilisation policy more effectively coordinated between the world's major economic and currency areas and an institutional design at international level, in order to ensure that foreign exchange markets do not again become the source of misdirected economic trends. There is of course no royal road to this end, but progress must be made if future financial market crises are to be averted.

While this kind of institutional framework to enhance exchange rate stability is founded on the existing monetary policy cooperation between G 7 countries, it serves also to intensify such cooperation. In contrast to earlier phases of monetary policy cooperation, a mandatory consultation machinery between the three major currency areas on the basis of constant surveillance of exchange rate trends should be capable of averting any substantial exchange rate misalignment in its initial stages. Greater exchange rate stability between the "big three" is also essential for enhancing financial market stability in the emerging economies. Moreover, well-founded decisions on suitably stable currency regimes for these countries cannot be taken until the core area itself is sufficiently stable.

4 The Euro as a stimulant of further international cooperation on monetary policy

The introduction of the Euro will reinforce the trend towards a multipolar structure in the international monetary system. The impact of this will be felt not only by the USA and the dollar, which will in future be sharing its formerly dominant position in the financial markets with the European currency, but by all other countries as well. At global level, the Euro will be more of an alternative to the dollar than were the D-mark and the other internationally traded EU currencies. The Euro is likely to lend fresh momentum to the ongoing trend towards currency diversification in official reserves, in investment, in the billing of international trade and in foreign exchange transactions. Whatever course the future process of adjustment may take, and whether or not the Euro will prove able to benefit from its potential as alternative to the dollar, it should be ensured that any concomitant turbulence in the foreign exchange markets is avoided (cf. Henning 1998). This will call for international cooperation on economic and monetary policy alike. It will also assign a new global responsibility to economic policy-makers in the USA and the monetary union. If there are substantial shifts in investments between the dollar area and the Euro area, it will be the task of economic policy-makers in both areas to take measures to counter unrest in the financial markets. The necessary coordination as between partners of approximately equal strength is likely to differ from that pursued in the G 7 world of the eighties.

But there can be no disputing the fact that the international system is best served if each of the major players keeps its own house in order. Macroeconomic policy must accordingly be geared to attaining strong, employment-promoting growth while maintaining price stability. The USA and the EU are largely in agreement on this. The extent to which this consensus also applies to price movements in the foreign exchange markets is less evident. The introduction of the Euro could prove a means of deepening transatlantic relations in this respect. To this end it must be acknowledged that the world economy is better served by policy cooperation between the major currency areas of the world than by a strategy of benign neglect of misalignments in foreign exchange markets.

References

Cochrane, John H., New Facts in Finance, CRSP – University of Chicago Working Paper, June 7, 1999

Deutsche Bundesbank, 1998: Zur Indikatorqualität unterschiedlicher Konzepte des realen Außenwerts der D-Mark, Deutsche Bundesbank Monthly Report, November, p. 41 ff.

Eatwell, John; Taylor, Lance, 1999: International Capital Markets and the Future of Economic Policy: A Proposal for the Creation of a World Financial Authority, Internet Publication (www.newschool.edu/cepa)

Eichengreen, Barry, 1999: Toward a New International Financial Architecture – A Practical Post-Asia Agenda, Institute for International Economics, Washington, D.C.

Fama, Eugene F.; French, Kenneth R., 1992: The Cross-Section of Expected Stock Returns, The Journal of Finance, Vol. 47, No. 2, June 1997, p. 427 ff.

Furman, Jason; Stiglitz, Joseph E., 1998: Economic Crisis: Evidence and Insights from East Asia, Brookings Papers on Economic Activity: 2: 1998, p. 1 ff.

Filc, Wolfgang, 1997: Das Ende der Effizienzträume, Hamburger Jahrbuch für Wirtschafts- und Gesellschaftspolitik, 42. Jahr, p. 99 ff.

Filc, Wolfgang, 1998a: Mehr Wirtschaftswachstum durch gestaltete Finanzmärkte, International Politik und Gesellschaft, 1/1998, p. 22 ff.

Filc, Wolfgang, 1998b: Theorie und Empirie des Kapitalmarktzinses, 2nd enlarged and revised edition, Stuttgart

Frömmel, Michael; Menkhoff, Lukas, 1999: The International Efficiency of Financial Markets and Macroeconomic Equilibrium. In: Filc, Wolfgang; Köhler, Claus (eds.): Macroeconomic Causes of Unemployment: Diagnosis and Policy Recommendations, Publications of the Institut für Empirische Wirtschaftsforschung, Vol. 36, Berlin

Haugen, Robert A., 1995: The New Finance: The Case Against Efficient Markets, New Jersey

Haugen, Robert A., 1996: Finance From a New Perspective, Financial Management, Vol. 25, No. 1, p. 86 ff.

Hellwig, Martin, 1998: Systemische Risiken im Finanzsektor. In: Duwendag, Dieter (ed.): Finanzmärkte im Spannungsfeld von Globalisierung, Regulierung und Geldpolitik, Berlin, p. 123 ff.

Henning, C. Randall, 1997: Cooperation with Europe's Monetary Union, Institute for International Economics, Washington, D.C.

UNCTAD, 1998: Trade and Development Report, Geneva

Williamson, John, 1983: The Exchange Rate System, Institute for International Economics, Washington, D.C.

Discussion of Wolfgang Filc's "Functions of economic policy in promoting the efficiency of the international financial system"

Bernhard Eckwert

Chemnitz University of Technology, D-09107 Chemnitz, Germany

This paper deals with a question of topical interest. It is written in a provocative style and contains an unconventional solution concept. In this way I found the paper congenial because its style eases considerably a discussant's task to stimulate a controversial debate.

The financial sector has been the most rapidly evolving part of the global economy for years. While the changes in the financial sector have significantly facilitated and stimulated international trade and capital movements, it appears that they have also facilitated the transmission of financial disturbances across countries and currency areas. The currency crises in South-East Asia, East Europe and South America we have seen in the past years are often taken as evidence for the increased fragility of the international financial system in an integrated global economy. These crises were not confined to the currency markets but they involved the whole financial sectors of the countries concerned and they rapidly spread into the real sectors as well.

Wolfgang Filc argues in his paper that the volatilities on the financial markets, in particular on the foreign exchange markets, result in non-acceptable economic turbulences for the whole economy. Therefore the government has the obligation to intervene into the price formation process on the financial markets in order to make sure that these markets support sustainable economic growth and high employment. Mr. Filc suggests the following mechanism: A comittee of experts watches over the international financial markets and sets target zones for the bilateral exchange rates. The criterion for choosing the target zones should not be linked to the supposed equilibrium rates. Instead the criterion should be based on the adequacy of the exchange rates, e.g., in the sense of purchasing power parity or interest parity. If the target zones are defended by appropriate economic policy measures they will serve as a guide of orientation for the actors on the financial markets. In this manner the private agents will be enabled to interpret price signals in a more reliable way than would be possible in the presence of eratically fluctuating prices. In addition, the performance of financial markets improves in terms of informational efficiency, because the markets reflect the opinion of a comittee of experts rather than the opinion of mislead speculators. The markets gain additional stability and will no longer be a trigger of worldwide economic turbulences.

The statements contained in this paper are highly controversial and I disagree with most of them. While, as a thought experiment, the expressed ideas have intellectual appeal, from a more practical perspective I feel that the author has lost his way. In my view this holds true with respect to the problem diagnosed in the paper as well as with respect to the proposed measures designed to solve the problem.

Let me start with the diagnosis. In order to make possible a reliable diagnosis the problem to be solved needs to be formulated more clearly. In this regard complaints about global economic turbulances and, in particular, about turbulances on the financial markets and foreign exchange markets are of little help. Mr. Filc's paper offers a solution; it is less than clear, however, whether there is a problem which would require such a solution.

The currency crises in South-East Asia and East Europe were no random events; rather they were caused by developments in the real sectors of the affected economies. E.g. the currency crisis in Russia was soon followed by a default of the Russian government on its internal and external debt. It is misleading to think of financial crises as random erratic turbulances. A financial crisis is a symptom of, or a signal for, misdirected developments in some sectors of the economy. Such signals must not be suppressed by regulatory intervention. Otherwise misdirected trends in the real economy will be detected only with delay, or may escape the attention of policy makers altogether, thereby becoming much harder to rectify. Price volatility alone is no indication for economic instability and does not justify subjecting price formation processes to the control of a state authority. Stability of the financial system does not necessarily imply that prices within the financial sector must be stable. On the contrary, the responsiveness of the prices plays a key role for maintaining the stability of the financial system. The volatile performance of the US Dollar on international currency markets during the past 15 years in combination with the extraordinary robustness of the American financial system provides ample evidence for this fact.

The international currency markets have calmed down in the meantime. Due to their size the currency areas of the Euro, the US Dollar, and the Yen are largely immune against speculative currency attacks. Also, in the medium run, the financial crises in South-East Asia, East Europe and South America will probably have a benign impact on the affected economies. The transition period is, of course, painful. Yet, the process of economic recovery, which was helped by structural reforms of the banking sector and of the domestic capital markets, has already begun and seems to be well under way.

Turning from the diagnosis to the cure of the problem, Prof. Filc advocates policy measures which exert tight control over the formation of prices on the foreign exchange markets. Prof. Filc argues that financial markets are informationally inefficient and, hence, the price signals on unregulated financial markets lack reliability. For that reason, the political authorities advised by an international comittee of experts, should set up crash barriers for prices on the foreign exchange markets.

Some remarks on the theoretical background and on the implementation of these suggestions are in order.

First, the paper correctly states (and reiterates again and again) that financial markets are less than fully informationally efficient. This does not imply, however, that the financial system fails to communicate *any* information. If it is true that an unregulated financial system eliminates at least part of the informational asymmetries across agents, then the resulting equilibrium risk allocation may still be preferable to what can be achieved through state control. Making things worse, interventions into the price formation process will necessarily lead to price distortions, i.e., discrepancies between exchange rates and fundamental values. These distortions are inevitable because as yet the fundamental factors by which exchange rates are determined in equilibrium are unknown. It is more than unlikely that policy makers are able to determine the 'correct' prices more accurately than the market does.

A second remark relates to the hypothesis of the author according to which prices on the foreign exchange markets have a tendency to fluctuate erratically. If the exchange rates were to move eratically then these movements would constitute unsystematic (i.e. insurable) risks for the global economy. In such a case the problem of real sector instability would disappear immediately if (unbiased) insurance markets are organized. Yet, even if exchange rate fluctuations constitute systematic risks, any attempt to stabilize exchange rates would still be pointless. Since in this case exchange rates merely respond to fluctuations in the real sector of the economy any policy which succeeds in stabilizing the exchange rates will necessarily create additional volatilities elsewhere in the economic system.

The rationale for the recommendations in the paper is based on the assumption that the comittee of experts will always agree on upper and lower reference values for exchange rates. The conjecture that the committee will always reach a consensus, even in turbulent times, is obviously of debatable merit. Furthermore, if it becomes necessary to reset reference values, i.e., if the old reference values turn out to be inadequate, then the new ones are very likely to be inadequate too. This is almost inevitable because it is explicitly not intended that reference values are in line with actual market trends. If inadequate reference values are being established repeatedly, the credibility of the committee of experts will soon become damaged and, once again, markets are left without reliable orientation.

Even worse: the establishment of inadequate reference values will heat up speculation, and hence volatility, on the foreign exchange markets. Typically, wild currency speculation sets in if an exchange rate approaches a reference value, because market participants become encouraged to bet on central bank interventions. The currency crises in South-East Asia did not occur as the result of fluctuating exchange rates. Quite on the contrary, they originated because overly rigid exchange rates provided incentives for speculative investor behavior.

Summarizing, I feel that the paper contains some interesting starting points for the development of ideas about policies aimed at stabilizing the international financial system. Yet, in its current form the analysis does not significantly go beyond a cure of symptoms. In the long run, a policy concept solely based on direct intervention in the price formation processes on the financial markets is bound to fail. Such a policy will aggravate the very same problems it is supposed to solve, i.e., it will promote the emergence of speculative currency attacks and thereby increase the fragility of the international financial system.

Part II:

Banking systems and restructuring

Universal banks – A reconsideration

Vincenz Timmermann

University of Hamburg, Institute for International Trade, and Economic Integration, Von-Melle-Park 5, D-20146 Hamburg, Germany

As regards the role of the banking sector in economic development, numerous important contributions have been made in the literature of economic theory and economic history.[1] Today, I wish to focus on one aspect of this discussion, namely on the role and importance of the universal banking system.

In the process, I shall take the following steps: first, I shall deal with the universal banking system and with the experiences made with this system in the past. For obvious reasons, I shall confine myself to the German universal banking system, according to which in my opinion, the benefits and disadvantages may be illustrated. In a second section, I wish to follow up the arguments put forward against the universal banking system. Finally, in a third section I shall attempt to answer the question as to whether the universal banking system, bearing in mind all that we know about it, may be able to stand its ground against other banking systems.

1.

I should like to begin with a brief definition: An universal bank is a banking institution which, "conducts all banking operations apart from the issuing of notes and mortgage bonds" [2]. In other words, unlike specialized banks in the so-called separation bank system, universal banks are not characterized by any form of specialization as deposit-taking banks *or* as credit institutions *or* as long-term finance institutions; instead, universal banks are engaged in all fields providing money and capital: they conduct deposit-taking *and* loan operations of various maturities,

---

1 Contributions relating to economic theory were made above all by *J.A. Schumpeter* („Theorie der wirtschaftlichen Entwicklung (1911)", 5th. ed., Berlin 1952, pp. 105 and pp. 140) as well as by *J.G. Gurley and E. Shaw* ("Money in a Theory of Finance", Washington 1960), while contributions concerning economic history were derived particularly from *A. Gerschenkron* ("Economic Backwardness in Historical Perspective", Cambridge 1962, pp. 5) and *R. Cameron et al.* ("Banking in the Early Stages of Industrialization", New York 1967; "Banking and Economic Development", New York 1972).

2 *H.E. Büschgen*, „Universalbanken oder spezialisierte Banken als Ordnungsalternativen für das Bankgewerbe der Bundesrepublik Deutschland unter besonderer Berücksichtigung der Sammlung und Verwendung von Kapital", Cologne 1970, p. 7.

bond issues, the company promotion business, money transactions and dealings in shares and securities.

In my opinion, the immense importance of universal banks for Germany's economic development is attributable to special features, which I consider worthy of emulation:

- The one special feature is the granting of *unsecured, personal loans*.
- The other consists in long-term *investment financing*, with which the company promotion business, bond issues and participation are inextricably linked.

The German banks were the first to link up the two specialities of unsecured personal loans and long-term investment financing in a particularly successful manner.

At this juncture, I wish to add some comments on unsecured personal loans: The origins of this extremely successful banking practice – like the spadework of many a financial innovation – are to be found in *Scotland.*

This business practice is characterized by two processes closely linked to one another: within the scope of this system, on the one hand it is true to say that *unsecured personal loans* are granted by the banks. However, in return, the borrower must settle *all* his money transactions via 'his' banker providing the loan in question. The borrower is granted credit facilities without having to furnish collateral security; the bank is provided with full information on the borrower's business performance and his financial activities. *Adam Smith,* in the second chapter of volume two of his book, "The Wealth of Nations", reports that the banks in Scotland were already granting loans without demanding collateral security in his day and age (i.e. in or about 1776).[3] *Werner Sombart* characterizes this credit form as "the elevation of persons without any financial assets to the status of entrepreneurs, in the process of which the coincidences of earlier days, in which the exercise of such entrepreneurial activities was dependent on the possession of monetary wealth, were eliminated." [4]

The second special feature of the universal banking system, which has been so successful in Germany, is long-term investment financing. This also includes the incorporation of companies, the issuing of securities and even the participation on an enterprise, rarely with the intention of a long-term participation from the outset, more frequently of a temporary nature, i.e. as long as not all equities are as yet capable of being placed.

This comprehensive form of investment financing was first practised on the European continent in *Belgium*, namely by the "Société Générale de Belgique" established in 1822; this institution is considered the first European commercial bank of this new category since this bank (which, incidentally, was already operating as a joint stock bank at the time) also conducted securities operations from

---

[3] *A. Smith,* "An Inquiry into the Nature and Causes of the Wealth of Nations" (1776), ed. by J.R. McCulloch, Edinburgh 1846, pp. 123.

[4] *W. Sombart,* „Der moderne Kapitalismus", Volume III: „Das Wirtschaftsleben im Zeitalter des Hochkapitalismus" (1902), 3rd ed., Munich 1928, p. 220.

the very outset.[5] The bank attempted to solve the liquidity problem arising from the transformation of maturities by issuing its own bonds as contra items to loans outstanding and to participations in enterprises. This attempt – and all further trials with such so-called "Crédit Mobilier Banks" in France and Italy failed owing to the fact that these banks spent too much time relying exclusively on the (initially) very risky financing of housing and industry, completely neglecting the deposit-taking business in the process.

By contrast, the major German banks operating branches, above all the 'big banks' of Berlin (in 1851 the *Disconto-Gesellschaft*, in 1856 the *Berliner Handels-Gesellschaft*, in 1853 the *Bank für Handel und Industrie* in Darmstadt, in 1870 *Deutsche Bank* and in 1872 *Dresdner Bank*) were meticulous in maintaining deposit-taking from the very beginning; the large German banks had learnt their lessons from the difficulties encountered by the Belgian, French and Italian "Crédit Mobilier" banks. By establishing banking branches and sub-branches throughout Berlin and other German cities, the deposit-taking business was used to establish the preconditions for lending operations catering for various maturities: to an ever increasing extent, equity capital became part of reserves while the actual working funds of the universal banks were above all time deposits and savings.

The development in the direction of universal banks in Germany was also promoted by the fact that German private banks were not entitled to issue notes. From the beginning, however, they were always keen to process *all* their clients' banking transactions. Since they were not allowed to issue notes, they had to develop other methods of monetarization and financing, which very soon took them back to the Medieval Italian giro system which was meanwhile being practised only in particularly important trading centres such as Amsterdam, London and Hamburg:[6] If numerous traders and merchants operated a current account with one particular bank, it was possible for substantial proportions of their receivables and liabilities to be offset *internally* against one another within the bank in question; furthermore, if banks also maintained accounts with one another, it even became possible for internal settlements in the nature of a modern clearing system to be intensified; at any rate, fewer banknotes were needed for business transactions.

The rediscovery of the giro system and the financial innovation of bank clearing very soon led to a significant expansion in current account transactions, the concomitant increase in depositing money constituting an important contribution to the industrialization of Germany.

Thus, by way of summary the special features of German universal banks are as follows:

---

[5] Cf. *K.E. Born*, „Geld und Banken im 19. und 20. Jahrhundert", Stuttgart 1977, pp. 102 and pp. 171.

[6] In Hamburg, the 'Hamburger Bank', the first German giro bank, had been established as early as 1619. Cf. *O. Veit* in this regard, „Grundriß der Währungspolitik", pp. 467; *Landeszentralbank* in der Freien und Hansestadt Hamburg (ed.), „Die Notenbank in Hamburg: Wie sie wurde, was sie war und was sie ist", Hamburg 1981, pp. 7.

First of all, there is the unsecured, personal loan, i.e. the bank opens a current account for its client, allowing him to overdraw this account to a certain extent previously agreed; in return, the client agrees to conduct *all* his banking transactions via 'his' banker. Secondly, we have investment financing, if necessary involving a *direct participation* of banks in particularly risky investments made by their customers.

According to *Alexander Gerschenkron*, by means of their active engagement on the market the private banks, followed later by the big joint stock banks, had to act as substitutes for entrepreneurs and private capital, both of which there was a lack of in those days.[7]

Indeed, the German universal banks accompanied the business "from the cradle to the grave", so to speak: they were actively engaged in the *foundation* of companies, they had a say with regard to any *extensions* and major innovations, *capital increases*, mergers and finally – if applicable – also in *liquidation*. Thus, the banks in Germany actually became an important source of capital and entrepreneurial expertise – at least in the early stage of industrialization. It was only later, when substantial profits were being realized by industrial enterprises (in turn making self-financing possible) that industry became less dependent on banks.

However, it would be wrong to devote our interest in the German monetary and credit system exclusively to the *big joint stock banks*, as is so often the case, and to credit these above all with the laurels for financing economic development in Germany[8]. In doing so, one would overrate the influence of the German big banks since there were numerous industrial enterprises in Germany long before the large-scale, really efficient joint stock banks came into being; these were only established around 1870. Thus, it was only towards the end of the 19th century that the large credit institutions and branch banks were able to participate in the foundation of industrial companies introducing capital-intensive innovations, such as the mining corporations, the pipe construction works, railway and telegraph companies. However, the high capital requirements in coal and iron ore mining and in the metal industry proved to be far in excess of the means at the small private banks' disposal. Even though the *small credit banks* were at a disadvantage relative to the major joint stock banks as regards the foundation of industrial companies and the security issuing business, they clearly enjoyed advantages in current lending operations: their knowledge of local conditions and the local markets and, accordingly, of the business affairs of their clients and the latter's credit standing, made it possible for banks to grant or refrain from granting personal and unsecured loans, as the case may be.

The way in which a French journalist described this special feature of the German banking system and its significance for economic development is described in

---

[7] Cf. *A. Gerschenkron*, "Economic Backwardness in Historical Perspective", Cambridge 1962, pp. 14.

[8] A warning against this erroneous conclusion is also given by *K. Borchardt*, „Die Industrielle Revolution in Deutschland", Munich 1972, pp. 104.

a report which he forwarded to his newspaper in France.[9] While in Barmen (today known as Wuppertal-Barmen) he spoke to the directors of two banks, the *"Barmer Bankverein"* and the *"Bergisch-Märkische Bank"*, and these gentlemen told him that the industry of the region in Germany known as the "Bergisches Land" owed its success above all to the "blindly trusting and almost limitless credit made available by the banks to the diligent captains of industry". In France, as a rule the banks generally did not grant unsecured credits to industry and trade. Apparently, in Germany this was a fairly common custom. In Germany, if a merchant's skill and prudence induced a banker to consider him trustworthy, the merchant could obtain as much money as he needed. In return, the firms entrusted the bank providing the funds with all their money transactions. Against payment of 1 or as little as ¼ % over the Reichsbank discount rate, any diligent manufacturer could obtain as much capital as he required. Krupp would probably have gone bankrupt 20 times over if the bankers had not loyally supported him; the same applied to Thyssen. How would the remarkable chemical factory of Friedrich Bayer at Elberfeld (which, founded by a minor businessman, now ranks in first position worldwide) ever have attained such a stage of development but for the support of the banks? So much for the report of the French journalist, who, as a contemporary witness, so impressively describes the special features of the German banking system which I mentioned earlier.

2.

Following this outline of historic experiences with universal banks in Germany as shown in studies by economic historians but also in travel reports, biographies of industrial pioneers as well as in anniversary writings compiled by German banks and industrial companies, I now wish to deal with the arguments put forward in more recent literature against the German universal banking system.

German universal banks have been reproached time and again for exerting too great an influence on the economy, this influence being derived from several sources: from normal day-to-day lending operations, industrial participations, seats on supervisory boards and proxy voting rights. Critics of the German universal bank system conclude that this leads to a conflict of interests on the part of banks, a tendency towards greater market power and engenders conduct which has the effect of stifling competition.

Indeed, the close relationship between German banks and industry constitutes a special problem of the German universal banking system, particularly in the eyes of foreigners. As an external sign, references are frequently made to the large number of supervisory board seats of industrial companies held by representatives of banks.

---

[9] *Jules Huret*, „In Deutschland" (1907), in: K. Hackenberg (ed.), Wuppertal (year of publication not stated), pp. 29.

In addition, critics of the German banking system often assert that the formation of large groups and cartels in Germany and the general concentration of industry in Germany had actually been promoted by the banks; the latter had urged their clients to merge and amalgamate since the security of their loans had increased in the process. According to these critics, the banks could hardly be interested in very intensive competitive relations among their clientéle. Simultaneously, the interests of major banking customers had also developed in favour of having large and efficient bankers for their business needs. Accordingly, the concentration of banks and industry served mutual interests: industry required big banks for their immense financing requirements; the banks, in turn, needed large enterprises in order to secure their large-scale loans.[10]

The assertion that the German universal banking system was beneficial above all to the banks in making the latter strong and influential does not hold water. Granted, it is true to say that big banks and large-scale industry also developed in Germany. However, in Germany a reasonable balance of power between the banks and industry evolved in the 19th and 20th centuries. Part of the time the banks had a stronger influence on industry, while at other times industry had the upper hand. Thus, not only do banking representatives have seats on industrial companies' supervisory boards but industrial representatives also have seats on the supervisory boards of banks.

By and large, the participation of banking representatives in the supervisory bodies of industrial enterprises is appreciated because this makes information and financial know-how available on the one hand, ensuring on the other that there is a competent counter-balancing effect vis-à-vis the representatives of other interests in the supervisory bodies concerned. Furthermore, it must not be overlooked that as a rule, the representatives of various banks sit alongside and opposite one another on these supervisory bodies and exercise voting rights; in the process, the influence of individual banks is partially neutralized.

Thus, to me the objections to the universal banking system appear to have been grossly exaggerated, perhaps disregarding some abuses which have developed in Western industrialized countries in the course of a long period of application without any effective legislative regulations having been enacted to remedy the situation. However, these excesses (such as the unrestricted exercise of the banks' proxy voting rights, the seats on supervisory boards, or the exaggerated shareholdings of individual banks) can be regulated in terms of appropriate statutory provisions.[11]

---

[10] In this connection, it is pointed out to the reader that the close relationship between the big banks and large-scale industry clearly led to preferential treatment being given to large enterprises over smaller ones. Thus, e.g. by *H. Neuburger and H.H. Stokes*, "German Banks and German Growth", 1883-1913, An Empirical View, in: The Journal of Economic History, No. 34 (1974), pp. 710.

[11] Cf. *U. Immenga*, „Beteiligungen von Banken in anderen Wirtschaftsbereichen", 2nd ed., Baden-Baden 1978, pp. 145.

3.

In the light of what has been said thus far, it is tempting to conclude that the universal banking system clearly is the best possible solution for a country intending to restructure its banking sector. Before such a conclusion can be drawn, however, the following must be borne in mind:

From the research conducted in economic history to date, and from our own experience, we know that given a diversity of cultural and institutional conditions in various countries and during various times, very different banking systems have evolved to produce efficient solutions: small individual banks and major banks operating branch networks, highly specialized institutions and universal banks.

No country can adapt the banking system of some other country without making any changes, simply by imitating the other country's organization, business practices and modes of conduct. Several examples may be cited as evidence. Even after achieving their independence, many former colonies in Asia and Africa have retained the banking systems imposed by their colonial masters although these banking systems failed to correspond to their own circumstances and requirements. Thus, most former colonies have adapted the Anglo-Saxon separation system. Such a system of highly specialized banks functioned well in the conditions prevailing in Great Britain, where borrowers were generally in a position to provide adequate collateral security. By contrast, in the poorer countries of Asia and Africa there was a dearth of wealthy merchants and traders.

The French banking system was hardly suited to poorer countries either since French banks abroad confined their activities above all to the collection of savings in the former colonies. In addition, these banks – like the French banking system as a whole – were much too preoccupied with Paris as a banking centre; thus, local lending was sadly neglected.

A completely different approach was followed in *Japan*, where various elements of American, British and German banking systems were initially introduced; it was only after and to the extent that the blueprints taken over from abroad had been tried and tested for several years under Japanese conditions that these concepts were adapted to Japan's circumstances and finally established. In the process, Japan has been exemplary in demonstrating how individual parts of the banking systems of other countries can be taken over and adapted to fit in with a country's own needs and conditions.

Thus, in my view the motto should be "adapt rather than imitate". In other words, a banking system which has been successful elsewhere should not be emulated or taken over unchecked; instead, useful elements should be selected and adapted to the own particular needs and conditions of the country concerned.

Incidentally, not only does this apply in the economic sphere but also in the political arena. Furthermore, it applies to a banking system such as the German one which, at first glance, has all the advantages on its side but was itself derived by adapting elements of other banking systems.

This brings me back to the question stated at the outset: can the German banking system – as a whole or at least material elements thereof – stand its ground against other banking systems today?

I believe the answer is "yes", and in doing so, I am thinking of the following special features of the German universal banking system:

- the granting of personal, unsecured loans;
- the application of the 'crédit mobilier' principle of long-term investment financing;
- the strong emphasis on deposit-taking;
- the continued development of current account transactions and the bank clearing system.

Specially for countries not in a position to rely on a prosperous middle class and on wealthy merchants and traders, the universal banking system in principle is more suitable than the Anglo-Saxon separation system. The German economist Adolf Weber is credited with characterizing these two systems in a manner which I consider very apt. Weber is said to have stated that German banks were created for people who needed money while English banks were for people who had money.

The credit category known as the unsecured, personal loan makes it possible for all proficient and venturesome enterprises to make investments, even if such enterprises are short of the necessary assets. The crédit mobilier principle of long-term investment financing likewise is a valuable enrichment for countries intending to restructure the fabric of their monetary and credit systems. On the other hand, the high risks involved in the foundation and extension of companies as well as in the introduction of technical innovations must be supplemented by a very active deposit-taking scheme. The accumulation of savings (be they ever so modest) and the efficient allocation of investible funds can be performed in universal banks making optimum use of all the experience, knowledge of the market and information available "under one roof", as it were; this is particularly the case if no efficient capital market is available as yet, meaning that the banks have to help out with interim loans or preliminary financing, or take custody of stocks until ready for placement.[12]

Bearing in mind all we know about universal banks, not only have these assumed substantial risks themselves in the past; they have also always provided private and institutional investors with good facilities for holding diversified portfolios, mobilizing venture capital in the process.

In other words, on the one hand the bank client is presented with the complete range of banking services as if he were in a supermarket; on the other, the client commits himself to a particularly close relationship with 'his' banker. In the case of personal loans, it will be difficult for him to change banks: this could be seen as a disadvantage but could nevertheless be kept within acceptable limits provided there is a well-functioning system of competition among the banks.

---

[12] Cf. *W. Hankel*, „Währungspolitik", Stuttgart 1971, pp. 252.

On the whole, therefore, in my judgement the German universal banking system represents a banking category whose adaption – even if not in its entirety, at least in its principal elements – is also worthy of recommendation to other countries.

References

Borchardt, K., Die Industrielle Revolution in Deutschland, Munich 1972.

Born, K.E., Geld und Banken im 19. und 20. Jahrhundert, Stuttgart 1977.

Büschgen, H.E., Universalbanken oder spezialisierte Banken als Ordnungsalternativen für das Bankgewerbe der Bundesrepublik Deutschland unter besonderer Berücksichtigung der Sammlung und Verwendung von Kapital, Cologne 1970.

Cameron, R. et al., Banking in the Early Stages of Industrialization, New York 1967.

Cameron, R. et al., Banking and Economic Development, New York 1972.

Gerschenkron, A., Economic Backwardness in Historical Perspective, Cambridge 1962.

Gurley, J.G., Shaw, E., Money in a Theory of Finance, Washington 1960.

Hankel, W., Währungspolitik, Stuttgart 1971.

Huret, J., In Deutschland, (1907), in: K. Hackenberg (ed.), Wuppertal (year of publication not stated).

Immenga, U., Beteiligungen von Banken in anderen Wirtschaftsbereichen, 2nd ed., Baden-Baden 1978.

Landeszentralbank in der Freien und Hansestadt Hamburg (ed.), Die Notenbank in Hamburg: Wie sie wurde, was sie war und was sie ist, Hamburg 1981.

Neuburger, H., Stokes, H.H., German Banks and German Growth, 1883-1913, An Empirical View, The Journal of Economic History, No. 34 (1974), pp. 710.

Schumpeter, J.A., Theorie der wirtschaftlichen Entwicklung, (1911), 5th ed., Berlin 1952.

Smith, A., An Inquiry into the Nature and Causes of the Wealth of Nations, (1776), ed. by J.R. McCulloch, Edinburgh 1846.

Sombart, W., Der moderne Kapitalismus, Vol. III: Das Wirtschaftsleben im Zeitalter des Hochkapitalismus, (1902), 3rd ed., Munich 1928.

Veit, O., Grundriß der Währungspolitik, Frankfurt a.M. 1961.

Efficiency of the banking system: The Italian case

Gianandrea Goisis

Istituto di Scienze Economiche e Statistiche, University of Milan, I-20122 Milano, Italy

Abstract. This essay focuses on the situation of the Italian system in a European perspective. Several parties blame the limited size, the poorly diversified production, and the excessive capacity of this system. In the author's view, recent ECB statistics and other empirical evidence seem to point out that the recent poor results of the Italian banking system mostly depend on a low credit quality and on a limited diversification of production. On the other hand, there are doubts with respect to the possibility to calculate univocal statistics for the Italian banking system, in the light of the marked difference observed between the Northern and Southern regions of the Country.

1 Introduction

A review of the economic results achieved by the Italian banking system cannot help arousing some concern, with data pointing out to net margins on assets and equities among the lowest in the EMU, as "confirmed" by very high operating cost-income ratios (see Appendix, Tables 1, 2, 3, 4).

An expected tough competition on the European market, reaching beyond national boundaries, calls for a thorough analysis of the causes for such disappointing results.

A few matters, apparently crucial in this respect, should be tackled in order to carry out this review, based on recent statistics published by the ECB and other institutions.

1) These include, most importantly, the issue of the size adequacy of Italian banks, even though this does not really deserve the ongoing emphasis Monetary Authorities and press media are putting on it. As a matter of fact, a larger size is thought to promote achievement of scale and scope economies, especially if this is accomplished without too much increasing the number of branches. The combination of information centres and administrative facilities and, more generally, the elimination of duplicates at a centralized and decentralized level, as well as, on the other hand, the sharing of experiences and innovative financial products, could ensure these benefits. A set of empirical estimates, mostly performed by means of translog multiproduct functions, seem to confirm this assumption, for our country

more than for others [Conigliani, 1992; Goisis, Parravicini, 1993; Focarelli et al.,1998; Piloff, Santomero, 1998]. Indeed, according to several indexes – including the share of assets, loans, and deposits of the first five major Italian banks – there seem to be no dominating banks in Italy, unlike in other countries (e.g. France, Germany, and the UK), capable of taking on a "global player" sector [Desario, 1995] role at an international level (see Table 5). At the moment two planned mergers (see Table 6) could change the situation.

In this respect, however, an appropriate distinction should be made between the convenience of creating few large players or of indiscriminately raising the scale of assets of each banking entity (and this is often not done in Italy!). A few German banks (e.g. Deutsche Bank), for example, have a considerable size and worldwide standing, but the 3.576 German credit institutions seem to make up a banking system with a smaller average size than in Italy, where after all there are only 935 credit institutions, and where 169 out of the 402 mergers and acquisitions that took place in the EMU area from 1995 to 1998 were recorded. Based on ECB data (however still to be confirmed), the average assets of Italian credit institutions have been estimated at approximately 3.234 billion lira, vs. 2.597 for German institutions (and, on the other hand, 4,508 for French institutions). If an impression-based approach, such as "survivorship", was then applied to calculate scale economies, a sub-optimal size could not be assigned to the Italian system as a whole.

In addition, while the profits of "major" Italian institutions seem to lag behind those of all other size groups, those of "minor" institutions are higher than the system's average – although this indicator is based on impacts that reach well beyond scale economies. Non-conclusive data on the existence of scale yields also emerge from a review of average operating cost structures (see Tables 7 and 8).

The recent assumptions, most assertively expressed in early 1999, on mergers of some of the main Italian institutions seem to herald the setting up of entities that could rank among the first 10 European institutions in terms of assets and equity.

The recent financial Consolidation Act[1], promoting take-over bids and concentration in general, should strive towards the creation of larger banks. However it should be noted that mergers and acquisitions are only successful if executives' intentions are in agreement and if duplication of functions, which are not subject by their own nature to a scale-proportional growth, is actually prevented [Smith, Walter, 1998, Berger 1998].

2) Secondly, specialized production in the Italian banking system also deserves some thinking. Note, in this respect, that the income from activities other than interest contribution only accounts for 29% of the total in our country, vs. an average of 34.8% in other EMU countries, and a 53.2% peak in France (see Table 9).

Considering that the ongoing fall in interest rates, currently under way within the European monetary area, increasingly makes traditional collection and lending ac-

---

[1] T.U. Finanza ,1998.

tivities less profitable – the rates required by banks in Italy fell from 13% in 1995 to 8% in 1998 – a change in behaviours is needed [Fazio, 1998; Profumo, 1997] in order to enhance indirect collection, asset management activities, bankinsurance, shares and bonds trading, and generally all innovative activities allowed by the Consolidation Act on banks as of 1993, acknowledging the existence of the so-called "universal bank"[2].

3) The internationalization degree of our banking system should also be discussed. To some observers, it is characterized by a poor representation of both Italian institutions abroad and of foreign institutions in Italy [Rossignoli, 1998]. As far as the latter case is concerned, the strict rules on the opening of branches (removed in the late 1980's) and the present applicability of the so-called "silent approval" rule (less binding but in any case a limit) may certainly have hampered the access of foreign competitors to our markets.

However it should be noted that foreign branches or subsidiaries only account for 7.2% of the total assets of the banks operating in our country, vs. 52.1% in the UK and 36.1% in Belgium (see Table 10), on the other hand there are lower values for Austria and Germany (3.6% and 4% respectively) and slightly higher for France (9.3% in 1996). In addition, foreign institutions increased their presence in Italy significantly from 1995 to 1996 (+31%). The values of penetration of Italian banks into foreign markets (measured in terms of "total assets of branches and subsidiaries of domestic institutions in foreign countries as a percentage of total domestic assets") – apparently more significant – amount to 15.3% and growing, also for the 1996-1997 period, though lagging behind those of France and Germany (29.4% in 1996 and 27.1% respectively). While the internationalization of our banking system is certainly under way there are still excellent opportunities for growth.

4) On the other hand, thinking about the current distortions of the Italian banking system, even the fourth "plague" that many have charged it with, i.e. a production capacity surplus, does not seem to be occurring, in many respects. As mentioned, there were only 935 institutions in our country in 1997, vs. 3.576 in Germany and 1.291 in France. Their number in absolute terms is even lower than in Austria (955).

There are 0.44 branches (see Table 11) per 1.000 inhabitants (with an 80% increase compared to 1980) vs. a European average value of 0.48, 0.57 in Germany and 0.58 in Austria. There are six employees per 1,000 inhabitants vs. a EMU average (unweighted) of 9.73, 9.16 in Germany and 6.89 in France. Considering the average salary of bank employees as a percentage of total average salaries, a value of 219.5 was recorded for 1996, vs. an average value of 145, which heavily seems to account for the high costs of banking products in Italy and for the job losses currently affecting this sector [Ciocca, 1999].

---

[2] T.U. Banche, 1993.

5) Last but not least, there seems to be a definitely abnormal ratio in our country between the amounts allocated in view of coping with credit losses and bank incomes net of allocations, i.e. approximately 64.3%, or twice as much as in the EMU (see Table 12).

This data points out to the operators' inability to assess credit quality on one hand, and outlines on the other an institutional environment unsuited for "bad loan" recovery; the long time required, especially in some Italian regions, to end the trials or settle bankruptcy is also a well-known issue sector [Goisis, Parravicini, 1999]. In addition, until recently the public nature of a number of Italian banking institutions (and of the most important among them) has certainly promoted inappropriate mingling of political pressures and economic decisions, thus contributing to the fall in the number of bank profits. Consideration of a number of long-established "bad loans" may lead to charge more recent balance sheets with the (negative) results of past choices. It should be noted, however, that some southern regions experience dramatically different conditions compared to the rest of the country sector [Bagella, 1997; Cusimano, 1997, Bianchi, 1996]. Bad loans in the South and Islands amounted in 1997 to four times as much as their value, as a percentage of loans, in north-western Italy (see Table 13).

This discussion on credit quality leads to express clear reserves on the possibility to judge the Italian credit system globally. Significant differences in productivity and product quality, in fact, produce dramatically different economic results (see Table 14).

Generally applicable credit policies, with no distinction between non-homogeneous domestic areas (and this also applies to countries other than Italy), may therefore hardly be put forward.

In conclusion, the high cost per product unit and the low operating results observed in the Italian banking system, at an aggregate level, should be attributed to poor product diversification and to low-quality credit, giving place in turn to significant overdues, rather than to a generally inadequate size. The phenomenon of overdues is (and particularly was) encouraged by political pressures and ineffective administrative and judicial credit recovery practices.

Now that the big gaps between required and paid interest rates which had allowed to conceal this inefficiency are no longer observed, an improved and updated training of executives and personnel at large is required in order to cope with European challenges. In this respect the high employment cost, compared to European standards, appears quite unusual, though typical of Italy's experience; in the present tough job market, it brings in fact to the forefront the trade off between job protection and salaries.

Banks should become true "enterprises", give up their privileges and at the same time remove protection, in order to establish a "contestable markets" equilibrium without predetermined functions and dimensions sector [Berionne, 1998]. Moreover, the difference between regions in our banking system poses a natural hindrance to enforce strict common rules.

Legal developments have occurred: customs should now improve and implement them.

2 More remarks on the banking system in the South

As already mentioned, Southern Italy and the Islands (briefly the "South") represent the main weakness of the Italian banking system. Thus, in the light of the deep differences compared to the North, it makes little sense to draw up national statistics providing an average of different situations. The efficiency of Unicredit, Banca Commerciale Italiana and Rolo, in fact, greater than the European average, clashes against the comatose state of several institutions, that still need to recover from a dramatic lack of efficiency, often due to their public status, by which they are subject to an interference that is fully incompatible with their institutional economic nature.

These conditions also result from inspections carried out by the Bank of Italy (in charge of checking stability and efficiency of the credit system) that pointed out, in 1998, to deeply diversified judgements. As shown in Table 15, inspections carried out in the South are concluded with 61% negative judgements vs. 11% for the North and 25% for the Centre. On the other hand, the North achieves 67% fully positive judgements vs. 5% for the South and 38% for the Centre.

These observations, referred to official controls, confirm the impression resulting from a review of overall data. In addition, the intrinsic weakness of the Southern banking system, which undoubtedly depends on its own structure, as well as on economic problems, is one of the main factors determining charged interest rates, by far higher than the Italian and European average values (see Table 16 and Figure 1). Rates in Calabria, for example, are 50% higher than in Lombardy, to the detriment of regional economies that are already in trouble for structural economic reasons. On the other hand, legislation on usury interest rates, in force since 1996, establishes common thresholds regardless of the regions where the institutes operate, and may therefore cause serious problems to weaker sectors and regions, which may be denied credit at rates that do not fully cover the related risk.

It may not be ignored that general unemployment rates in the South are three times as high as in the North, productivity levels are by far lower and so are, consequently, private incomes and consumption.

Only public consumption and public expenditure in general seem to be homogeneous, with an income and expense deficit that would lead to exclusion of the same from the system if compliance with Maastricht parameters were assessed by regions (see Table 17).

In this situation the Bank of Italy is supporting the acquisitions of Southern banks by Northern banks.

These acquisitions aim at promoting know-how transfer, the strengthening of the assets of institutions and the achievement of scale and scope economies, also through product diversification and enlargement of the existing network.

According to the Bank of Italy's data, 36 of the 71 Southern banks subject to mergers or acquisitions from 1985 to 1997 were joined with Northern banks and 18 with Central banks. No Southern banks acquired banking institutions in other areas.

However, acquisitions may not solve the problem: an action is also required on the environment and on Southern institutions. While criminality hampers, among others, the banks' economic activities and great caution is required, here more than anywhere else, to avoid appearing as supporters of criminal activities and money launders, the problem of civil justice, particularly slow and captious in Southern regions, is also quite serious (see Table 18). Estate building judicial auctions, that usually last approximately 8 years in the North, with serious impacts on the accounts and leanness of the banking system, may take up to 15 years in the South. This obviously affects loan terms and may exclude an increasing number of potential users from the same.

These environmental difficulties, may finally result into financial saving transfers from backward regions (more in need of the same) to more advanced ones, also following up acquisition of Southern institutions by Northern banks. Southern banks may turn into saving collectors for the North, since the higher charged interest rates (paid ones are lower in the South) do not make up for the credit risk.

In fact, it may be convenient to induce the acquired Southern banks to finance directly Northern enterprises or indirectly by transferring part of their deposits to their northern group-leader.

It is therefore a matter of outlining solutions for the reorganisation of the Southern banking system, based on improved techniques and at the same time related to a more general economic and social modernisation, possibly resulting into virtuous interactions.

Appendix: Tables and figures

Table 1 Selected bank profitability ratios: Return on equity (net income as a percentage of equity)

	1995	1996	1997
AT	8.1%	9.6%	
BE	12.9%	15.3%	15.3%
DK (1)	18.5%	16.1%	15.1%
FI	-7.9%	8.0%	15.2%
FR	3.6%	4.8%	7.7%
DE	12.6%	12.3%	
GR (2)	24.4%	16.7%	
IE	20.2%	20.1%	18.4%
IT	3.7%	5.1%	3.4%
LU(2)	19.9%	22.3%	23.0%
NL	17.0%	17.6%	
PT (2)	7.7%	10.7%	13.1%
ES	9.2%	9.7%	10.6%
SE	21.1%	24.0%	13.0%
UK	28.6%	25.6%	26.4%
Average EU-14 (5)	10.0%	11.0%	
Average EU-15	10.1%	11.1%	
Average EU-11 (5)		12.2%	12.2%
USA (1)	19.3%	19.6%	22% (2)
Japan	-5.0%	0.2%	
Switzerland	8.4%	1.7%	

Notes: (1) Commercial banks and savings banks; (2) commercial banks; (3) total commercial banks, foreign commercial banks, savings institutions; (large commercial banks; (5) the average EU-14 figures exclude IE, the average EU-11 figures include all countries which delivered 1997 data.

Source: ECB, "Possible Effects of EMU on the EU Banking Systems in the Medium to Long Term", February, 1999.

Table 2 Return on assets (net income as a percentage of total assets)

	1995	1996	1997
AT	0.4%	0.4%	
BE	0.3%	0.3%	0.4%
DK (1)	1.3%	1.3%	1.0%
FI	-0.4%	-0.4%	0.8%
FR	0.2%	0.2%	0.3%
DE	0.5%	0.5%	
GR (2)	1.1%	1.1%	
IE	1.4%	1.4%	1.0%
IT	0.3%	0.3%	0.3%
LU(2)	0.5%	0.5%	0.5%
NL	0.7%	0.7%	
PT (2)	0.6%	0.6%	0.8%
ES	0.8%	0.8%	0.9%
SE	1.3%	1.3%	0.7%
UK	1.1%	1.1%	1.1%
Average EU-14	0.5%	0.5%	
Average EU-15	0.5%	0.5%	
Average EU-11			0.7%
USA (1)	1.6%	1.6%	1.8% (2)
Japan	-0.2%	-0.2%	
Switzerland	0.5%	0.5%	

Notes: (1) Commercial banks and savings banks; (2) commercial banks; (3) total commercial banks, foreign commercial banks, savings institutions; (large commercial banks; (5) the average EU-14 figures exclude IE, the average EU-11 figures include all countries which delivered 1997 data.

Source: ECB, "Possible Effects of EMU on the EU Banking Systems in the Medium to Long Term", February, 1999.

Table 3 Cost-income ratio (overheads as a percentage of total income)

	Cost-income ratio		
	1995	1996	1997
AT	69.5%	69.1%	
BE	67.5%	65.7%	63.9%
DK (1)	54.0%	56.9%	59.2%
FI	112.2%	88.6%	73.4%
FR	65.6%	69.9%	68.7%
DE	63.8%	63.8%	
GR (2)	64.3%	68.1%	68.1%
IE	59.3%	57.6%	58.3%
IT	68.2%	67.1%	69.0%
LU(2)	46.5%	46.5%	43.3%
NL	67.3%	67.3%	
PT (2)	64.9%	64.3%	57.7%
ES	63.2%	62.2%	61.4%
SE (3)	71.6%	64.3%	64.0%
UK	63.8%	62.3%	60.9%
Average EU-14 (5)	65.5%	65.4%	
Average EU-15	65.5%	65.3%	
Average EU-11 (5)		63.9%	62.9%
USA (1)	63.7%	63.3%	60.8%(2)
Japan (2)	66.5%	74.3%	
Switzerland	56.4%	66.1%	

Notes: (1) Commercial banks and savings banks; (2) commercial banks; (3) total commercial banks, foreign commercial banks, savings institutions; (large commercial banks; (5) the average EU-14 figures exclude IE, the average EU-11 figures include all countries which delivered 1997 data.

Source: ECB, "Possible Effects of EMU on the EU Banking Systems in the Medium to Long Term", February, 1999.

Table 4 Net interest margin (net interest income as a percentage of average total earning assets)

	Net Interest Margin		
	1995	1996	1997
AT	1.8%	1.7%	
BE	1.3%	1.3%	1.2%
DK (1)	3.2%	2.7%	2.4%
FI	2.3%	2.3%	2.1%
FR	1.3%	1.2%	1.0%
DE	2.0%	1.9%	
GR (2)	2.6%	2.3%	
IE	2.9%	2.5%	1.9%
IT	4.4%	4.1%	3.8%
LU(2)	0.7%	0.7%	0.7%
NL	1.8%	1.8%	
PT (2)	2.6%	2.3%	2.3%
ES	3.4%	3.2%	2.9%
SE (3)	2.8%	2.4%	1.8%
UK	2.6%	2.4%	2.3%
Average EU-14 (5)	2.0%	1.9%	
Average EU-15	2.0%	1.9%	
Average EU-11 (5)		2.5%	2.3%
USA (1)	3.8%	3.9%	4.0%(2)
Japan (2)	1.6%	1.3% (4)	
Switzerland	1.4%	1.3%	

Notes: (1) Commercial banks and savings banks; (2) commercial banks; (3) total commercial banks, foreign commercial banks, savings institutions; (large commercial banks; (5) the average EU-14 figures exclude IE, the average EU-11 figures include all countries which delivered 1997 data.

Source: ECB, "Possible Effects of EMU on the EU Banking Systems in the Medium to Long Term", February, 1999.

Table 5 Concentration: Loans of the five biggest credit institution as a percentage of total loans

	1995	1996	1997	% change 1985-1995	% change 1995-1996	% change 1996-1997
SE	90.06	86.45	87.84	+43.76	-4.01	+1.61
NL	78.50	78.10	80.60	+16.99	-0.51	+3.20
GR	80.75	78.65	76.90	-13.32	-2.60	-2.23
DK	79.00	85.00	75.00	+11.27	+7.59	-11.76
PT	73.00	76.00	75.00	+21.67	+4.11	-1.32
BE	61.00	63.00	66.00	+12.96	+3.28	+4.76
FI	59.93	57.98	56.23	+20.63	-3.25	-3.02
FR	46.80	48.60	48.30	-3.90	+3.85	-0.62
IE	47.50	46.40	46.80	-0.42	-2.32	+0.86
ES	43.12	42.54	42.13	+22.85	-1.35	-0.96
AT	34.01	33.38	39.31	+17.77	-1.85	+17.79
LU	15.13	30.06	28.63		+98.68	-4.76
UK	25.00	26.00	26.00		+4.00	0.00
IT	26.30	26.60	25.90	+58.43	+1.14	-2.63
DE	13.83	13.26	13.71		-4.12	+3.39
EU average unweighted	51.60	52.80	52.56		+2.34	-0.46

Notes: (1) Commercial banks and savings banks; (2) commercial banks; (3) total commercial banks, foreign commercial banks, savings institutions; (large commercial banks; (5) the average EU-14 figures exclude IE, the average EU-11 figures include all countries which delivered 1997 data.

Source: ECB, "Possible Effects of EMU on the EU Banking Systems in the Medium to Long Term", February, 1999.

Table 6 The ten biggest banks in Europe (assets in billions of Euro)

BNP-PARIBAS- SG (planned) – (France)	861.866
DEUTSCHE BANK-BANKERS TRUST – (Germany)	660.078
UBS-SBS (Switzerland)	638.606
CREDIT SUISSE (Switzerland)	433.128
HONG KONG SHANGAI BANK (United Kingdom)	432.925
CREDIT AGRICOLE (France)	384.045
ABN AMRO (Holland)	375.035
BARCLAYS BANK (United Kingdom)	354.730
SAN PAOLO – BANCA DI ROMA (planned) – (Italy)	286.873
INTESA COMIT – (planned)	286.166

Source: Author elaborations on data "Corriere della Sera", March 20, 1999, and "Il Mondo" july 31th, 1998

Table 7 Returns on assets and overheads – Italy 1997

	OVERHEADS AS A PERCENTAGE OF ASSETS	NET INCOME AS A PERCENTAGE OF ASSETS
MAJOR BANKS	2.36	-0.43
BIG BANKS	2.18	0.41
MEDIUM BANKS	2.13	0.26
SMALL BANKS	2.37	0.25
MINOR BANKS	2.83	0.32

Source: Author elaborations on data Banca d'Italia, Relazione del Governatore 1997, Roma, 1998.

Table 8 Return on equity in Italian banking system

Dimensions	1991	1992	1993	1994	1995	1996	1997
Major	7.35	1.86	2.09	-0.46	-1.95	-0.59	-4.77
Big	-	5.02	2.07	0.21	2.35	4.24	4.50
Medium	11.76	4.70	3.46	2.02	-0.61	1.53	2.40
Small	5.22	3.99	3.51	1.95	3.48	3.87	2.69
Minor	4.34	4.02	4.68	-0.39	2.33	3.77	3.07
All banks	7.09	3.55	2.69	0.54	0.27	1.80	0.40

Source: Author elaborations on data Banca d'Italia, Relazione del Governatore, Roma, different years.

Table 9 Non interest income contribution (non interest income as a percentage of total income)

	1995	1996	1997
AT	39.4%	41.0%	
BE	29.2%	30.7%	37.1%
DK (1)	32.8%	32.1%	31.8%
FI	43.2%	49.5%	45.6%
FR	45.5%	47.0%	53.2%
DE	21.0%	21.0%	
GR (2)	52.4%	55.5%	
IE	29.8%	32.1%	33.8%
IT	20.2%	24.9%	29.0%
LU(2)	34.5%	38.3%	44.1%
NL	33.3%	35.9%	
PT (2)	24.0%	31.1%	33.4%
ES	23.1%	26.6%	29.2%
SE (3)	35.0%	41.6%	48.6%
UK	42.9%	38.5%	38.8%
Average EU-14 (5)	31.4%	32.5%	34.8%
Average EU-15	31.4%	32.5%	34.8%
Average EU-11 (5)		31.7%	34.7%
USA (1)	33.7%	35.0%	38.2%(2)
Japan (2)	1.9%	-10.2%	
Switzerland	56.7%	59.6%	

Notes: (1) Commercial banks and savings banks; (2) commercial banks; (3) total commercial banks, foreign commercial banks, savings institutions; (large commercial banks; (5) the average EU-14 figures exclude IE, the average EU-11 figures include all countries which delivered 1997 data.

Source: ECB, "Possible Effects of EMU on the EU Banking Systems in the Medium to Long Term", February, 1999.

Table 10 Market share of total foreign branches and as a percentage of total domestic assets (sorted by the market share of total branches/subsidiaries in 1997)

	TOTAL B+S			% change	% change
	1995	1996	1997	1995/1996	1996/1997
LU	99.7	99.9	99.9	+0.31	0.00
IE	40.6	45.6	53.6	+12.42	+17.36
UK	51.6	50.6	52.1	-1.92	+2.82
BE	28.4	26.5	36.3	-6.46	+36.73
GR	18.6	22.1	21.9	+18.59	-0.91
ES	11.8	11.4	11.7	-3.64	+2.99
PT	9.4	7.7	10.5	-17.48	+36.05
FR	12.2	9.8		-19.67	
NL	9.8	8.5	7.7	-12.91	-9.53
FI	6.5	6.3	7.1	-3.98	+13.38
IT	5.4	7.1	6.8	+31.11	-3.81
DE	4.2	4.0	4.3	+4.57	+8.82
AT	3.5	3.6	3.3	+4.05	-7.50
SE	1.7	1.2	1.6	-26.79	+26.83

Notes: (1) Commercial banks and savings banks; (2) commercial banks; (3) total commercial banks, foreign commercial banks, savings institutions; (large commercial banks; (5) the average EU-14 figures exclude IE, the average EU-11 figures include all countries which delivered 1997 data.

Source: ECB, "Possible Effects of EMU on the EU Banking Systems in the Medium to Long Term", February, 1999.

Table 11 Capacity indicator: Number of branches per 1.000 capita, number of bank employees per 1.000 capita and average wages in banking as a percentage of total average wages

	branches/1000 capita 1997	bank employes/1000 capita – 1997	average wages (a) 1996
ES	0.97	6.29	153.28
LU	0.75	45.75(b)	182.00
BE	0.72	7.57	172.78
AT	0.58	9.43	
DE	0.57	9.16	
FR	0.44	6.89	
IT	0.44	6.00	219.50
NL	0.44	7.19	136.10
DK	0.42	8.10	117.00
PT	0.41	5.97	160.00
FI	0.32	5.21	116.68
IE	0.32	6.29	118.00
UK	0.32	9.07(b)	133.00
SE	0.29	4.93	133.00
GR	0.24	5.25	106.00
EU average unweighted	0.48	9.73	145.61

Notes: (a) The EU average is unweighted and calculate on the basis of the number of countries available in the year.(b)LU: not show in the chart for reasons of scaling; UK: including staff of members of the British Bankers' Association and staff employed by building societies.

Source: ECB, "Possible Effects of EMU on the EU Banking Systems in the Medium to Long Term", February, 1999.

Table 12 Net provisions as a percentage of preprovisioning income (loan loss provisions as a percentage of net income minus loan loss provisions)

	1995	1996	1997
AT	56.6%	52.1%	
BE	34.8%	28.9%	18.9%
DK (1)	35.1%	28.5%	24.3%
FI	3.8%	-6.3%	1.1%
FR	74.9%	64.6%	49.6%
DE	39.0%	39.0%	
GR (2)	15.7%	39.7%	
IE	9.6%	8.2%	8.7%
IT	65.5%	49.5%	64.3%
LU(2)	11.6%	4.8%	18.5%
NL	17.7%	18.9%	
PT (2)	41.2%	40.5%	30.4%
ES	33.9%	25.9%	18.4%
SE (3)	-11.1%	2.0%	34.4%
UK	20.5%	15.1%	13.6%
Average EU-14 (5)	45.4%	39.3%	
Average EU-15	44.9%	38.8%	
Average EU-11 (5)		31.4%	32.6%
USA (1)	15.0%	17.2%	17.3%(2)
Japan (2)	134.2%	97.8% (4)	
Switzerland	58.1%	90.0%	

Notes: (1) Commercial banks and savings banks; (2) commercial banks; (3) total commercial banks, foreign commercial banks, savings institutions; (large commercial banks; (5) the average EU-14 figures exclude IE, the average EU-11 figures include all countries which delivered 1997 data.

Source: ECB, "Possible Effects of EMU on the EU Banking Systems in the Medium to Long Term", February, 1999.

Table13 Bad loans in different areas

	Change %		Bad loans/loans	
	1996	1997	1996	1997
north-west	1.6	1.3	5.8	5.3
north-east	1.9	-3.1	6.6	6.0
Middle	7.0	3.0	9.4	9.6
South and Islands	23.3	-8.0	24.2	21.8
Italy	11.7	-2.5	10.1	9.4

Source: Author elaboration's on data Banca d'Italia, Relazione del Governatore 1997, Roma, 1998.

Table 14 Economic results of banks as percentage of total assets

	North-West		North-East	
	1996	**1997**	**1996**	**1997**
Interest income contribution	2.36	2.02	3.15	2.79
Non Interest income contribution	1.09	1.13	1.22	1.28
Total contribution	3.45	3.15	4.37	4.07
Cost income ratio	2.24	2.16	2.69	2.57
Net income	0.27	0.28	0.54	0.59
	Middle		**South**	
	1996	**1997**	**1996**	**1997**
Interest income contribution	2.35	2.14	2.81	2.83
Non Interest income contribution	0.92	0.95	0.79	0.92
Total contribution	3.27	3.09	3.60	3.75
Cost income ratio	2.21	2.17	3.02	2.89
Net income	0.20	-0.62	-0.95	-0.03

Source: Author elaboration's Banca d'Italia, Relazione del Governatore 1997, Roma, 1998.

Table 15 Banks inspections in 1998

Judgement	North	Middle	South	Total	Major, Big and Medium	Small and Minor	Coop.ve credit banks
Good	67,3%	38,8%	5,3%	42,7%	33,3%	37,2%	44,8%
Partially good	21,7%	26,2%	33,3%	28,1%	50%	30,2%	26,4%
Bad	11%	25%	61,4%	29,2%	16,7%	32,6%	28,8%
Total	100%	100%	100%	100%	100%	100%	100%

Source: Author elaboration's on data Banca d'Italia, Relazione del Governatore, 1998, Roma 1999.

Table 16 Charged and paid short term interest rates by the Italian banks – Regional data, 1998

Area	Charged Interests	Paid Interest	Difference
Total	6,70	1,96	4,74
North West Italy	6,17	1,88	4,29
Piemonte	6,38	1,63	4,75
Valle d'Aosta	7,90	1,93	5,97
Liguria	7,32	1,68	5,39
Lombardia	6,04	1,99	4,05
North East Italy	6,56	1,83	4,73
Trentino Alto Adige	6,90	1,68	5,22
Veneto	6,75	1,89	4,86
Friuli Venezia Giulia	6,46	2,08	4,38
Emilia Romagna	6,30	1,72	4,58
Central Italy	7,22	2,24	4,98
Marche	6,73	1,77	4,96
Toscana	6,88	2,06	4,82
Umbria	8,29	2,07	6,22
Lazio	7,47	2,39	5,08
Southern Italy	8,54	1,67	6,87
Campania	8,36	1,69	6,67
Abruzzo	8,40	1,89	6,51
Molise	9,27	1,79	7,48
Puglia	8,35	1,82	6,53
Basilicata	9,15	1,46	7,49
Calabria	9,68	1,61	8,07
Insular Italy	9,23	2,15	7,08
Sicilia	9,31	7,25	7,06
Sardegna	9,10	1,98	7,12

Source: Author elaboration's Banca d'Italia, Bollettino Statistico.

Table 17 Taxes and public expenditure – estimated – 1997

Area	Taxes (per capita)	Public Expenditure (per capita)	Taxes - Public Expenditure	Taxes - Public Expenditure/Incom e %
Piemonte	16.632.000	13.719.000	2.913.000	+ 7,6%
Valle d'Aosta	20.391.000	23.115.000	-2.724.000	-6,2%
Lombardia	19.993.000	13.521.000	6.472.000	+15,0%
Trentino Alto Adige	16.598.000	18.217.000	-1.619.000	+3,7%
Veneto	16.313.000	13.067.000	3.246.000	+8,1%
Friuli Venezia Giulia	17.620.000	16.696.000	924.000	+2,3%
Liguria	17.062.000	17.248.000	-186.000	+0,004%
Emilia Romagna	18.487.000	15.066.000	3.421.000	+7,9%
Toscana	16.269.000	14.602.000	1.667.000	+4,6%
Umbria	14.029.000	15.651.000	-1.622.000	+5,05%
Marche	14.616.000	14.124.000	492.000	+1,4%
Lazio	18.313.000	15.057.000	3.256.000	+8,6%
Abruzzo	12.366.000	14.460.000	-2.094.000	-7,1%
Molise	10.719.000	15.480.000	-4.761.000	-19,0%
Campania	9.749.000	12.467.000	-2.718.000	-12,5%
Puglia	9.738.000	12.150.000	-2.412.000	-10,1%
Basilicata	9.011.000	14.921.000	-5.910.000	-28,0%
Calabria	8.357.000	14.049.000	-5.692.000	-29,6%
Sicilia	9.583.000	14.219.000	-4.636.000	-21,4%
Sardegna	11.259.000	14.743.000	-3.484.000	-13,7%
Unweighted National Average	14.355.000	15.128.000		

Source: Author elaboration's on data Ragioneria dello Stato, Roma, 1997.

Table 18 Bankruptcies declared and closed in Italy in 1995, regional data

Area	Bankruptcies declared	Bankruptcies closed	Ratio between Bankruptcies closed and declared
Piemonte	924	922	0,997
Valle d'Aosta	27	24	0,888
Lombardia	2575	2038	0,791
Trentino Alto Adige	140	124	0,885
Veneto	1017	881	0,866
Friuli Venezia Giulia	336	271	0,806
Liguria	469	322	0,686
Emilia Romagna	908	817	0,899
Toscana	1338	706	0,527
Umbria	224	174	0,776
Marche	382	268	0,701
Lazio	2156	1178	0,546
Abruzzo	400	216	0,540
Molise	74	15	0,202
Campania	2142	643	0,300
Puglia	796	339	0,425
Basilicata	76	13	0,171
Calabria	302	206	0,682
Sicilia	1395	363	0,260
Sardegna	335	79	0,235

Source: Author elaborations on data Istat, Introducing Italy, Roma, 1997.

Figure 1 Charged interest, paid interest, difference between charged and paid interest

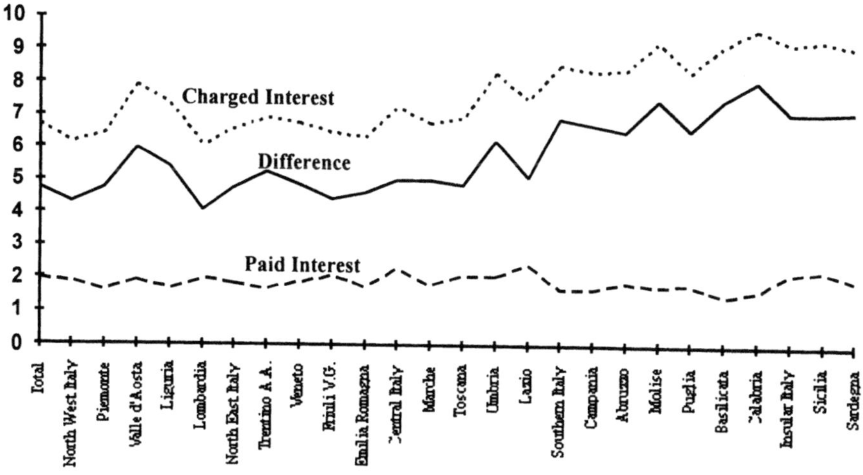

References

Bagella, M. (1997), "Credito, efficienza del sistema bancario e crescita: un confronto fra le regioni del Sud Europeo", in L. Paganetto "Mezzogiorno e Mezzogiorni d'Europa", pp. 105-117 Il Mulino, Bologna.

Berger, A.N. (1998), "The Efficiency Effects of Bank Mergers and Acquisitions: a Preliminary Look at the 1990s Data", in Amihud, Y., Miller, G. "Bank Mergers and Acquisitions", Kluwer Academic Publisher, Boston.

Berionne G. (1998), "Scenari e prospettive strategiche per le banche italiane: capire la transizione", Ned, Milano.

Bianchi, T. (1996), "L'Europa, il Mezzogiorno e le banche", Rivista Bancaria, 52, March-April, pp. 25-31.

Ciocca, P. (1999), "Concorrenza e concentrazione nel sistema finanziario italiano", Banca d'Italia, Bollettino Economico, 32, February, pp. 58-65.

Conigliani, C. (1992) "La concentrazione bancaria in Italia", Il Mulino, Bologna.

Cusimano, G. (1997), "Il sistema bancario nelle due Italie: alcune evidenze empiriche", Rivista Bancaria,, Minerva bancaria, n. 3.

Desario, V. (1995), "La concentrazione del sistema bancario", Bollettino Economico della Banca d'Italia, 25, pp. 119-125.

ECB (1999), "Possible Effecys of EMU on the EU Banking System in the Medium to Long Term".

Fazio, A. (1998) "Il sistema bancario italiano in Europa", Banca d'Italia, Bollettino Economico, 31, october pp. 34-39, Roma.

Focarelli D., F. Panetta, C. Salleo et al. (1998), "Bank of Italy", Research Department, September.

Goisis, G., Parravicini, P. (1993), "Economie di scala e da produzione congiunta nel sistema bancario italiano", Rivista Internazionale di Scienze Economiche e Commerciali, 40.

Goisis, G., Parravicini, P.(1999), "Tassi d'interesse usurari e mercati regionali del credito: un'analisi in termini di efficienza", Rivista Internazionale di Scienze Sociali, I, pp. 4-28.

Piloff, S., Santomero, A. (1998), "The Value Effect of Bank Mergers and Acquisitions", in Amihud, Y., Miller, G. "Bank Mergers and Acquisitions", Kluwer Academic Publisher, Boston.

Profumo, A.(1997), "L'UEM ed il sistema bancario italiano", Rivista Bancaria, 53, November-December, pp. 213-229.

Rossignoli, B. (1997), "Profili strutturali e funzionali dell'attività internazionale del sistema bancario italiano", Rivista Milanese di Economia, n. 64, pp. 38-54.

Smith, R.C., Walter, I. (1998), "Global patterns of Mergers and Acquisitions Activity in the Financial Service Industry", in Amihud, Y., Miller, G. "Bank Mergers and Acquisitions", Kluwer Academic Publisher, Boston.

Discussion of Gianandrea Goisis's "Efficiency of the banking system: The Italian case"

Hermann Locarek-Junge

Lehrstuhl für Betriebswirtschaftslehre, insbes. Finanzwirtschaft,
Dresden University of Technology, D-01062 Dresden, Germany

1 Message of the paper

A review of the economic performance of banks in countries throughout Europe (see ECB 1999) shows strengths and weaknesses, with some countries – among them Italy – having quite bad net margins and cost-income ratios.

In a closer look at Italian banks, G. Goisis (this volume) points to some matters which may have influenced bank performance in Italy and have been the reason for the disappointing results. These include

- *size inadequacy* (many small banks, and no huge bank),
- *specialised production* (mostly interest dependent business, which makes banks sensitive to declining interest rates and margins),
- *low internationalisation* (poor representation of Italian banks abroad),
- *high credit losses* compared to bank incomes net of allocations (bad loans).

On the other hand, the Italian Banking System does not suffer from being overbanked, as the country has only 935 bank institutions (fewer than Austria) and 0.44 branches per 1000 inhabitants (compared to Germany: 0.57, Austria: 0.58, European average: 0.48).

A detailed analysis of the figures by region gives other interesting insights about the distribution of bad loans over Italy. The average quotient of bad loans is 9.4% for Italy as a whole, but "only" 5.3% and 6.0% for *North-West* and *North-East*, close to the average (9.6%) for the *Middle*, and 21.8% for the regions *South and Islands*. Therefore Goisis states: "This discussion on credit quality leads to express clear reserves on the possibility to judge the Italian credit system globally." (Goisis 1999). This is an interesting and important finding and I strongly support this view. However, at this point another question has to be raised as a consequence, which has not been answered by the paper.

2 Efficiency of the banking system: What is it?

The comparative analysis of the Italian banking system within EU banking systems shows that there are a lot of problems with the usage of averages for countries, as in Italy there are huge differences by region or maybe also on a bank by bank basis.

Net margins on assets and equities in Italy are *on average* among the lowest in the EMU. However, this might not hold for the *North* or for large banks compared to small banks. Therefore questions about efficiency (size adequacy, concentration, market share, loan losses) probably can not be answered at all by computing averages by country.

Even if we try to compare European banks by average cost and profitability (success) ratios: Should we refer to statistical data, as they only would show the past and history of European banks, or should we try to compare the future of European banks in European countries?

This immediately raises several additional questions: What is *Efficiency of the Banking System* compared with bank efficiency? What do sums and averages tell us? Should we talk about benchmarking? Should we talk about competition in the „Euro" banking system, the future of the European banking system or even challenges for European banks and institutions?

In an interesting recent paper William White of the BIS (White 1998) raises this sort of questions. His thesis is, that continental European banks may be about to enter a period of enhanced competition, and that the starting point for many banks, see e.g. Italian banks, is not particularly strong.

When we try to answer the question about the relative position of Italian or other national banks in the EMU now and in the future, we have to know the correct questions before we can get the answers. Otherwise we are close to the story of Douglas Adams (Adams 1995) in the Science Fiction novel "Hitchhiker's Guide to the Galaxy", which I want to quote here:

> 'Alright', said the computer. 'The Answer to the Great Question of Life, the Universe and Every- thing is Forty-two'.
> 'Forty-two!' yelled the scientist [...]. 'Is that all you've got to show for seven and a half million years' work?'
> ‚I checked it very thoroughly', said the computer, ‚and that quite definitely is the answer. I think the problem, to be quite honest with you, is that you never actually have known what the question is. So once you do know what the question actually is, you'll know what the answer means.

The main task in the evaluation of banking systems therefore, in my opinion, is to find the correct questions. Let me suggest two of them:

- What are the underlying forces for change in the EU banking system?
- What should *all* European banks do to meet the challenges?

As stated above, White (1998) has identified some of the major forces for change in his recent paper.

3 Underlying forces for change

3.1 Developments in technology

The banking systems find themselves in a state of rapid technological and intellectual development. New financial products, which require advanced risk management technologies such as exotic options, credit derivatives and asset backed securities currently mark the frontiers of finance. They also represent challenges for banks which call for solutions.

On the pure technological side, ATM, Electronic Banking and Internet Banking are the developments in computer science and automation technology, which require new concepts in bank marketing.

Both developments, market orientation and advanced financial instruments as well as technological breakthroughs and broad acceptance of computer based bank access pose the additional question: Is the concept of branch banking still viable?

3.2 Changing role of the state

In the past, the most important goal in the design of national banking systems was stability. However, with increasing globalisation and international competition, efficiency of banks and banking systems becomes more and more important and even dominating. In many countries this goes hand in hand with reduction of state ownership as well as deregulation and liberalisation of the national markets. In the EU, the Second Banking Coordination Directive and the Capital Liberalisation Directive have set the framework for this development.

3.3 Demographic change

Another current driving force, although well known for many years is the fact that the population in many developed countries is growing older on average. This calls for new bank products, e.g. private pension plans to support or replace public social security (unfunded pension schemes), asset management offers, specialised mutual funds etc.

Many banks, e.g. most Italian banks, have a dominating savings and loan business and the interest dependent income currently is the major source on bank profitability. The current customer structure sees the young active customer (*young poor*), workers, families, in the focal point of the bank activities. This structure may shift to the older, the retired (*old rich*) and the inactive customers who need bank advice, e.g. for retirement planning and structuring or re-balancing their assets.

3.4 Concern for shareholder value

In the past, national authorities have protected banks against international competition, because they had to carry the huge burden of bank regulation to guarantee a safe national banking system. The result was a stable but often inefficient system. The ratio of bank shares to general stock price indices has declined in many European countries and the rates of return of European banks have been below their competitors for many years. However, there are signs that this culture is beginning to change. We have seen hostile take-overs in several national markets within continental Europe (e.g. France, Netherlands), and even across national borders (e.g. France and Belgium). National governments seem somewhat more comfortable with the concept. Mergers, take-overs, and share-buybacks increase the pressure from shareholders to change the system in favour of higher efficiency and better financial performance.

3.5 Introduction of the Euro

Although many voices could be heard during the recent years that the Euro will be the cause of dramatic change in the European banking system, this is not quite correct. Other than being a cause, the Euro might be considered as a catalyst for the other forces described above, as it will "stimulate the growth of a much larger and more liquid securities market in Europe, [.. which is..] expected to pose a significant competitive challenge to banks offering traditional forms of intermediated credit." (White 1998, p. 8-9).

Increased competition from outside Europe will also be caused by the Euro because one common currency means better economies of scale for international activities of US or UK banks and some global banks (i.e. Citicorp and HSBC) which seek a platform in the common financial market.

4 Meeting the challenges

As has been stated above, the future relative position of Italian, German, French etc. banks within Europe, the future efficiency of the national banking systems, and their position in international competition depends on their flexibility to react to the forces of change.

Banks have to lower costs and improve market communication by using electronic banking devices (multichannel banking). The national governments have to create systems of competitive and compatible regulation. Banks have to restructure their business to service the older generation, and to lower their dependencies from interest sensitive business.

Higher efficiency will protect single banks from unfriendly take-overs. However, some mergers and co-operation agreements will be necessary to generate the essential size and economies of scale. We have seen mergers in the past, there are some current activities, and there is a good chance that these activities will continue throughout Europe.

References

Adams, Douglas: The Hitchhiker's Guide to The Galaxy, London, Pan Books, 1995.
ECB (ed): Possible Effects of EMU on the EU Banking Systems in the Medium to Long Term, February 1999, http://www.ecb.int/pub/pdf/emubnk.pdf.
Goisis, Gianandrea: Efficiency of the Banking System: The Italian Case, this volume.
White, William R. The Coming Transformation of Continental European Banking? BIS, Working Paper, June 1998, http://www.bis.org/publ/work54.htm.

Institutional changes in economies in transition and stability of the banking system

Chuluunbaatar Enkhzaya

Dresden University of Technology, Faculty of Economics, D-01062 Dresden, Germany

1 Introduction

The main criteria of a successful banking reform are first, at the macroeconomic level, a positive flow of financial resources to the enterprise sector, and second, at the microeconomic level, the efficient allocation of available resources.

Despite of the significant progress in reforming the economy as a whole and the financial sector as a special in a few years time, it is still too early to speak of stabilised banking systems in economies in transition (EITs). The goal should be the efficient allocation of financial resources. But banking systems in transition are characterised by systemic problems which are the reason for inefficient allocation. These systemic problems[1] should be addressed by decision makers at any level. The individual behaviour of decision makers has a great impact not only on the definition of strategies and policies but also on the enforcement or implementation of economic policies. How and by which means can and do the policymakers deal with widespread bad loan problems in banks, with the ceding of state property and with the supervising of banks activities? These problems threaten the stability of the sector as a whole.

In order to analyse the flaws by the implementation of the banking system reforms, the present work deals with the question of what is the impact of institutional changes on the stability of a banking system. The focus is mainly set on the institutional issues that relate to the creation of a stable banking sector, and especially to the role of individual behaviour. The statements and the examples made here refer to such countries like Poland, Hungary and Mongolia. They are however generally applicable.

In the next section, section 2, the aspects of stability of the banking system will be discussed after making a short overview of the banking reforms. Section 3 will try to address which institutional changes take place during the transformation. Section 4 will deal with institutional changes in the banking system during transition and with the way in which and when they influence the stability. Finally in section 5, we will sum up the major tasks and challenges for a "well-measured"

---

[1] It means the way how the system is organized.

liberalisation of the banking sector in order to permanently ensure the stability of the banking system. In conclusion, it will be remarked that the development of a stable banking system is not an overnight task and needs a long-term comprehensive approach.

2 The banking system in transition with respect to its stability

Early in the beginning of political transition (in some cases before, such as in Poland or Hungary) state-owned commercial banks were established by separating the commercial portfolio and segregating the clientele of the monobank, on sectoral (Hungary, Mongolia) or regional (Poland) principles. As joint-stock companies with almost state ownership these banks were (and partly are) the financial source of the state budget. Under socialism they could not be a true financial intermediary, which collects private savings and efficiently channels them to borrowers in the capital market. So one could say there was no banking sector in true sense. Consequently as Hillman and Ursprung (1999: 135) say, it is more a matter of establishing the banking sector rather than of reforming it. And (i) sound and competitive banks, which could spread risk and gain trust by depositors, are needed to establish a market-oriented banking system, as well as (ii) an appropriate legal framework for their activity.

As far as the last point is concerned, the formal legal framework was more or less established in the EITs. A new democratic constitution, a new commercial law, banking laws, and bankruptcy law were passed in a relatively short time. To begin with there was a single banking law (as for example the Banking Law of Mongolia 1991) regulating both, the central bank activities and the commercial banking activities. But the further developments progressed, the more extensive the laws became, so that they were separated (as for example Law of Bank of Mongolia and Banking Law of Mongolia, 1996). Since then, the laws have been amended (as for example Banking Law of Mongolia, amended last in 1998). In addition, several special laws have been passed, such as a law on investments, law on payment systems etc. But the enforcement of these laws remains weak. This could be explained by missing properly functioning organs like courts, public prosecutor's offices, police, registers and other supervision authorities.

The situation of the banks is rather difficult. The state-owned banks are characterised by a bad loan portfolio and a mostly bad customer base of mainly state-owned enterprises, both owned by the previous regime. So not only the debtor should be protected, but also the creditor: "[...] the bias towards protection of the debtor instead of the creditor in the first phases of transition can indeed have very harmful effects on the intermediation function of banks in the economy" (OECD, 1998: 45). It is to be mentioned that in many EITs bank credits are now the only financial source for the real sector. And it is not exceptional that a few big banks are the key lenders to the biggest companies. The situation of the newly established private banks is not much better. Because of continued predominance of state-owned banks, private banks have generally kept their balance sheets small to reduce risk and have focused on fee-generating transactions (Borish, Ding, Noël, 1997: 1205) such as international settlements, currency exchange etc.

Banks in transition are still not able to fulfil their significant role in the economy at the microeconomic level: the efficient allocation of savings throughout the economy. The main weaknesses are that banks are still not equipped to measure risks, have staff problems, are strongly influenced by politics and have credibility problems with their depositors.

The literature delivers the opinion that privatisation would solve these problems of inefficiency of financial intermediation. Certainly privatisation is a significant way to define property-rights and to allocate resources efficiently. But this does not automatically mean the disengagement of the state in banking governance and the ability of bank managers to take market oriented decisions. The acceptance of the state and of the rest of the population is herewith not taken for granted. As Bonin et al. (1998: 2) point out "privatisation goes beyond a formal change in ownership structure. It must be accompanied by a change in control as well". Lessons from some advanced EITs like Poland and Hungary show that the control is one of the complicated issues to implement.

A control system or a regulatory structure which is able to create confidence and to complete the market is needed. It could permanently ensure the *stability* of the banking system, make it more confident, create trust, which is important, especially in EITs. An instability occurs if there is a danger „that disturbances in financial markets and institutions will generalise across the financial system, so as to disrupt the provision of payment services and the allocation of capital" (Davis, 1992: 285). And the consideration of this aspect of control system is for ensuring the stability of the banking system a key point in this sense. In economies with a history of strict control past it seems to be quite difficult to realise that a certain control mechanism is necessary to bring the market and credibility together to a sustainable success.

Experiences from EITs rise questions like: Is the decision making process the reason for lack of trust? Why are optimal decisions not taken? Is there a lack of political support? Lack of political support is a real problem. But there are some positive examples from EITs, where"[...] certain special circumstances played an important role in getting the Polish programme pushed through quickly – in particular the solid political platform provided the officials responsible for its design and implementation" (OECD, 1998: 41). Besides financial problems (financing the banking reform) the political willingness to sustain the reforms is one of the most important tasks. And what about the willingness of individuals to stand by? To answer these questions, the next section will take a close look at issues of institutional changes which underlie the individual behaviour and are rather important in economies in transition, in changing societies.

3 Institutional changes

As institutional economics makes clear, institutions influence the economic performance, the effective allocation of resources, by increasing or decreasing the costs of transaction. Institutions are "the rules of the game in a society" (North, 1992: 477) and consist of (i) *formal rules*, (ii) *informal rules* and (iii) the enforcement of them.

These three items build the subjective framework of individual's decisions. Formal rules can be set by politics more or less automatically with laws which guarantee well-defined property-rights, competition and decentralised decision-making. But it takes time to evolve the informal rules, because they consist of conventions to co-ordinate problems, as well as norms of behaviour complemented by self-imposed codes of conduct. Customs and traditions are the terms we colloquially use to denote the existence of the informal rules.

The opinion of individuals about whether rules are fair or unfair are of crucial importance for the enforcement of the "game" they play. This "individual perception about the fairness and justice of the rules of the game" is considered by North (1992: 479) as *ideology*. "Ideologies underlie the subjective frameworks that individuals possess to explain the world around them" (North, 1992: 485), we use these culturally conditioned ideas to receive and interpret information. Ideology develops an informal framework to structure human interactions. The negative attitude of individuals about the fairness of the rules creates uncertainty, and consequently affects the enforcement.

Thus, the subjective model which is used to make choices is an "interplay among the evolution of culturally conditioned ideas, the constraints imposed by the existing institutional framework, and the consistency or inconsistency between perceived and predicted outcomes" (North, 1992: 487). This subjective model of individuals in economies in transition is characterised by the old patterns of behaviour (because of elements of old economic system). These old patterns of behaviour and the existing distortions of incentive structures make market instruments not bring the wanted results (Theurl, 1997: 142, 155).

Therefore it is of crucial importance in times of transition to complement the "automatic" changes in formal rules with informal constrains and their enforcement. This means, it is not enough to define the property-rights by privatising the state-owned enterprises or state-owned banks. As Bonin and Wachtel (1999: 93) argue, "a necessary condition for privatisation to be deemed a success is that state remain a passive investor only [...] without any direct involvement in the conduct of the banking business". Similarly, to induce competition, it is not enough to lay down laws and regulations which bind the banks to ensure their deposits or to build up reserves. The true competition is only then reached if the mental model of individuals include these requirements as a feature for a "good" bank. Only in that case they can function as an incentive for banks to improve they facility to compete.

4 Institutional issues of stability of the banking system

In some EITs, especially in advanced ones in Eastern Europe, the formal part of institutional structure of a banking system is set (see Solarz, 1998: 150). But as far as the informal part concerns as well as the question, whether the actions lead the pursued results, the situation is becoming difficult. Blejer and Škreb (1999), Bonin and Wachtel (1999), Borish, Ding and Noël (1997), Hillman and Ursprung (1999) carried out studies of experiences with the main procedures of banking reform in context of the role of individuals and the state as a whole.

The question of how governments, banks and enterprises adapted themselves to the new commercial system, and of how banking systems have evolved since the establishment of two-tier system is most interesting in this context. Because the kind of stability to be reached in a concrete banking system depends not only on legal system but also on the preferences and culture. In accordance to them have the economic agents different risk aversion, different art of risk sharing arrangements.

The main procedures of a banking reform are bank restructuring, rehabilitation and privatisation. Whereas advanced economies in transition in Eastern Europe have made progress towards opening up the banking market to private competition – as the growing share of private banks assets, loans, deposits and capital shows - Mongolia is for example far from making significant steps in privatisation of its banks. Nevertheless in all countries the privatisation of the larger state banks was slower than privatisation of the enterprise sector. Borish, Ding and Noël (1997: 1196) explain: "Privatisation of banks has been slow owing to a lack of political consensus, as well as because of the financial or structural problems faced by these banks, which render them unattractive to potential purchasers. More often, privatisation has stalled because the state is openly reluctant to privatise some banks, such as savings banks [...]" And even in privatised banks with a majority private ownership there is no true control: because the state can retain control over many banks via blocking shares, explicit veto rights or "other" obligations of owners or bank managers.

Thus, despite of the developed and recommended ways and methods of the banking sector reform (detailed investigations see Bonin and Wachtel (1999)) bank restructuring, rehabilitation and privatisation are faced with strong resistance of the economic agents, including politicians, bank managers themselves and state-owned (or controlled) enterprises. It is their individual interest and personal gain not to restructure or to privatise the bank.

Even in cases, where some group of people staked their claim to property, it was not automatically respected by others. In fact it seems to be the recognition that enterprises or banks once belonging to the state – to the "hole nation"- are now a property of private individuals is problematical. In Mongolia, there were cases of using the popular outrage of the population to renationalise the biggest department store of Ulaanbaatar or separate one of the biggest state owned banks shortly after its merger with a private bank. But the success of the privatisation of livestock in

Mongolia, with its centuries old tradition of livestock breeding[2], teaches us that the existence of institutions (and remarkably the existence of both formal and informal rules with their enforcement mechanism) is a significant factor. Residual informal rules from pre-revolutionary times survived the socialist era could be quickly refreshed.

We have the same problem with the regulatory framework of the banking system: it is not a question of norms and standards but a question of enforcing these standards. In most of the advanced EITs like Poland and Hungary the framework of banking regulation is adjusted to western standards, which does not necessarily mean a successful functioning of banking supervision[3].

The reforms of economic liberalisation were not automatically accompanied by changes in (governance or management) incentive structures that are necessary for a successful transformation to a market-based system (see Borish, Ding and Noël, 1997: 1187). Even in advanced economies, the question of incentive structures still remains a relevant problem to the present situation. However characterised as they are by short-sighted decisions, lack of credibility of economic policies, a lesser ability in risk-measuring and a lack of trust and honesty, the change in incentive structures is more important for economies in transition in general and for ensuring permanently the stability of their banking system in particular.

Much of the literature on banking reform in EITs is engaged with problems of restructuring and privatisation[4]. A great deal is written on various aspects of the banking reform process itself. Nevertheless the literature does not explain why these strategies or norms were only partially implemented and did not bring the expected results. There are no recommendations to policy makers about how to ensure the implementation of reforms, and thus the stability (that is to avoid systemic risk).

The experiences from EITs show that it is the action of individuals preventing the efficient implementation of economic policies or reforms. They are lead to behave in this way by incentives or *incentive structures* which already exist but which should be changed. This means co-ordination of individual actions so as to "design a mechanism that will elicit truthful revelation of individual preferences, leading to the production of an efficient outcome" (Campbell, 1995: 314).

The new institutional economics call this idea creating incentive compatible institutions. This means, institutions which prevent *opportunistic behaviour*. Adapted from Williamson (1993: 56), opportunism means "self-interest seeking with guile, to include calculated efforts to mislead, deceive, obfuscate, and otherwise confuse."

In the case of reforming and stabilising the banking system, it is the alteration of incentive structures within the bank as well as within the economy. As Buch (1993: 6) points out, "reforms should aim at establishing correct and consistent incentives within the already liberalised sectors". For this purpose it is very im-

[2] See Schmidt (1995).
[3] See Bonin et al. (1998) and Buch (1996b).
[4] See Buch (1996b) and Hein (1995).

portant to accept the changes of the ideology which underlie the development of informal rules. In the case of Mongolia (Enkhzaya, 1999: 20) there are three of them: (i) the instinct for collective action to gain a collective profit and consequently individual profit which remains from pre-revolutionary times, (ii) the ideology which honours the state and everything belonging to it, shaped by socialism, doing everything for state or for the "whole nation", and (iii) the new ideology of selfishness and of individual rationality[5]. We should note that these ideologies could exist simultaneously (incentive mix), and this makes things more difficult and challenging.

The practical evidence is the harmonisation or co-ordination of changes in formal and informal rules. To put it differently, a *"well-measured"* liberalisation of economic system in general and of the banking system in particular.

5 Well-measured liberalization

The principle of the well-measured liberalisation is directed to the question as to whether the process of liberalisation is in line with the institutional capability of the banking system. The keys of institutional capability are incentive compatible institutions; institutions which do not allow opportunistic behaviour.

At the centre of this well-measured approach lies the idea of harmonising reform steps (formal rules) in accordance with the changing of informal rules in order to reach an equilibrium. It needs a complex new equilibrium as North (1992: 486) says. Whereas in neo-classical economic theory only one equilibrium exists, there are multiple equilibria in a world with transaction costs and acceptance of the role of ideology. You can copy the formal rules, but without accepting the informal rules and their changes this will not result in an efficient allocation of resources.

Changing institutions make adoption of economic reforms necessary. The adjustment of reform stages to institutional changes in order to permanently ensure the stability of the banking system shall be the challenge of future policies. As institutional changes are different from country to country there is no universal or „prefabricated“ formula for shaping the adjustment. Some EITs, especially countries of Central Asia, had because of the history no elements of behavioural structure of financial markets at all, like risk aversion. So they should be established.

This leads to the problem of measuring the current state of the institutional changes. Buch (1993: 30) worked out some proxy-variables for measuring the behavioural changes, which are however coupled together with the enforcement of formal rules (the implementation of bankruptcy rules, the privatisation of banks, solutions to the problem of non-performing loans in the balance sheets of banks).

In addition, the understanding of the specific and crucial role played by state is of great relevance. The state should not fulfil the role of an efficient allocator but he should create the institutional framework for efficient allocation in order to permanently ensure the stability of the banking system despite of the inherent risks.

---

[5] See Schmidt (1995) and Braun (1997).

This means the disengagement of the state from bank governance. It is also important that banks should be satisfactorily monitored and supervised without the state having an ownership stake. Thus the main task is that the banking sector should be depoliticised.

Finally, building credibility and confidence during transition is a crucial issue. It is an intertemporal problem and long-term comprehensive tactics (proceedings) are required. Trust and credibility (reputation) should complete the market. Thus OECD (OECD Proceedings, 1998: 12), "[...]solving a spreading banking sector crisis cannot be left to the financial markets on their own, especially not in economies in transition, where weaknesses in the institutional fabric in general and in supervision in particular, can easily aggravate otherwise containable problems". Thus, it is important:

(i) on the one hand, to ensure self-regulation by market and
(ii) on the other hand, to build trust and credibility for successful complementation of market.

6 Conclusion

Informal rules and ideological constrains underlie the subjective model of individual behaviour. Thus there is a need, as well as for formal changes to the law (to make the private ownership of banks possible or to liberalise interest rates), for simultaneous changes of formal and informal rules. The incentive structures should be correct and consistent, they should not allow opportunistic behaviour. The reform steps must be harmonised with the changes of informal rules in order to permanently ensure the stability of the banking system. The role of the state as non-allocator and its disengagement from bank governance are of crucial importance hereby. Ensuring self-regulation by the market and building of trust (confidence) and credibility are the key words for sustainable success.

The processes of financial transformation, banking reform, and establishing an institutional framework are very controversial (especially concerning informal rules and its enforcement). Even in developed economies, the question of incentive structure and incentive compatibility is an unsolved problem.

The tasks differ significantly from country to country depending on its institutional differences and the policy objectives of governments. For EITs in Eastern Europe it is a little easier regarding policy objectives and the future development concept as they can refer to EU-membership conditions. Meanwhile other post socialist countries in Central Asia are still searching for their own ways, their own appropriate concepts.

Thus, it will take some time until the banking system in EITs will be able to avoid systemic risk, that is to ensure a stability.

References

Ábel, I., Siklos, P. and Székely, I. (1998): Money and Finance in the Transition to a Market Economy, Cheltenham, UK, Northampton, MA, USA: Edward Elgar.

Blejer, M., Škreb, M. (1999): Financial Reforms and Economic Transition: An Overview of the Major Issues, in: Financial Sector Transformation: Lessons from Economies in Transition, Blejer, M.I and Škreb, M. (eds.) – Cambridge: Cambridge University Press, 1-18.

Bonin, J., Mizsei, K., Székely, I. and Wachtel, P. (1998): Banking in Transition Economies: Developing Market Oriented Banking Sectors in Eastern Europe, Cheltenham, UK and Northampton, Ma, USA: Edward Elgar.

Bonin, J. and Wachtel, P. (1999): Toward Market-Oriented Banking in the Economies in Transition, in: Financial Sector Transformation: Lessons from Economies in Transition, Blejer, M.I and Škreb, M. (eds.) – Cambridge: Cambridge University Press, 93-131.

Borish, M.S., Ding, W., and Noël, M. (1997): The Evolution of State-owned Banking Sector during Transition in Central Europe, in: Euro-Asia Studies, Vol. 49, No.7, 1187-1208.

Braun, H. (1997): Historische Wurzeln spezifischer Transformations- und Entwicklungsprobleme der Mongolischen Republik, in H. Pohl and R. Gömmel (eds.), Sozial und Wirtschaftsgeschichte, Stuttgart: Franz Steiner Verlag, 84, 512 –543.

Buch, C. (1993): An Institutional Approach to Banking Reform in Eastern Europe, Kiel Working Papers, No. 560, February 1993, The Kiel Institute of World Economics.

Buch, C. (1996a): Creating Efficient Banking Systems: Theory and Evidence from Eastern Europe, Tübingen: Mohr.

Buch, C. (1996b): Banken in Transformationsprozeß – eine Bestandaufnahme für Polen, Tschechische Republik und Ungarn, in: Kieler Working Papers, The Kiel Institute of World Economics, 70-101.

Campbell, D.E. (1995): Incentives: Motivation and the Economics of Information, Cambridge: Cambridge University Press.

Davis, E. P. (1992): Debt, Financial Fragility, and Systemic Risk, Oxford: Clarendon Press

Enkhzaya, Ch. (1999): Zur institutionenökonomischen Begründung der Bankenregulierung, Working Paper, 10/1999, Dresden University of Technology.

Hannig, A. (1998): Finanzsystemreformen – Konzept, Erfahrungen und Perspektiven am Beispiel Boliviens, Köln: Weltforum Verlag.

Hein, M. (ed.) (1995): Bankensysteme in Ostmitteleuropa, Berlin: Berlin Verl. A. Spitz; Wien: Verl. Österreich.

Hillman, A.L and Ursprung, H.W. (1999): The Trials and Tribulations of Banking in Transition Economies: A Political Economy Perspective, in: Financial Sector Transformation: Lessons from Economies in Transition, Blejer, M. and Škreb, M. (eds.) – Cambridge: Cambridge University Press: 132-149.

North, D. (1992): Institutions, Ideology, and Economic Performance, Cato Journal, Vol.11, No.3, Cato Institute.

OECD (1998): Financial Market Trends, No. 69, February 1998.

OECD Proceedings (1998): The New Banking Landscape in Central and Eastern Europe: Country Experience and Policies for the Future, OECD.

Schmidt, S. (1995): Mongolia in Transition: The Impact of Privatization on Rural Life, Saarbrücken: Verlag für Entwicklungspolitik, (Bielefelder Studien zur Entwicklungssoziologie, 62).

Solarz, J. K. (1998): Transformation of the Banking System in Poland in Comparative Perspective, in: Systemtransformation in Mittel- und Osteuropa und ihre Folgen für Banken, Börsen und Kreditsicherheiten, Ulrich Drobnig (ed.) – Tübingen: Mohr Siebeck.

Theurl, T. (1997): Monetäre Transformation: Konsistenzfallen einer sich wandelnden Wirtschaftsordnung, in: Institutionelle Probleme der Systemtransformation, Cassel, D. (ed.) – Berlin: Duncker und Humblot: 141-163.

Williamson, O.E (1993): The Economic Analysis of Institutions and Organisations – in General and with Respect to Country Studies, OECD, Economics Department Working Papers, No. 133, Paris.

Discussion of Chuluunbaatar Enkhzaya's "Institutional changes in economies in transition and stability of the banking sector"

Jan K. Solarz

Research Department, National Bank of Poland, PL-00-919 Warzawa, Poland

Chuluunbaatar Enkhzaya gives a comprehensive overview of the state of the debate on the stability of banking systems in transition. I have hardly any critical comments to make and prefer therefore to supplement Mrs. Enkhzaya's paper somewhat and to stress some of the views of Mrs. Enkhzaya with which I in general agree.

There is a contradiction between "stability" and "transition" in static analysis. Only a dynamic analysis of the banking sector can resolve the contradiction between the concepts of stability and the changes required by transition from a planned to a market economy. Creative destruction of the status quo is a main element of transition. "Shock therapy" overcame "shortage economy" in Poland in months, but establishing the institutional framework of a market economy in Poland will take decades.

Stability of banking systems in transition meets some universal conditions:

- disinflation to change inflationary expectations to expectations of price stability,
- change of the economy's ownership structure; private ownership is the main source of fiscal discipline,
- change of the state's role in the economy; the key is a small government with budgetary surplus,
- political mobilisation and integration into the West.

Stability of the banking system also needs to fill many universal lags and gaps. We observe more stability of the banking systems in countries that reformed real socialism, such as Hungary and Poland, than in countries that have no experience in the transformation of their economies, such as the Czech Republic or the USSR. Accumulation of knowledge on the market mechanism in planned economies creates a favourable environment for private economic activity. After ten years of transformation the gap in skills is close up.

Stability of the banking system also needs a proper sequencing of changes. In the first step, we expect regulatory slack. All standard regulation of market oriented banking cannot be implemented on this stage. On one side, it creates many small and undercapitalised banks, on the other it opens space for financial innovation in countries with shortages of capital. In the second step, we overcome the bad debt problem. In Poland we implemented a decentralised approach, imitating US regulations. As a result, enterprises too big to fail pay debt to banks, but do not serve their tax obligations and social security remuneration. In the next step, we observe mergers and acquisitions in the banking sector. Consolidation of the banking sector is an element of the adaptation of our credit institutions to membership in the EU.

Main elements of the stability of banking systems in transition are trust in local banks and state guarantee for deposits. An increasing participation of foreign capital in our banking sector lowers trust in local banks. People do not trust global banks. The put their savings in banks with state guarantee.

Year 2000 will be crucial for the stability of our banking system. In this year, the state guarantee for deposits will end and full liberalisation of capital movement will be the obligation from our OECD membership. As far as the stability of banking systems in transition is concerned, the mandatory changes may create inherent instability. The only way to avoid this is to build a solid institutional infrastructure of the financial system.

An advanced institutional infrastructure of the financial system consists of:

- good corporate governance in credit and investment institutions,
- all types of financial intermediary institutions and consolidated supervision of these,
- a bank oriented financial system,
- reform of the state
  - administrative reform, decentralisation of the state budget,
  - social insurance reform, introduction of pension fund reform,
  - medical care reform,
  - educational system reform.

Transformation challenges the stability of the banking system in Poland. We are on the way to find proper answers to this new type of challenge. We need more situational than universal solutions for our problems. Maybe, we shall be forced to slow our institutional reforms and ensure macroeconomic stability first. An effective protection against instability needs responses in different dimensions. Short-term response required free exchange rate policy. Monetary policy is a longer-term phenomenon. Transformation of institutional infrastructure is a long-term process. Mix of instruments and time perspectives is only one way in finding proper solutions to change the state and the banking system at the same time. The great social cost of a general financial crisis, so it is argued, requires special treatment of transformation in the banking sector. Stability first, transformation next. This is our solution to the problem of internal dynamics of banking systems and transformation.

Central banking and financial stability in transition economies

Jens Hölscher

University of Brighton, GB-Brighton BN2 4AT, United Kingdom

1 Introduction

The transition towards a market-type economy has experienced substantial setbacks in economic development due to crises of the financial sector.

The aim of this account is to advance the understanding of the dilemma that low interest rates are needed for promotion of growth and high rates of interest are imperative in order to secure macroeconomic stability. The minimum of stability within this context requires the absence of capital flight, i.e. interest rates high enough to compensate eventually existing devaluation expectations. High central bank lending rates have to prevent depleting of existing reserves in foreign currency and following crises. If the lending rate as such is given by this market constellation, a sound financial system can contribute to growth without jeopardising stability through declining spreads.

The following section takes up the issue of banking crises and macro-economic instability by a discussion of the anatomy of a typical financial crisis to show the peculiar importance of the financial sector for 'real' output. For this anatomy it is shown that the 'legacies of the past' implicate a disadvantageous start position for banking in transition, which is the main cause for the vulnerability of the sector. The second step of the section enlarges the underlying question of the analysis in so far, as now not only the financial sector's contribution to stability, but also to growth as the overall economic aim of the transition process is tackled. The section concludes that growth promotion through the financial sector can only be expected by decreasing interest rate spreads.

The third section presents stylised facts of monetary policy in transition economies, which are candidates of EU-Enlargement to the East. As a means of reference transition economies are presented within the framework of the EU Maastricht criteria. As far as central banking is concerned, priority is given to exchange rate policy with its differing forms of options and practices. In the conclusion central banking in transition economies is seen within its infant state.

2 The relevance of financial systems for stability and growth

The pre-eminent relevance of the financial sector for stability and growth lies in the fact, that in difference to for example the agricultural sector, a crisis within the financial sector can lead to a general decline of production and output. The infliction of the macro-economic level rather than adjustments of relative prices between industries and sectors within the economy causes the particular importance of banking and finance for stability and growth. The financial sector can principally be described as the market place for stocks of wealth with an asymmetric relationship between borrowers and creditors. A crisis that goes along with the devaluation of assets would reciprocally lead to a revaluation of debt, the so-called 'debt deflation' (Fisher 1933). Accordingly the rate of interest for this debt service as the flow category generated by the stock of debts will rise and the 'real' economy needs to earn this service by surplus production.

These macro-economic impacts, the financial sector might have, are independent from the micro-level of the role of the financial sector for corporate governance, which will be analysed later.

2.1 Financial sector and macroeconomic stability

The way, in which the financial sector can contribute to macro-economic stability is in the first place not to undergo a crisis, i. e. to be robust. This 'soundness' of banking and finance is best regarded as institutional infrastructure, in which markets function. Such an institutional infrastructure would go beyond legal framework such as contract, bankruptcy and competition law and would include a regulatory framework of financial markets like in other key industries like telecommunication, gas, water and energy. As the argument for regulation of these other key industries, namely certain cost structures that would lead to the emergence of monopolies, the argument for the regulation of financial services would be, that "macroeconomic stability is an intermediate public good whose provision cannot be contracted out to the private sector" (Buiter et al. 1997, p. 20). Although the theory of public goods has been shattered since Coase showed that even lighthouses were run efficiently by private firms, a closer look at the anatomy of financial crises will show the need for state activity.

2.1.1 The anatomy of financial crises

Although reasons for financial crises can be manifold, four main reasons can be located within the domestic economy. First of all an increase in interest rates initiated by the central bank for whatever good other reasons can lead to credit rationing, in which case some investment projects will not be financed by banks although they would be profitable under the conditions of higher interest rates. According to the contribution of Stiglitz and Weiss (1981), in such a situation the borrowers with high-risk projects will succeed to obtain loans and the banking sector as a whole will reduce its volume of lending in order to reduce the level of risks. Based on the assumption of asymmetric information between borrowers and lenders (here banks) an increase in interest rates will increase the financial instability through rising adverse selection. The rate of interest is not operating as market clearing price and in anticipation of a theory of a financial crash it is even possible that a slight increase in interest leads to a decline in the volume of lending and subsequently of investment and the level of aggregate economic activity. Then declining incomes would cause a cumulative process of a fully fledged economic crisis.

It has to be added that the rise of the interest rate might not be home-made, but initiated by the rise of the interest rates of one of the key currencies or globally rising interest rates, which can not be buffered by exchange rate policy. The exchange rate itself can be the reason for the start of a financial crisis, because international capital movements can enforce a devaluation of the exchange rate in such a degree, that cannot be counterbalanced by improved competitiveness of exports. To show this possibility of external shocks figure 1 separates external and internal reasons of financial crises. Although the figure does not explicitly show it, it should be mentioned that an exchange rate revaluation can cause external destabilisation, too. In that case the increasing overvaluation would drive the balance of trade into deficit and increase foreign indebtedness.

The second reason for financial instability is described as 'deterioration of bank's balance sheets'. This can be caused directly by an increase in the rate of interest as this process as such devalues 'real' assets like the net value of a firm against nominal assets like bonds. Usually a deterioration of the balance begins with unexpected defaults of loans for enterprises with insufficient collateral to cover for the losses. A particular form of the same principle is a decline in the stock market, which alone would decrease the value of collateral as the net market value of firms would decrease. It is mentioned as a third reason for a financial crises, as the dynamics of a stock market crash alone can cause defaults of banks and might affect the banking sector as a whole.

The fourth and most fundamental reason for a financial sector crisis is an increase in uncertainty. An increase in uncertainty would foster the desire to hold liquidity and subsequently increase the price for giving up liquidity. The rise of the liquidity preference therefore would lead to an increase in interest rates and implicate the consequences outlined above. Moreover the degree of uncertainty can grow to such an extent, that no interest rate might be able to attract individuals to hold liquidity and domestic money at all. Subsequently capital flight into abroad and into 'real' assets like land due to uncertainty would normally be associated with political instability.

Whether one or all reasons above would be responsible for the financial crises the sequence would normally show rising informational asymmetries between creditors and debtors. The synopsis of the anatomy of a financial sector crisis mentions increasing adverse selection and increasing moral-hazard behaviour as result of the four major reasons causing the crisis. This would not be a change of individual behaviour as such, but an adjustment of a behaviour assumed for normal conditions to a serious situation caused by the higher degree of instability within the financial sector. Rising intransparency alone would lead to a higher demand for loans, for which there was never the intention to be paid back. This is to illustrate that it is not the people, who begin to panic, but that a change of circumstances due to the above reasons has the consequence for the economy as a whole.

The sequence of such a behaviour of the economy would be a crisis within the banking sector in the first place. If this is a serious crisis the assumption would be, that it is not possible to contain it in the national financial system and it would spread over the borders. This would happen by some pressed personal computer buttons following a change in the choice of currency by some international asset portfolios. This reaction, which is sometimes executed even without pressing a button but by a computer programme alone, would increase the supply of domestic currency and subsequently cause it devaluation. This devaluation would push import prices and lead to an inflationary impulse for the afflicted economy.

The fourth step in the sequence of the anatomy of financial crises then is the crisis of the balance of payments. In order to stop the capital flight and to defend the domestic currency the central bank will have to rise interest rates astronomically. This in turn will even accelerate the domestic banking crisis and might lead to its collapse. The balance of payments crisis might go along with the imposition of capital controls, which will feed further devaluation expectations.

The fifth step will finally consist in the falling production leading the sixth step of falling real income or rising unemployment respectively. The step six will be the sharper, the higher the proportion of foreign debt of domestic enterprises is, as the devaluation of the domestic currency will increase the value of that debt and cause bankruptcies.

The worst case scenario would be a seventh step of a global devaluation race as experienced in the 30s of the 20th century.

Consolidation of financial crises would be some kind of bail out, either externally by international institutions such as IMF or Worldbank or internally by the state. In reality we normally find a combination of both ways of consolidation ending up in an increase of foreign debt and state debt. The problem with this type of consolidation is that some economies might be so poor that they find themselves caught within a debt trap in the aftermath of a financial crisis, because the burden of the debt service is too high to be matched by capital inflows, i. e. foreign investment, and export surpluses. The general fallacy of consolidation by bail out and liquidation is that incentives are set to borrow and lend carelessly.

2.1.2 Stability oriented policy conclusion

In view of the anatomy of financial crises government intervention is unlikely to succeed within the course of the crisis itself, in particular as cumulative dynamics have to be assumed, which are not reflected by figure 1.

Figure 1 Anatomy of a financial sector crisis

I. Reasons
external:
– exchange rate devaluation
– globally rising interest rates
internal:
– increasing rates of interest
– deterioration of bank's balance sheets
– stock market declines
– increasing uncertainty
II. Sequence
1. initial factors
– increasing adverse selection
– increasing moral-hazard behaviour
2. banking crisis
3. capital flight, currency devaluation, inflation
4. balance of payments crisis
5. decreasing production
6. decreasing income
7. deflation
III. Consolidation
– external: 'bail out', increase of foreign debt
– internal: liquidation, 'bail out', increase of government debt

Priority therefore has to be given to setting the rules of the game by the state, a case of classical German-type of *Ordnungspolitik* (see Hölscher 1998). An order for financial sector stability would then consist of two main components: setting of generally binding standards and tough supervision of the financial sector. However, there are at least two features that make this approach to financial markets more difficult as in goods markets. Firstly financial markets are global markets and standards for trafficking in finance ought to reflect this nature by being globally applicable, although there is not a global institution in place to supervise such global rules. Secondly financial markets proved to be extremely innovative in their products and legislation as well as supervision can easily end up in a position of being always one step too late for being in control of the situation.

Even if the possibility of setting standards is assumed, the harder part would be maintaining those standards (see Goodhart 1997). Normal moral hazard behaviour is particular relevant within the financial system, because a system of incentives and sanction has to reflect that the state itself is a major player of the system partly due to deposit insurance but principally by the institution of the central bank. Independent auditing is one way of approaching the problem, but still leaves the details of who would be in charge for hire, fire and pay of this auditor unresolved. As the realisation of some kind of *Ordnungspolitik* proves to be difficult for the case of financial sectors, the question remains, what type of regulatory policies are required.

Three types of regulatory policies can be distinguished for the financial sector: The first and most obvious policy is monetary policy itself, which means in the extreme case of a collapsing financial sector caused by bank runs that the central bank acts as 'lender of last resort' in order to prevent an asset deflation like experienced in the 1930s. Such a policy can only be the exception of the rule, as it has *per se* destabilising inflationary effects.

Secondly the formal regulation of the financial sector itself is a traditional but effective approach to promote stability. Banking activities are subject to licensing like for example driving as well as permanent monitoring like for example the weather. Normally market entry is not free, nor is market exit. Rules for certain ratios within the balance sheet as well as market behaviour could be the basis of the (temporary) close of institutions. Competition policy would be part of this regulation policy.

Finally the protection against foreign causation of domestic financial crises would require some auditing of exposure against foreign exchange risk (see Buch/Heinrich, p. 24), although it must be stated that the balance of payments position of a country can only be influenced by macro stability, i. e. exchange rate policy as it is subject of the third section.

2.2 Financial sector and economic growth

The case of transition economies is even more challenging, as here not only stability but growth is required. Dynamic growth rates are the prime aim of economic transition in order to catch up to western countries. Therefore the relevant question for a sound financial sector is not only how to support monetary stability, but how can the financial sector promote growth.

If the basic decision to invest is taken as choice of demand for credit to finance the investment project or not to invest, the general condition for investment would be that profit expectations exceed the cost of investment finance, i. e. the rate of interest. For the sake of simplicity profit expectations of the entrepreneurial sector are assumed as exogenous. Furthermore interest rate policy of the central bank is assumed to be instrumental for matching the inflation target of macroeconomic stability and can not be used for encouragement of investment by low interest rate policy during transition. Now the relationship between growth and the financial sector in the transition to fully fledged market economies is isolated and the contribution of the financial sector to growth can only be to supply lowest possible lending rates. As the restrictive assumption of this approach is the impossibility of a low interest policy of the central bank, lower lending rates can only be achieved by a decreasing spread of deposit and lending rates within the financial sector. The soundness of the financial sector would be indicated by narrow spreads.

Although it has to be mentioned that high interest rate spreads can contribute to the stability of the financial sector itself by allowing to build up (hidden) reserves or to write off bad assets, this would not change the main line of the argument brought forward here. In the dynamic context of system transformation the process of declining spreads would indicate the success in cleaning up the banks' portfolios. From an equilibrium analysis point of view this process would enter some type of steady state, when world market spreads are achieved. This also implies that such banks would then be able to compete with foreign financial institutions.

3 Monetary policy in transition economies[1]

Recent financial turbulence of 1997/98 found differing responses of national economies in transition (see Hölscher 2000). Here the analysis concentrates on implications for monetary policy of the EU accession countries. Although not even this set of transition countries may substantiate a homogenious set of economies the common overruling policy aim of EU entry constitutes the dominating orientation of monetary policy.

3.1 The Maastricht Convergence Criteria

How the applicant countries would currently fare regarding the Maastricht Criteria[2] is shown in Table 1 (values in bold indicate that they surpass the reference values used as a benchmark)[3].

---

[1] See Vinhas De Souza/Hölscher 1999 for an indepth elaboration of the subject.

[2] Some numerical benchmarks, aiming to guarantee the stability of the new single currency area, were defined in the framework of the Maastricht Treaty, the four so-called *EMU or Convergence Criteria*, which aim to ensure monetary and fiscal stability in the joint currency area: their assessment is not obligatory for application countries at this stage of the process. Two of these are monetary, one is linked to currency rate stability, and the final one is fiscal. They are: i) *The Inflation Convergence Criterion*, defined as an inflation rate which should not exceeds by more than 1.5 % the average inflation rate of the three best-performing countries; ii) *The Interest Rate Convergence Criterion*, meaning that the average long-term nominal interest rate should not be more than 2% above the average interest rate of three countries with the lowest inflation rate; iii) *The ERM Criterion*, which postulates that the currencies of future EMU members should be have been the ERM (Exchange Rate Mechanism) without devaluation or revaluation for at least two years; iv) *The Excessive Debt Criterion*, which is composed of a budget deficit component, which declares that a country's budget deficit should not exceed 3% of its GDP, and of a stock of debt component, which states that the stock of outstanding government debt should not exceed 60% of that country's GDP (on otherwise be in a descending sustainable trajectory towards these benchmarks).
Additionally, an „operational" element was also set, concerning the legal and institutional features of the national Central Bank (CB), namely, its independence from government interference, a mandate towards price stability, the prohibition of monetary financing of deficits, and the availability of a set of market-based instruments that enable the CB to conduct monetary policy actions.

On the face of it, the fiscal situation for these countries, on general terms, is better that the average fiscal situation for either the Euro area or the whole set of EU members, with only Bulgaria, Cyprus, Hungary, Malta and Slovakia breaching either one of these criteria.

The inflation criterion, as a result of the surprisingly fast deflationary process of the past few years and of the introduction of tighter monetary policies[4], is now also respected by most of the countries, but, on the other hand, the associated interest rates criterion is still broken by virtually all the candidates.

Concerning the exchange rate stability criterion, none of these countries is, of course, an ERM member, but roughly it can be said that the currency board countries, plus Cyprus, the Czech Republic, Slovakia and Latvia have had relatively stable currencies lately, and that Poland, Hungary and Slovenia have had moderate currency devaluations. Only Romania seems to have experienced serious exchange rate instability recently.

The actual fulfilment of the additional operational criterion of an independent Central Bank (CB) is a controversial question: some of those countries (namely, Bulgaria, Estonia and Lithuania) don't have an actual CB, but a mere currency board, which is by definition an independent organ, but, also by definition, one that does not have the means to engage in open market operations. In most of the others, in spite of the fact that their CBs are now assured a great degree of legal independence (in some cases, like Poland and Slovenia, this is even enshrined in their Constitutions), the actual relationship between the CB and the government *and* the Parliament can be one of conflict (see Radzyner, O. & Reisinger, S., 1997, and Äimä, 1998), with the latter trying, more or less systematically, to influence the former. Also, in several cases, the monetary financing of government deficits is still permitted.

The interpretation of the mostly positive figures above must be careful. The transition process is still ongoing in virtually all the former centrally planned economy countries[5]. This implies that the twin long-run processes of transition and of catching-up with the EU average development level shall imply both higher average domestic inflation and interest rates for the time being which, on their turn, will imply continuous pressures for the appreciation of the real exchange rate. Also, concerning the budgetary criteria, the apparently healthier fiscal situation masks the fact that the

---

[3] The values presented are a compilation of the most recently available figures from several difference sources. *They are presented here as merely indicative*. The exchange rate criterion is not illustrated here, because none of the countries is an ERM member so far.

[4] And with some help of the deceleration brought about by the emerging markets crisis that started in 1997 and reached Eastern Europe in 1998 (see Hölscher 2000).

[5] Throughout this study we shall concentrate on questions related to the transition economies of Central and Eastern Europe. This is justified by the fact that much more studies and information have been produced about these economies than about Cyprus and Malta, which are economies nearer EU/EMU standards with a consequent smaller need to adjust. Turkey as new candidate is not included in this study.

Table 1 EMU criteria for the candidate countries

Countries	Inflation Rate	Discount Rates	Deficit or Surplus as a Share of the GDP	Public Debt as a Share of the GDP	Monetary Authority Status
Bulgaria	-4.1	**4.7**	1.3	**95.0**	Currency Board Arrangement.
Cyprus	2.5	**8.5(d)**	**-3.4**	55.0	NonIndependent Central Bank (b).
Czech Republic	2.4	**6.0**	-1.6	40.0	Legally Independent Central Bank (b).
Estonia	3.1	**4.8(a)**	-0.3	7.0	Currency Board Arrangement.
Hungary	**8.9**	**19.3**	**-4.7**	52.0	Legally Independent Central Bank (b).
Latvia	1.9	**9.0**	0.7	6.0	Legally Independent Central Bank.
Lithuania	0.0	**4.2**	-1.3	13.0	Currency Board Arrangement (b),(c).
Malta	3.2	**8.1**	**-9.9**	52.0	NonIndependent Central Bank (b).
Poland	**6.3**	**15.5**	-2.5	50.8	Legally Independent Central Bank.
Romania	**48.6**	**35.0**	-2.6	18.0	Legally Independent Central Bank (b).
Slovakia	**6.7**	**8.8**	**-5.5**	54.0	Non Independent Central Bank (b).
Slovenia	**6.0**	**8.0(d)**	-0.3	25.0	Legally Independent Central Bank (b).

Source: Business Central Europe, EU, 1999; (a): Interbank rate; (b) Lending to Government is still permitted; (c) Capable of engaging in some types of open-market operations; (d) Ceiling on domestic interest rate.

transition process has meant a *still incomplete shift* from government consumption towards social transfers, which brutally reduced the GDP share of government expenditures. This, added to unavoidable future financial commitments for structural reforms, and coupled with still incomplete tax reforms, could indicate a future worsening of their fiscal position.

3.2 Exchange rate policy: Current linkages to the Euro

The reaching of the EMU macro convergence criteria for the new entrants has to be seen as a set of mid-term goals, to be achieved in a sustainable and permanent basis, adequately supported by micro reforms. In practice, the convergence to these benchmarks will be reached through paths that will be largely national, and, therefore, specific to each of the candidate countries[6].

The relationship of the set of monetary and fiscal targets in the criteria with the exchange rate regime is one of dependence and concordance with the macro setting of reforms. The exchange rate regime is **not** an independent aim by itself, and cannot be seen as such. This is not only the position of the Commission, but of the national governments themselves (among others, see EC, 1998; Nemenyi, 1998; Polanski, 2000). As such, the analysis of the subject separately from the wider macro framework is artificial.

As a general rule, most transition economies adopted, at some point early in their transition process, macroeconomic stabilisation programs[7] with some form of exchange rate anchor. Most of these initial peg strategies where later abandoned or softened, in face of growing external imbalances, either relatively swiftly, as is the case in Poland, or spectacularly, in the midst of a speculative attack, as was the case in the Czech Republic.

It must be noted that the learning curve of these countries (some of them newly independent, namely, Estonia, Latvia, Lithuania, Slovakia and Slovenia, which had to build national institutions virtually from scratch, including their monetary authorities)

---

[6] The time span required for the convergence process of Eastern European countries, according to an IMF study (see Fischer, S. at al., 1998), using the average development level of the Southern EU member countries (Greece, Portugal and Spain) as a benchmark would be: 28 to 29 years for Bulgaria, 11 to 15 years for the Czech Republic, 16 to 17 years for Estonia, 20 to 22 years for Hungary, 23 to 25 years for Latvia, 33 to 24 years for Lithuania, 18 to 23 years for Poland, 34 to 36 years for Romania, 15 to 19 years for Slovakia and 19 to 24 years for Slovenia. In other terms, it will be a generation-long process, even with sustainable macro policies.

[7] These macro programs encompassed, of course, several different policy actions. On the monetary side, one of the main initial concerns was the elimination of the monetary overhang: centrally planned economies traditionally generated a surplus of legal tender, given the limited amount of goods and services available for consumption. A substantial part of this overhang was held by households outside of the former mono-bank financial system. The liberalization of prices and external trade, besides the macro balance and allocative micro-efficiency issues involved, aimed at eliminating part of this surplus.

had to be very steep: hardly ten years ago, the currently universal two-tier bank structure was not only absent, but irrelevant. The CB, for all practical purposes, was a department of the Ministry of Finance, and its only real function was to produce the means of exchange to allow the trading of plan-determined quantities among individual consumers[8].

The development of the institutions able to carry out monetary policy actions, as well as the development of the necessary instruments to carry it through took time. Initially, more blunt direct monetary control instruments were used (interest rate and credit caps, high reserve requirements, „moral persuasion", etc.) since i) the monetary authorities themselves hadn't learned how to use modern monetary policy tools[9], ii) the transmission channels for the proper use of those tools, namely, working financial markets where absent in these economies (and still are today, but to a much lesser degree) and iii) the lack of stable relationships among the CB's target variables and its instruments. Only more recently market-based indirect monetary policy instruments – repos, lombard facilities, government securities auctions – have been introduced[10].

The primary goal of a central bank is to maintain price stability. This can be accomplished through direct or indirect strategies. To try to meet an inflation target indirectly assumes some sort of stable links between the final target and an aggregate(s), which the central bank attempts to influence. These aggregates are the so-called intermediate targets, but inflation is the final target. There are two possible types of indirect strategies, one based on a stable rate of exchange between the domestic currency and the currency of a low inflation country, and the other based on controlling the growth rate of a domestic money supply aggregate. The use of any type of pegging regime is, therefore, equivalent to the use of indirect inflation targeting. Nevertheless, it is usually considered that only one type of exchange rate strategy is sustainable on a long-term perspective: the free float[11]. All other strategies are unstable to exogenous shocks and ultimately collapse[12].

---

[8] Among the state enterprises and government departments, not even this mean of exchange function of money was necessary: barter – inter-unit transfers of goods and services for settlement – was used instead.

[9] Which, even in Western Europe, were only slowly and progressively introduced between the 1950s and the 1990s.

[10] It is estimated that, on average, only three years separated these two distinct phases: it was a much faster process that its counterpart in Western Europe (See Radzyner & Riesinger, 1998).

[11] A full fixing (like the Euro) merges the national currency in a composite currency that floats itself: in these terms, a full fixing to the Euro is actually a floating regime, from the point of view of the aggregate.

[12] Due to the following weaknesses of peg regimes:
– it is very difficult to determine the equilibrium exchange rate of a national currency in a peg;
– under a peg, monetary policy has limited ability to absorb shocks;
– the economy becomes vulnerable to shocks in the country to which the national currency is pegged;

The extreme case of the peg strategy is the currency board arrangement (CBA), which requires the official foreign exchange reserves to be – at least – equal to the amount of domestic currency issued (at a given fixed exchange rate): under a strict CBA, there is no actual domestic monetary policy, since both the monetary base and the level of interest rates are endogenously determined. Modified CBAs, though, may perform limited monetary policy actions, through the use of some types of CB-like instruments, like lender-of-last-resort (LLR) facilities or limited open-market operations.

Usually, the choice of a CBA is linked to the need to give credibility to a stabilisation policy, or, in the case of Eastern Europe, to sheer inexperience in terms of conduct of monetary policy by the monetary authorities of these countries.

Among its stated advantages, a CBA entails automatic balance-of-payment adjustments (essentially in the same way that a gold standard exchange system would operate: in case of a deficit in the capital and current accounts, money supply is reduced, causing, *ceteris paribus*, the interest rate to rise, which will lead to i) reduced domestic activity and reduced imports, and to ii) an increase in foreign capital inflows,). It should also result in reduced inflation expectations (depending on the anchor currency chosen). Finally, it should also, in principle, encourage sound fiscal policy (the dismissal of monetary policy leaves fiscal measures as the only counter cyclical macroeconomic tool)[13].

Among its drawbacks, a CBA means not only the loss of monetary policy as a counter cyclical tool, but it can actually be *procyclical* (reinforcing economic booms and troughs). The lack of LLR features by the monetary authority increases both the short run probability and effects of financial sector crisis (regardless of the beneficial long run effects caused by the reduction of moral hazard). The need to perform active policy actions is heightened in periods of market instability, as was clearly the case in Eastern Europe after last year's Russian crisis, and during the series of Baltic banking crisis of 1993-1995. A CBA also discourages the development of domestic money and capital markets.

Nevertheless, the most fundamental problem of a CBA lies in the question of how to get out of it. There is no optimal staircase from virtually the absence of monetary policy under a CBA regime towards a fully-fledged and even independent central bank.

Since the application countries have, at the moment, several different ways of linking their national currencies to the Euro area, we will make a condensed presentation of those different linkage strategies. The current arrangements are resumed in Table 2.

– the destabilising effects of capital inflows, when a misaligned fixed exchange rate violates the uncovered interest rate parity condition (by creating exploitable „risk-free" interest rate differentials), forcing the CB to costly and ultimately ineffective sterilisation operations.

[13] It must be noted that this last feature is not automatic, since the CBA does not endogenize fiscal policy.

The transitional linkage strategies and the degrees of preparation – and, indeed, the very perception of the need to already start preparing – for an eventual integration into the Euro area varies widely from country to country.

This shall necessarily change, as the need to prepare for it becomes clear in the next few years. The European Commission, during the ongoing negotiation process, through the pre-accession treaties, with the advice and technical support from the European Central Bank, will have to define a more clear and gradual monetary integration strategy for these countries. Until then, their disparate, even informal linkages with the Euro area – shadow and sliding pegs, free and dirty floatings, currency boards – shall remain.

The question is, whether all the application countries shall, with time, converge to a common optimal strategy for their progressive integration into to the common currency monetary framework or whether currency competition will continue until the very end.

For the national economies the initial convergence rate to the Euro is crucial for their competitiveness. Competition among them makes sense, assuming that, at the set up of EMU for these countries, market exchange rates will be the basis of the Euro convergence rate. However, any joint convergence strategies for the applicant countries should, nevertheless, be necessarily specific to the individual countries' national conditions.

4 Conclusion

In transition economies central banks had to be founded from scratch. There was no tradition of monetary policy, neither was there an institutional infrastructure of commercial banking and finance. Given the importance for a sound financial system to achieve stability and growth within the transition from planned to market economies institution building in the area of banking and finance was at the core of economic reform. External stabilisation through exchange rate regimes vis-a-vis the European Union was an option to „import" stability for those transition countries, which are nominated as EU accession candidates. These post socialist economies had the privilege of a (more or less) credible peg to the Euro as a shield for institution building. After ten years of transition they meet a large fraction of the Maastricht criteria. Central banking had to revert to robust exchange rate policies ranging from currency boards to managed float regimes to progress to these milestones. Many countries still have a long way to go to arrive at a fully fledged monetary economy.

Table 2 Current exchange rate linkages

Countries	Currency	Exchange Rate Regime	Date of Introduction
Bulgaria	Lev	Currency Board regime (anchor changed from the DEM to the Euro in 01/1999).	July 1997
Cyprus	Pound	Peg with interventions bands (+/- 2.25%) towards the Euro.	1992
Czech Republic	Koruna	Managed float, with informal shadowing of the DEM/Euro.	May 1997
Estonia	Kroon	Currency board regime (anchor on the Euro).	June 1992
Hungary	Forint	Sliding peg with intervention bands (+/- 2.25%) towards a basket made of Euro and the USD (70%, 30%).	March 1995
Latvia	Lats	Peg with the International Monetary Fund's (IMF) SDR, with intervention bands (+/- 1%).	October 1993
Lithuania	Litas	Currency board regime (the anchor is the USD).	March 1994
Malta	Lira	Sliding peg with no intervention bands, towards a basket of Euro, GBP & USD (56.8%, 21.6% and 21.6%,).	1989
Poland	Zloty	Sliding peg with intervention bands (+/-12.5%) towards a basket made of Euro and the USD (65%, 35%).	May 1995
Romania	Leu	Managed float.	1991
Slovakia	Koruna	Managed Float.	October 1998
Slovenia	Tolar	Managed float with informal shadowing of the DEM.	October 1991

Source: IMF, EU.

References

Äimä, K., „Central Bank Independence in the Baltic Countries", Review of Economies in Transition, n° 3, Suomen Pankki (Bank of Finland), 1998.

Begg, D., Monetary policy in Central and Eastern Europe: Lessons after half a Decade of Transition, IMF Working Paper WP/96/108, 1996.

Buch, C., Heinrich, R. P., Banking and balance of payments crises – On possible causes of the twin crises, The Kiel Institute of World Economics, Kiel Working Paper No. 848, 1998.

Buiter, W., Lago, R., Stern, N., Promoting an effective market economy in a changing world, EBRD working paper 23, 1997.
EBRD, Transition Report, London, 1997.
EBRD, Transition Report, London, 1998.
Fisher, I., The Debt-Deflation Theory of Great Depressions, in: Econometrica, Vol.1, pp. 337-57, 1933.
Fischer, S., Sahay, R. & Végh, C., „How Far is Eastern Europe from Brussels?", IMF Working Papers, WP/98/53, IMF, 1998.
Gabrisch, H., Pohl, R. (Eds.), EU Enlargement and its Macroeconomic Effects in Eastern Europe, Macmillan Press: London, St Martin's Press: New York, 1999.
Goodhart, C. A. E. (1997): Setting standards is just the first step: Maintaining them is the harder part, paper presented at the University of Birmingham (mimeo).
Hölscher, J. (Ed.), Financial Turbulence and Capital Markets in Transition Countries, London: Macmillan Press, New York: St Martin's Press, 2000.
Hölscher, J., Owen Smith, E. Pugh, G., „The DM-Undervaluation and Germany's Economic Performance", University of Birmingham, Discussion Papers in German Studies, 1999.
Hölscher, J., Zur Formierung marktwirtschaflicher Ordnungen in Zentralosteuropa, in: Konjunkturpolitik, 4, 1998.
Hölscher, J., „Economic Dynamism in Central-East Europe: Lessons from Germany", in: Communist Economies & Economic Transformation, Vol. 9, No. 2, 1997.
Horvath, J. & Jonas, J., „Exchange Rates Regimes in The Transition Economies: Case Study of the Czech Republic 1990-1997", ZEI Working Papers, B11, 1998.
Masson, P., „Monetary and Exchange Rate Policy of Transition Economies of Central and Eastern Europe after the Launch of EMU", IMF Policy Discussion Paper No. 99/5.
Nemenyi, J., „Challenges of Monetary Policy in the run-up to European Union Accession", 1998, mimeo.
Melo, M. de, Denizer, C., Monetary Policy During Transition – An Overview, The World Bank, Policy Research Working Paper 1706, 1997.
Mishkin, F. S., International Capital Movements, Financial Volatility and Financial Instability, paper presented to the annual meeting of the 'Verein für Socialpolitik', Bern 1997 (mimeo).
OECD (Ed.), The New Banking Landscape in Central and Eastern Europe, OECD Proceedings, Paris, 1997.
Polanski, Z., „Poland and International Financial Turbulence of The Second Half of The 1990s", in Hölscher, J. (Ed.), Financial Turbulence and Capital Markets in Transition Countries, London: macmillan Press, New York: St Martin's Press 2000.
Radzyner, O. & Reisinger, S., „Central Bank Independence in Transition: Legislation and Reality in Central and Eastern Europe", Österreichische Nationalbank, 1998.
Stern, N., Stiglitz, J., A framework for a development strategy in a market economy: Objectives, scope, institutions and instruments, Working paper 20, European Bank for Reconstuction and Development, London, 1997.
Stiglitz, J. E., Weiss, A., Credit Rationing in Markets with Imperfect Information, in : American Economic Review, Vol. 73, pp. 912-27, 1981
Turnovec, F. (ed.), Czech Republic 1997 – The year of crises, CERGE-EI: Prague 1998.
Vinhas de Souza, L., Hölscher, J., Exchange Rate Linkages and Strategies of new EU Entrants, in: Bohata, M., Turnovec, F. (Eds.): Transition, European Integration and Institutional Change, CERGE of Charles University, Prague 1999.

Part III:

Public sector banks

The Saxon savings banks association

Saxony's response to the challenges posed by competition in the banking sector

Georg Milbradt

Sächsisches Staatsministerium der Finanzen, D-01076 Dresden, Germany

By passing the "Act to Restructure the Saxon Savings Banks and Landesbank Sachsen including Sächsische Aufbaubank" in March 1999, the state of Saxony has embarked on a new route to further develop the traditional public owned savings bank system in the light of proven principles and adapt it according tocurrent technical and economic challenges. Saxony has traditionally played a key role in the history of Germany's public-law banks and the savings bank system in particular. Some of the early milestones in this development include:

- 1826 establishment of the savings bank in Leipzig,
- 1908 establishment of the first regional association of savings banks,
- 1909 establishment of the first German clearinghouse for savings banks.

The de-facto nationalization of the savings bank system and its inclusion in a single-level state bank system under East Germany's communist regime meant that the Saxon savings banks lost their role as stand-alone banks. In fact, they largely degenerated into mere outposts ("payment offices") of the state bank, primarily collecting capital for the state and handling payments. It was not until the breakup of the state bank and the conversion of the savings banks into independent financial institutions in 1990 that they were able to catch up on trends in Western Germany. Over the past few years, the 22 savings banks currently operating in Saxony and the newly established Landesbank Sachsen – Girozentrale – have made a key contribution to rebuilding the Free State of Saxony. They are normal banks which additionally fulfil a particular public duty. It is precisely this duty, performance of which is in the particular interests of the general public, that forms the basis of the existence of public banks. Public duties may be varied and manifold and change over time. In Eastern Germany, in particular, the existence of local banks with a special commitment to fostering local and regional development is of particular importance. This is the difference between the situation in Eastern Germany and in Western Germany where a highly developed economy and an efficient financial services sector put the particular role played by public banks into perspective, encouraging critics to doubt the necessity of Germany's unique savings bank system.

Without a doubt, the Eastern German savings banks have effectively supported development in the Eastern German states over the past few years, testifying to the special role they play. Over the past few years, the number of employees has almost doubled. Their track record in terms of the economic benefits gained is extremely impressive, too.

The very positive performance of the trades in Saxony, for example, remains closely linked with the services provided by the savings banks. A genuine employment miracle has taken place in this segment. Whereas prior to German reunification around 65,000 people were employed in this sector of the economy, this number has since risen to approx. 500,000. This means that there has been an almost eight-fold increase in employment. This achievement – the increase in trade businesses from 23,000 to just under 50,000 and the growth in employment – is due to a large degree to the support and assistance provided by the savings banks.

The ongoing reconstruction of the Saxon economy bears a certain resemblance to trends recorded in the 19th century. The humus on which the economy grows is the plethora of small and medium-size businesses in which ownership and management responsibility are interwoven and which play an important role in their local communities. These small to medium-sized companies not only influence economic trends but also the social development of their environment. However, the beneficial influence of the small to medium-size businesses will only unfold if the banking sector assumes risks, particularly when successful SMEs hit the limits of their ability to finance their growth. Assuming responsibility for the development of local companies sometimes involves more than just granting loans. This is why the savings banks are also shareholders in venture capital companies which provide capital to promising companies. This is also true of Landesbank Sachsen, the regional financial institution. Landesbank Sachsen has, for example, supported a software company via a joint venture fund. Just recently, the equity interest was sold for over DM 100 million. These proceeds can now be ploughed back into new business activities which may not be quite as successful.

The Saxon savings banks and Landesbank Sachsen will and should continue to support the economic development of our state. The main advantage of these institutions is that they are familiar with the state and its inhabitants and are able to gauge risks reliably and do not need to depend solely on formal collateral. Another reason why they have a particular responsibility in the local and regional economic structures is that private-sector banks – with the exception of the cooperative banks – are not anywhere near as active in the new federal states as they are in Western Germany. Frequently, the savings banks alongside the cooperative banks are the only financial institutions in a given town or locality.

Unfortunately, the debate surrounding the justification of public financial institutions often ignores their important function as conduits of financial information. Having their own presence in the banking market gives local and state governments access to important general information including, for example, market development and competition intensity, profits and risks as well as the financing requirements of the private sector. This is information which would otherwise not be readily available and which can be put to good use in policy decisions relating to economic development. This is especially important against the backdrop of the single EU market which will have a key and partially divergent impact on regional economic structures. In particular, Landesbank Sachsen is able to provide up-to-date practical information on EU-related issues.

However, in addition to promoting the regional economy, the savings banks and the state bank are also a key decision-making factor in our state. A regionally oriented and economically successful public banking system can be very useful particularly in a state whose feeble economy is subject to remote decision-making from outside and is therefore particularly exposed to the risk of business relocation to other regions. Regionally oriented customers, in particular, like to deal with decision-makers at financial institutions based in the state itself. Quick and short decision-making paths are a key competitive edge for regional banks operating in an increasingly globalized environment.

The development of Hamburg as a banking centre illustrates this trend. While the number of banks based in the city increased by one third to 196 between 1970 and 1992, the number of domestic banks domiciled in Hamburg dropped by half to 52. The fact that the banks have their legal domiciles in this city does not, however, mean that this is where business policy is determined. Rather, decisions are in many cases made where the banks' parent companies are located.

In 1992, there were only ten banks with domiciles in Hamburg which also made business-policy decisions there – including Hamburgische Landesbank and Hamburger Sparkasse, which, however, is defined as a "free" savings bank. This means that more and more banking decisions are being made at other locations with the result that regional aspects are falling by the wayside. Accordingly, business is threatening to be relocated to the places where decisions are made, primarily Frankfurt am Main, leading to a loss of local banking resources and jobs.

This applies even more so to Eastern Germany. In the wake of reunification, an economic structure has emerged in which key decisions are made outside the state – frequently also by people who are not really familiar with this state. The regional balance which characterizes the economy in Western Germany does not apply in Eastern Germany – a fact easily revealed if you look at a list of Germany's 500 largest companies and the 500 top organizations, virtually none of which is domiciled in Eastern Germany. This is why I think that a key financial determinant of economic development must stay within Saxony to ensure a sufficient degree of independence. The existence of a public financial system exerting considerable influence on the market is of crucial importance for the future development of the Saxon economy and hence also the creation and retention of jobs in Saxony. In a purely private-sector banking sector, the quest for economies of scale would inevitably result in most decision-making centres being located in Western Germany. This is why the Saxon state government feels very strongly that the savings and state bank system needs to be secured on a regional basis under public law while maintaining the opportunity of playing an independent role of some weight in spite of the convergence of the European economy.

Competition in the German banking market with its roughly 60 million customers in 37 million households is becoming fiercer all the time. The sector is undergoing extremely dynamic change. Mounting internationalization and the new markets opening up as a result of the globalization process have boosted banks' business activities considerably. This trend is being spurred by developments in information and communications technologies. New market participants as well as changed strategies are fuelling competition.

In addition to this, in the near future banks will not only be competing with other banks in their direct vicinity but also with high-tech giants such as Microsoft, telephone companies, cable TV operators, Visa and MasterCard, retailers and midsize computer service providers. Who would have thought ten years ago that Volkswagen AG would set up its own bank and successfully attract investors' capital with appealing interest rates, thereby increasingly exerting pressure on the savings banks? Volkswagenbank today has just under 230,000 customers and manages deposits of DM 4.25 billion.

The banking market in the UK provides an example of what happens when nonbanks enter the banking market. In that country, non-banks and near-banks have drained deposits worth DM 17 billion from the traditional banks' balance sheets. It is assumed that the volume of deposits will increase to DM 60 billion over the next five years. The well-known British department store Marks & Spencer's has, for example, extended its range by offering customer loans, investment products, property insurance, investment funds, pension plans and life insurance. Unlike conventional banks, these non-banks and near-banks are frequently able to cross-subsidize the financial services at inexpensive rates within their groups.

The German savings bank system is well positioned to successfully come to terms with the challenges posed by the market and competition. Thanks to their regional links and customer proximity, the high esteem and confidence they enjoy on the part of customers and the public at large, savings banks are firmly rooted in broad strata of the population. In terms of business volume, the savings banks and state banks were the market leaders in 1998 with a share of 36%. Mention should also be made of cheque accounts relationships which play an important role in Eastern Germany where roughly 70% of the population have cheque accounts with a savings bank.

By working in collaboration with central institutions – e.g. Landesbausparkasse Ost AG – the savings banks are additionally able to operate as one-stop banks, offering their customers a full range of products and services typical of a large financial services company. However, the service-boosting and cost-cutting effects can only be achieved if the savings bank association – which comprises 594 savings banks, 12 regional associations and the DSGV (savings bank association of Germany) as the top association, 12 state banks, 13 state building societies and 40 public insurers as at December 31, 1998 – works smoothly and genuinely pools its resources. However, I have my doubts about this.

In this connection, what DSGV president Hoppenstedt said at the last conference of the savings bank management boards on November 3, 1998 is remarkable. I quote:

"If these partners do not work together properly – and this is still something which can be seen today – this is an enormous luxury costing us far too much money."

What is remarkable is that the same tenor can repeatedly be found in the speeches of the savings bank presidents over the past few years, pointing to a less than ideal division of labour between the savings banks, even though this very division of labour could potentially resolve many of their organizational problems. This finding made by president Hoppenstedt continues to apply in spite of the reforms which have been under discussion for years, e.g. a comprehensive McKinsey report in connection with the EU single market in 1992. According to a paper distributed by the city of Leipzig to the city council in 1998, the McKinsey report states the following:

"However, a sector with decentralized companies requires a joint strategic orientation to a far greater extent than before. Stronger decision and implementation skills mean that the decentralized units must refrain from certain activities – however this primarily concerns areas in which they in any case do not operate efficiently, e.g. product and system development. In numerous interviews, savings banks have appealed for greater strategic leadership and are willing to abandon other activities. It would be desirable for this view to be reflected in appropriate actions."

However, such action has not emerged to date. The savings banks' unsatisfactory business performance in 1998 is further proof of this. The DSGV president is correct in citing customers' greater yield awareness and aggressive competition by direct (non-)banks as the reasons for this. In this connection, particular mention should be made of the appreciably smaller interest margin, which dropped to 2.49% of average total assets in 1998, down from 2.68% in 1997. This decline is not solely due to generally low interest rates and has been evident for several years. Nor was it possible for this decline to be cushioned by increases in net commission income, which at 0.50% of average total assets has remained virtually unchanged. This figure came to 0.49% in 1997.

Whether this trend in the banking sector is to be welcomed or not is not the point. What is far more important is coming to terms with the new situation; a proactive approach is certainly preferable to merely reacting to events as they occur. The Saxon state government has taken the initiative by developing the Saxon Savings Banks Association model. In the services sector, in particular, and even more so in the financial services industry, standing still is tantamount to a step backwards. It should not be forgotten that experience in a wide variety of industries in Germany – e.g. new technologies and the photographic, motor cycle and electronics industries – has shown that belated action will result in a massive loss of jobs. There is agreement amongst the political parties and associations that something must be done. An example of this is the situation in Baden-Württemberg. In this state, the savings bank of the city of Stuttgart – the state clearing house – merged with Südwestdeutsche Landesbank and the market operations of L-Bank to form Landesbank Baden-Württemberg.

Saxony has taken a different course compared with Baden-Württemberg. The Saxon solution provides for a new joint company co-owned by the municipalities and the state governments with strategic management functions, to be known as Sachsen-Finanzverband ("Saxon Financial Association"). It is based on a principle of a partnership of equals between the municipalities and the state government. This is primarily reflected in the fact that a dual majority is required for all resolutions of fundamental importance passed by the shareholders (i.e. an overall majority including the majority of the municipal shareholders). The Association is a public-law body with share capital but is not classified as a financial institution. Its main function is to strategically pool the resources of the savings banks which have so far tended to operate in isolation. This means that joint activities will be more efficiently handled within the Association. Thus, Sachsen-Finanzverband is an instrument aimed at harnessing the considerable amounts of unused earnings potential identified by Ostdeutscher Sparkassen- und Giroverband and its advisors.

In brief, the Saxon Savings Banks Association works as follows:

The municipalities may voluntarily transfer responsibility for the savings banks, which will continue to be legally independent entities, to the Association; membership is not compulsory. The guarantees and liability assumed by a public-sector body for the debts of the savings bank in question will also be transferred to the Association. The shareholders, i.e. the state and the member municipalities, will be liable for the Association. In return for transferring guarantees, the municipalities receive shares in the Association's capital and interest-bearing loans according to enterprise valuations.

The savings bank governance – a management board and an advisory council – will remain unchanged. A representative of the Association will have a seat on the advisory council. Other than this, there will be no changes to the appointment procedures and composition. This means that municipal representatives will continue to be elected by the municipal or town council. The legally independent savings banks will continue to make their own business decisions with respect to operative customer business. This is in line with the principle of management-board responsibility stipulated by banking supervision legislature.

The Free State of Saxony will be contributing its shares in Landesbank Sachsen. Like the municipalities it will receive shares in the Association's capital and interest-bearing shareholder loans in return for contributing its shares in Landesbank Sachsen. The same procedure applies to Sächsische Aufbaubank.

The public mission is expressly provided for in the Restructuring Act under which the aim is not to maximize profit. In addition to the examples already given, the public mission is primarily reflected in the preservation of the branch network and hence broad-based availability of banking services to the public. Thus, the aim is not to close branches but to offer customers, particularly SMEs, attractive terms.

At the same time, the Saxon state government is quite aware that efficiencies need to be realized. Details in this connection must be determined on a partnership basis in a cooperation agreement still to be signed. Given that the primary goal of the Saxon solution is to ensure continued fulfilment of the public mission, earnings must be maintained and extended by improving the competitiveness of the savings bank system. This is the only way to ensure that goals of general public interest can be met as before. The regional principle is maintained. There is no formal or substantive privatization. Local trade tax liability and the previous donation and sponsoring activities will continue unchanged. In 1997, the Saxon savings banks spent an aggregate of approx. DM 18 million on donations and sponsoring.

According to the state government's calculations, the municipalities will receive DM 300 million in addition to donation and sponsoring funds, comprising the interest on shareholder loans and dividends with no restrictions as to their use and without being charged against municipal financial equalization payments. The current scope for making distributions to municipalities is far lower even for savings banks with a direct municipal guarantor (even taking account of the Restructuring Act).

The key to reaching these goals lies in a combination of the advantages of the decentralized structure of the savings bank system and the strategic management functions and coordination duties of Sachsen-Finanzverband.

In this connection, mention should be made once more of comments made by the savings bank organization decrying deficits in a whole range of different areas. This particularly concerns product ranges, consulting skills and securities business. The Saxon solution seeks to abandon the current "stand-alone structure" and replace the loose links with a tight system aimed at pooling resources. The aim is to reduce the defection ratio criticized by the savings bank organization; to the extent possible, business should be conducted within the "public-bank family" instead of being given to other banks. At present, this kind of consistent cooperation is not in place.

Under the Association system, decentralized business responsibility will remain with the managing boards of the savings banks. This means that lending and other customer decisions will continue to be made locally. The only loss of autonomy will occur in operative non-customer business, e.g. Custodian Account A business and liquidity management. It goes without saying that legislative requirements must also be complied with. The performance of non-market and non-customer activities by the Association or the state bank will allow savings bank executives to concentrate more on attending to the regional markets. In addition, duplicate work can be avoided in certain areas – e.g. the development of consulting concepts. This will preserve and tend to strengthen the savings banks' competitive lead thanks to local and independent customer services.

With the installation of a controlling department in Sachsen-Finanzverband, it will be possible to identify room for improvement in lending and securities business and to implement such improvements. In other words: improved analysis and pooled distribution tools will be used to boost market share. The greater distribution efficiency particularly aims to make better use of the considerable earnings potential identified in lending and securities business. We do not think that this can be achieved under the current stand-alone structure. This is suggested by the experience gained over the past few years as well as the appeals from within the savings bank association in both Western and Eastern Germany. Moreover, mention should specifically be made of savings banks' market share in lending business in 1997: loans to corporate and self-employed customers 20%, loans to private individuals 26%, loans to public-sector bodies 26%. What this means is that market share has been lost. Our response is to change or at least partially reverse this trend by means of improved distribution concepts. The strong customer ties – e.g. the high market share with cheque accounts – provides a good basis for this.

Finally, the abandonment of a stand-alone structure means that less liable equity will be required. Risks will be backed on a broader basis and spread more evenly. The Association will pool the corporate risks and perform an insurance function by diversifying risk. Thus, the risk arising from a mono-sector structure in a given region can be offset by strong performance in other regions.

To summarize, it can be stated that the Association system represents the attempt to combine the advantages of the present decentralized structure with the advantages of strategic parameters and size. The motto is "strength in unity". The basic decisions are made by the shareholders of Sachsen-Finanzverband subject to a majority of the municipalities' votes. This applies to the general guidelines for business and personnel policy, for example. In addition, the shareholders will decide on the planned performance-tied remuneration system for management boards. As the controlling system is located outside the banks, the examination of the activities performed by the management boards and the savings banks will be more transparent and easier to verify in greater detail. However, success will not be defined solely in terms of earnings. Rather, the savings banks will, of course, continue to be committed to serving public needs. To this end, a system of targets must be agreed upon in advance between the municipalities and the state government. It is not least of all in this connection that the Association system will substantially strengthen municipalities' powers towards savings bank management boards compared with the present situation. Ultimately, however, all this merely represents the introduction of normal corporate sector practice at public-law companies.

May I conclude by briefly outlining the progress achieved to date. The Act to Restructure the Public Banking System in the Free State of Saxony including Sächsische Aufbaubank GmbH came into effect in May 1999. The Saxon Association of Municipalities (Sächsischer Landkreistag) and the Saxon Association of Towns and Cities (Sächsischer Städte- und Gemeindetag) also take the view that the changes to the legislative procedure have dispelled the legal doubts and objections held by both bodies, particularly as a result of the aforementioned double-majority principle. Both bodies have recommended valuing the savings banks for the municipal owners. However, this does not necessarily mean that they will be applying for membership. This will ultimately be decided by the relevant district and municipal parliaments for the 22 Saxon savings banks.

The Association is the Saxon answer to the need to preserve public banks' competitiveness while retaining their particular regional duties. The system attempts to harness the advantages of size, particularly economies of scale and a united market approach, linking these with the classic advantages of local customer ties by replacing the previous loose collaboration between savings banks within the savings bank and clearing house associations and with associated companies by closer cooperation amongst the guarantors of this system, i.e. the municipalities and the state, and granting them extensive ownership rights.

References

Milbradt, Georg (1999), Sächsische Verbundlösung – Konzept für eine sichere Zukunft in Sachsen, in: Wertpapier-Mitteilungen, p. 1164 ff.

Milbradt, Georg (1999), Sachsens Antwort auf die Sparkassenfrage, in: Börsen-Zeitung April 10, 1999.

Milbradt, Georg (1999), Ein systemverträglicher Weg zur Sparkassen-Neuordnung, in: Börsen-Zeitung March 11, 1999.

Process of change within the universal banking system in Europe

Michael Weiss

Sachsen LB, Humboldtstraße 25, D-04105 Leipzig, Germany

The economic efficiency of universal banks is superior to that of other banking systems even today. This evaluation is supported by practical experiences. Still, this opportunity can be used to reinforce the above hypothesis.

First of all, the process of change effects not only the universal banks, but the other banks, too. The effects of globalization can be roughly divided into effects on the wholesale and on the retail sale businesses.

The phenomenon of globalization is not confined to the financial community only. It has caused major changes in other sectors, and the banks follow their customers through their structural changes. However, the effect is first and foremost felt in the larger customer businesses. The increasing transparency of capital markets results in more intensive competition, which can be described by using the French regional banks as an example.

Some time ago, French regional banks offered financing at a 100 base point margin. Recent competition, and more specifically the easier access to new markets, also for other banks, has reduced this margin to 10 base points. This means a major pressure on the players to adjust themselves. Globalization also makes former borders between sectors disappear. So, in our original core businesses we deal with companies from other sectors to an increasing extent today. Large companies act as banks themselves, and insurers also penetrate our market. The increasing importance of rating and risk management systems creates different classes within the banking business. Big companies do not accept banks as trading partners any longer if the banks do not offer adequate rating and risk management systems. Banks, which cannot offer such systems, will inevitably be relegated to the second, third or fourth divisions.

Customers demand more complex products and comprehensive solutions for their problems. There is an increasing pressure from government supervision, such as the sixth amendment to the German Banking Law (KWG), minimum trading standards, or the Basel equity capital agreement. This pressure, together with an increasing customer demand, means an increasing labour and cost expenditure on DP and risk management systems.

The retail business, too, is subjected to considerable changes, resulting in decreasing margins. Fierce competition with the direct banks causes a considerable shift in deposits. Also, non-banks and near-banks penetrate the market to an increasing extent, including the wholesale business as described above. The increasing use of new media, such as the internet, TV, and phone, opens up a new round of sharp competition. High yield expectations and a decreasing safety consciousness make some kinds of investment vehicles slide into insignificance.

Now, in the light of these trends, one could think that the universal banking system or universal banks would not be able to cope with these changes. Following the development in the industrial sector, the motto could be: let us reduce to the core business. However, this is more a policy statement than real analysis. On the other hand, it is obvious that universal banks suffer most from the above trends due to their wide range of activities. However, there is plenty of rope for banks that are sufficiently flexible.

So, the question is not universal bank versus investment bank, but rather how should universal banks be structured to guarantee sufficient flexibility. The universal bank of the future should provide a close-knit network of customized banking services. Universal bank does not mean: do it all by yourselves and all in one house. It is not only proper, but necessary for a universal bank to concentrate on profitable business lines, and to invest in creativity and problem-solving, because we are going to be paid for good resolutions to problems rather than for the mere bulk business. However, that does not mean at all that banks will withdraw from certain business lines. The point is: what businesses to focus on.

Flexibility needs a network to operate in, like a spider's web. There will be an increasing number of universal banks operating in such networks. This could be in the form of co-operation or concentration. The network type is more promising for medium-size and small units, such as the Sparkassenfinanzgruppe (the savings banks financial services group), to give you a good example. Operating in a network means co-operating, sharing fixed-costs, and creating competence centres. The use of advanced information technologies can provide major benefits here. Structures need to be adapted, and related changes must be seen as opportunities, and used. Teamwork, employee profit-sharing schemes, and new entrepreneurial concepts are just a few keywords here. The ability to operate in a network is based on the ability to integrate systems and to clearly define the interfaces between them. This is the only way for a medium-sized bank to cope with the changes in a network. If we manage to design and control a bank that is able to operate within a network, the universal banking system as outlined above will certainly provide benefits.

Public sector banks – Importance and restructuring

Discussion of Georg Milbradt's "The Saxon savings banks association"

Bernd Schips

KOF/ETHZ, Swiss Institute for Business Cycle Research, Weinbergstr. 35,
CH-8092 Zürich, Switzerland

Upon closer examination the role of public sector banks in a banking system in keeping with today's business and social developments has been under discussion for a long time already. For example, in 1964 Wolfgang Stützel submitted a detailed report commissioned by the Federal Minister of Economics which dealt with various questions in connection with this issue.[1] Stützel stated at the time that regional authorities would lose an important instrument of their independent regional planning and trade policies by dispensing with public sector banks. He also saw the necessity of the legal and economic system naming investment possibilities which completely discharge a diligent trustee (trustee investments), i.e. interest-bearing investment possibilities were to be offered and the state itself was to provide a guarantee for their creditworthiness.[2]

At first glance, this line of argumentation still appears reasonably convincing today. However, the question must be asked from a scientific point of view whether and to what extent a fundamental reassessment of the situation should be made in the light of the changes which have meanwhile taken place in the economic environment and especially in the banking industry and the conversion of the public credit institutions to what are actually all-purpose commercial banks, despite appreciating the fact that through the establishment of savings banks obvious gaps in the market were able to be closed in the past.

The historically occasioned special status of public credit institutions as banks with the task of serving the interests of the regional economy is becoming increasingly debated in the light of the development of most of the public sector banks into all-purpose banks and their range of services, which is comparable at first glance with those of other banks. The term "all-purpose bank" refers to traditional credit institutions that grant unsecured personal loans and finance long-term investments without neglecting deposit-taking business, which is linked to the house bank principle.

If public sector banks are regarded as "superfluous" institutions from an economic view nowadays, this is first and foremost a conclusion which has been drawn from the observation that in the meantime private banks usually maintain a sufficiently dense network of branches and offer all the bank services required to meet the basic

---

[1] Cf. W. Stützel, Bankpolitik – Heute und Morgen, 2nd edition, Frankfurt/Main 1964.
[2] Cf. W. Stützel, loco citato., p. 79f, Tz. 166.

needs of the population, the economy and the public sector. Furthermore, it is generally no longer possible to distinguish between the range of services offered by private banks and that of public sector banks.

On the basis of such an assessment of the market situation, the Monopolies Commission and the "Kronberger Kreis" have stressed, for example, that there are no legitimate reasons why the state should continue its business operations in the banking business today. The liability assumed by public sector banks for the debts of a public corporation and the assumption of a guarantor's liability are therefore called into question.

Although most of the public credit institutions have de facto developed into all-purpose commercial banks, this development is not to be judged as "bad" per se nor does it compel a review of the special legal status of these banks. Public sector banks which offer the same range of services as an all-purpose bank but fulfil a public duty in addition by waiving profits or by assuming increased risks are certainly imaginable in certain areas of their operations whilst performing the tasks assigned by each respective regional authority.

The subject under discussion here is being debated in many other European countries. In Switzerland, for example, there have also been fierce struggles in recent years concerning the status of the cantonal banks which have been provided with a state guarantee. In 1997, the EU carried out an examination of the status of the public sector banks in EU countries, provoked partly due to the debate held predominantly within Germany between the Federal Association of German Banks and the Association of Public-Sector Banks concerning the competitive situation between the private and public sector banks in Germany. This examination has been completed, but in my opinion, conclusions in the form of EU directives or recommendations cannot be expected.

In 1995, the Norwegian Bankers Association filed a complaint with the EFTA Surveillance Authority against the Norwegian house banks due to an infringement of the subsidy ban. The EFTA Surveillance Authority terminated the proceedings in 1997 without taking any further steps in the matter. However, a decision has not yet been passed concerning the subsequent action filed by the Norwegian Bankers Association at the EFTA Court of Justice due to formal defects in the treatment of the case by the EFTA Surveillance Authority.

Thus the entire area of tension in this debate ranges from an extreme, almost doctrinaire position, as is expressed for example by the statement made by the Monopolies Commission, to the firm belief that public sector banks are essential elements of regional and local measures to spur the economy from an economic policy viewpoint. In the case of the latter position, it is usually also assumed that there are no advantages attached to the state guarantee which might be regarded as inadmissible aid resulting in serious restrictions to competition. It must be mentioned in this connection that to my knowledge there have, in fact, been only a few individual cases in which it was able to prove that the special status of the public sector banks had led to distorted competition. However, as a rule it is explicitly or at least implicitly assumed when justifying public credit institutions that the task of these banks is to render services which are not included in the services rendered by private banks.

It is precisely the task of providing these banking services which is gaining importance in the economic debate at a time when there is an almost unlimited globalisation of financial markets. Political demands in relation to public sector banks, especially to better represent the interests of small and mid-sized companies, can be clearly heard. In future, banks should not only be places for people to go who have money but for those who need money. Especially small and relatively young enterprises experiencing rapid growth often encounter financing bottlenecks after being initially successful and require a detailed risk assessment, which is often only possible if there is in-depth knowledge of local conditions.

From a historical perspective, the task of providing banking services is an essential element of a public sector bank. The fact that a regional authority started banking operations through its own institution was originally only undertaken in the interests of the regional economy. The justification for banking operations was based in particular on providing banking services and granting low-interest loans. The state guarantee was then added to the task of providing banking services as a corrective in order to provide a guarantee to depositors for their credit balance despite the banking task.

The sustained series of bank mergers offer public sector banks, which are usually more familiar with local and regional conditions, the opportunity again today to fill vacant niches and gaps in the provision of loans. In the process of a banking concentration, public sector banks can certainly be accorded a compensatory function regarding competition policy.

However, there is still a danger that the banking task in connection with hidden subsidies might also pose a threat to the existence of a public sector bank. The state guarantee for all liabilities of a public sector bank is the distinguishing feature de lege lata and is also the main justification for exemptions from banking supervision in many countries. The state guarantee goes beyond merely providing a guarantee for liabilities – it is a de facto guarantee for the continued existence of a public credit institution. It is not possible to clearly determine whether public credit institutions gain any particular financing advantage due to this state guarantee. In my opinion, there are as many arguments in favour of this case as there are against it. However, it is worth discussing whether it would be possible for public sector banks to perform their competitive policy function just as well or perhaps even better without receiving special treatment from the legislator. Careful consideration of this question is important because the state guarantee for each regional authority and consequently for the taxpayer constitutes an indirect obligation. This is why the concerns of the taxpayer should be taken into due consideration in addition to ensuring the protection of creditors and that of the system, especially because the taxpayer cannot exert a direct influence on the risk that he also has to bear.

However, the fact should not be overlooked that a company always has a de facto state guarantee if the public sector holds an interest in it, irrespective of whether there has been a formal stipulation of this fact or not. The participation of public enterprises in the economic process is also in keeping with a leading political decision taken by the EU, which means that restrictions are not to be expected from that quarter as long as the banking operations of public sector banks do not cause serious restrictions to competition.

In its Amsterdam declaration in June 1997, the EU Council made the following statement concerning the debate on where to legally place the liability assumed by public sector banks for the debts of a public corporation and the assumption of a guarantor's liability: "The Conference has taken note of the view held by the Commission that the existing rules on competition of the Community allow full consideration of the services of a general business nature which are rendered by public sector banks in Germany as well as the privileges which are granted to these banks as compensation for the burden incurred by the provision of these services. In this connection, it shall be left to the organisation of this member state to decide on how it enables the regional authorities to perform the task of making an efficient and extensive financial infrastructure available in its regions. These privileges must not impair competitive conditions to a degree that exceeds the extent required in order to perform the special tasks and which run counter to the interests of the Community".[3] There is nothing more to be added to this statement. It complies with the comments which were made by Stützel in the sixties to a large extent and which I quoted at the beginning of this talk.

The "Saxon network solution" presented by the Minister of State, Mr Milbradt,[4] endeavours to do justice to the area of tension I have mentioned. To begin with, establishing that public sector banks in the new German states still play a different role in the banking sector than they do in the old German states meets with approval. The tasks of providing banking services and the assessment of their importance for the economy differ as a matter of course and there are also essential differences in the organisational tasks to be fulfilled. The basic idea of decentralised banking activities by a body which is familiar with local conditions in connection with a central "back office", although this term is to be understood here in the widest possible sense, i.e. by including strategic banking issues and considerations, sounds quite convincing in principle.

But are public sector credit institutions really necessary for this? The success of individual regional banks operating in a similar field of business in Switzerland and, above all, the success story of the agricultural credit co-operative movement speak against spontaneously replying in the affirmative to this question more so than they do in favour of it. Being located in the vicinity of customers, the security, the ability to constantly adjust to structural changes, the obligation of borrowers to become members of the agricultural credit co-operatives as well as having a strong headquarter in order to better meet capital requirements and the challenges of a constantly changing market are no doubt major factors which have contributed to the continued success of this part of the Swiss banking system. This development is continuing at a

[3] Cf. C. König, Zur Auslegung der Amsterdamer Erklärung im Hinblick auf die EU-Beihilfeaufsicht über Landesbanken, in: Wertpapier-Mitteilungen (1997), p. 1279f.

[4] Cf. G. Milbradt, Sächsische Verbundlösung – Konzept für eine sichere Zukunft in Sachsen, in: Wertpapier-Mitteilungen (1999), p.1164ff.

time when, in many areas, there is a strong decline in interest in what is known as the retail business due to profitability considerations and especially when many small and mid-sized businesses declare themselves to be having difficulties obtaining business loans, incidentally also from public sector cantonal banks. This part of the banking system, which is noticeable in this respect, i.e. individual, usually smaller regional banks and the agricultural credit co-operative organisation, have managed to hold up well especially in difficult times (e.g. during the price decline in the real property sector) and have reported predominantly lower bad debt charges than most of the public sector cantonal banks. Sound knowledge of local conditions, a high amount of flexibility and the use of scaled earnings through co-operation were sufficient for success. In my opinion, this experience should not therefore be completely left out of consideration when discussing the necessity of public sector banks.

The structure of the "Saxon network solution" is definitely in keeping with a large part of the concept of the successful model mentioned. The co-operation model chosen also ensures additional possibilities of procuring information for economic policy decision-makers through maintaining presence in the banking sector and can thus influence market developments which may be viewed as detrimental from a regional view. There are naturally also serious risks entailed in these fundamental opportunities for all parties involved, not least for the taxpayer, which means that the manner in which the concept can ultimately be implemented and further developed is of decisive importance for sustained success.

References

König, C., Zur Auslegung der Amsterdamer Erklärung im Hinblick auf die EU-Beihilfeaufsicht über Landesbanken, in: Wertpapier-Mitteilungen (1997), p. 1279f.

Milbradt, G., Sächsische Verbundlösung – Konzept für eine sichere Zukunft in Sachsen, in: Wertpapier-Mitteilungen (1999), p.1164ff.

Stützel, W., Bankpolitik – Heute und Morgen, 2nd edition, Frankfurt/Main 1964.

Part IV:

Quantitative explorations in financial systems

Causal links between financial activity and economic growth: Evidence from two-wave model estimations

Michael Graff

Dresden University of Technology, Faculty of Economics, D-01062 Dresden, Germany

Abstract. To clarify the causal links between financial activity and economic growth, a series of two-wave path models is estimated. It is shown that during the 70s and 80s finance was predominantly a supply-leading determinant of economic growth. The data suggest, however, that from about 1975-80, finance was far less beneficial – and possibly even detrimental – to growth.

1 Introduction

The causal relationships between financial activity and economic growth are still very far from being well understood by scholars of economics or related disciplines. The literature concerned with these questions can be loosely grouped into the following four categories.

Firstly, financial activity and economic growth are seen as *not causally related.* In this view, the observable correlation between them is spurious: economies grew, and so did their financial sectors, but the two followed their own logic.

Secondly, financial activity is taken to be the result of economic activity. Financial development is thus *demand-driven.* As the growing scale of economic activities requires more and more capital, institutional raising and pooling of funds for industry are substituted for individual fortunes and retained profits.

Thirdly, financial activity is seen as a *determinant* of economic growth. In this view, the line of causation runs from financial to real activity, where finance is one among other growth-inducing factors. Finance thus acts as a *supply-leading* growth device. Specifically, recent theoretical models give rationales for the assumption that well functioning monetary and banking systems and capital markets may be crucial for economic growth. The arguments vary, but Schumpeterian authors as well as some Neo-Keynesians usually stress the banking system's ability to create money and channel it into productive and innovative uses. Others claim that it is the information gathering and processing, which is accomplished by professional actors on credit and capital markets, that helps to improve the efficiency of capital allocation.[1]

---

[1] For a detailed survey cf. GRAFF (2000).

Fourthly, some scholars see financial activity as a potential impediment to economic growth. Thus, as in the previous case, the line of causation runs from finance to real activity; but the focus lies on the destabilising effects of financial overtrading and crises. Specifically, this view sees the financial system as inherently unstable. While some theoreticians are ready to include commercial banks into the sources of financial distress, most proponents direct their attention towards stock markets or international capital flows. This view – though hardly popular at the present time – is held by a wide range of distinguished economists ranging from SOMBART (1916, 1927) and KEYNES (1936) to DIAMOND/DYBVIG (1983), SINGH (1997), KRUGMAN (1996) and FILC (this volume).

Unfortunately, there is no simple procedure to determine which view is empirically adequate, since the factors that govern economic growth admittedly include many others besides financial development, and interactions among them are likely to prevail. Moreover, the existing cross-country data on financial activity are plagued by poor reliability and dubious validity.

Does economic history offer any lesson for the present? I think it does. First, as PATRICK (1966), GOLDSMITH (1969, 1987), CAMERON ET AL. (1967), and others have shown, in the now developed countries, modern financial systems generally evolved during the very early stages of their industrialisation.

Moreover, financial development – as measured by GOLDSMITH'S financial interrelation ratio (conveniently proxied by M2/GDP) generally levelled off after a few decades, reaching its fully developed stage[2] by the beginning of the twentieth century. These historical observations imply that in the process of industrialisation finance may have been supply-leading rather than demand-following.

In addition to this, the traditional financial sectors of the present LDC's are very similar to the financial systems of the DC's prior to their industrialisation. As many observers have noted (SHAW 1973, MCKINNON 1973, FRY 1995 – to name just the most prominent), financial dualism is the rule outside the developed part of the world: enclaves of modern finance, mostly located in the commercial centre, serve but a few export oriented firms, whereas the majority of economic transactions takes place in the traditional sector which – leaving aside local peculiarities – is basically functioning in the same way as it did in the now developed countries before their industrialisation. This observation implies that in the financially and economically less developed countries, there is a latent, but unexploited potential for growth.

What may matter in this context is that the sunk investment and well as the professional skills to operate a basic financial system providing a reliable means of payment as well as to ensure smooth financial intermediation between surplus and deficit units need not be extraordinary sophisticated and costly. Thus, unlike to

---

[2] Note, however, that financial interrelation ratios for developed economies vary considerably (from less than unity to up to three) from country to country due to different institutional frameworks such as government provision of pension schemes, structure of the housing market or the level of commitment to rules and norms in financial relations.

other economic activities, the LDC's might be able to exploit their growth potential by modernising their traditional financial sectors with financial technology that can be easily imitated and borrowed from the more advanced countries (cf. CAMERON ET AL. 1967).

2 Empirical analysis

The objective of the following empirical cross-country analysis is to investigate the asserted causal relationship from financial development to economic growth. To this end, a two-stage research strategy will be followed.

The first step is to construct for a large sample of countries and various years a new proxy for financial development (FD) which captures *the share of resources a society devotes to run its financial system* at any given time. In contrast to the usual indicators of financial repression/liberalisation and financial depth, which frequently suffer from ambiguity (expressing monetary and credit volumes as well as financial overheating and likelihood of financial crash), the FD-proxy suggested here relies on real inputs and stands for a well-defined macro-economic concept. Therefore, it is possibly more adequate for investigations into the sources of economic growth.

Moreover, while monetary indicators like M2/GDP are very hard to compare across time and space due to institutional diversity and change, the new FD-proxy is likely to be less sensitive to minor changes in institutional regulations, domestic and international shocks and business cycles.

Last but not least, since the shape and the scope of a financial system is firmly rooted in a country's history, this FD-proxy may be assumed to capture very basic characteristics of an economy's structure. Consequently, the FD-variable suggested here is probably less endogenous to current economic activity than the traditional FD-variables.

The second step is to investigate the causal structure between financial and real activity. To this end, I estimate a series a two-wave path models with the FD-proxy on the one hand and per capita income (as a proxy for the *level* of economic development) on the other.

2.1 A new proxy for financial development

The construction of the new variable FD for financial development is motivated by the interest to get a reasonably reliable and comparable quantification of *the share of resources a society devotes to run its financial system*.

While this intention bears some resemblance to the core argument of *transactions cost* and *institutionalist* economics (NORTH 1990, WILLIAMSON 1985), namely that aggregate transaction costs are very far from negligible and that financial institution are a major response to this problem, I depart from the closely connected evolutionist argument that prevailing institutions – having survived the selection mechanism of the market – are the 'adequate' solution. Instead, I regard the amount of resources devoted to run these institutions as an indicator of the effort to keep transaction cost (as well as frictions and market failures due to informational asymmetry that are mitigated by the financial system) low. This notion of financial development is thus very different from the common notion of financial depth; it signifies a *real* rather than a *monetary* phenomenon.[3]

The idea to measure the operating costs of a given financial system seems plain enough – why has this not been tried before?[4] I think a good part of the answer lies in the fact that no international statistics supply reliable and readily comparable data. The three indicators which I found suitable for consideration, (1) the share of manpower employed in the financial system, (2) the share of the financial system in GDP and (3) the number of banks and branches per capita, though distributed by distinguished institutions, are strikingly unreliable. Not only do the numerous footnotes indicate that the reported numbers are neither comparable across countries nor through time for a given country. Worse is that conceptual changes as well as retrospective recalculations sometimes appear in subsequent volumes *without any notice*. Moreover, missing values and obvious errors add to the trouble. Finally, these numbers have to be transformed into the desired ratios (normalised to labour force or GDP, respectively) by hand.

For a study of finance and development in a cross-sample of countries which intends to cover some twenty or thirty years, all mentioned variables are thus very far from satisfactory. What follows, therefore, rests on the assumption that the raw numbers can be transformed in a way that makes them reasonably reliable, complete and valid measures for the intended notion of 'resources for finance'.

The procedure chosen here is to identify the *common variance* of the three indicators using principal component analysis. If the operating costs of the financial system are reasonably well represented by the first principal component[5] the individual scores for this component may serve as a valid proxy for the interesting variable.

---

[3] I do not claim that the traditional notion of financial depth is not useful, but I believe that the degree of monetisation and the aggregate credit volume channelled through the financial system – i.e. the 'traditional' variables – and the amount of resources needed to run a given financial system stand for very different economic functions: While the former inform about the prevailing channels of finance, the latter measure the intensity of financial services.

[4] At least, to the best of my knowledge, there is no cross-country study that has attempted to do this.

[5] That is, if the correlations between the desired representations are high, but measurement errors, stochastic shocks have little common variance. To come close to this goal, a 'technical' condition is that the indicator variables have to be measured independently. This condition is satisfied here. Our three indicators for the size of the financial system are compiled from data published by ILO, UN and BANKER'S ALMANAC, respectively.

Practically, to prepare the raw data, the three normalised indicator-variables (share of manpower employed in the financial system, share of the financial system in GDP, number of banks and branches per capita) were carefully screened for obvious errors and incompatibilities. Next, the yearly values of the normalised variables were transformed into five-year averages for 1970, 1975, 1980, 1985 and 1990. Finally, operational rules had to be formulated how to treat missing values.[6] The remaining data for 93 countries and five points in time were pooled and standardised. Then, principal component analysis was applied to the resulting 465×3 matrix, delivering a first principal component representing 77% of overall variance.[7]

Finally, the individual scores for the first component were taken as the FD-proxy for further analysis.

We can thus proceed with a well-defined (μ=0, σ=1)-variable that assigns a specific value for financial development as defined here to all 93 countries in my sample through five points in time.

Sample and data

The sample consists of all countries for which the necessary data could be collected, with the exception of countries that are exceedingly small (population less than one million), of countries with centrally planned economies through most of the period 1970-90, countries in which oil exports accounted for more than 20% of GDP in 1985, and countries with war or civil war claiming a death toll exceeding 2.5% of total population during 1970-88. The exclusion of these countries is to acknowledge that it may make very little sense to run regressions across countries which are fundamentally different from usual conditions (cf. HARBERGER 1998).

The FD-proxy is computed as described above.

The real development proxy is per worker income Y/L. The usual proxy for labour (L) in studies similar to this one is the size of the population. While this may be adequate as long as the focus is on standard of living aspects of economic development, I rather refer to the size of the labour force proper for this productivity oriented study.[8]

---

[6] The general strategy was to estimate missing values in time by interpolation, extrapolation, trend analysis, and – where possible – by regression on exogenous variables, but to exclude all observations, where the majority of data would result from estimation rather than from original data.

[7] The variances for second and third principal component are 17% and 6%; and all communalities exceed 67%, indicating that the expected one-dimensional structure of the three variables is reasonable well represented by the first component.

[8] For further details and sources see appendix.

Causality

This section presents a path analysis with two variables, the new FD-proxy and per capita income Y/L, measured at t_0 and t_1.

The statistical method – path analysis with panel data – is established in biological research since the 30s, and sociologists have referred to it at least since the 60s (DUNCAN 1966, HEISE 1970). Economists, however, have concentrated more on time series bases concepts of causality, so that applications similar to the one presented here are not yet common in the economic literature. Some methodological remarks are therefore in order.[9]

The model is conveniently represented in the following path diagram (figure 1).

Figure 1 Two-wave path diagram

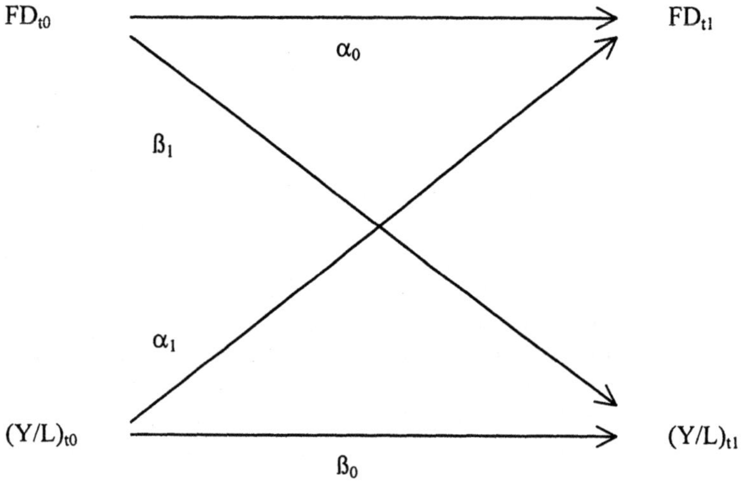

9 For a detailed description cf. FINKEL (1995).

Hence, the model consists of the following two equations:

$$FD_{t1} = \alpha_0 \, FD_{t0} + \alpha_1 \, (Y/L)_{t0} + \varepsilon,$$

$$(Y/L)_{t1} = \beta_0 \, (Y/L)_{t0} + \beta_1 \, FD_{t0} + \varepsilon.$$

Practically, the path coefficients are easily computed as the standardised partial correlations resulting from regressions of the t_1-variables on both t_0-variables.

The (sequential) structure of causation reveals itself in the estimates parameters α_1 and β_1. If neither of the two is significantly different from zero, there is no indication for causation in either direction; if both are, the model indicates mutual (bidirectional) causation. Significance for α_1 only implies unidirectional causation from Y/L to FD, which is consistent with the demand-following finance hypothesis, whereas significance for β_1 only implies unidirectional causation from FD to Y/L, which is consistent with supply-leading finance as defined by PATRICK.

Thus, contrary to the usual strategy to search for patterns of GRANGER-causality drawing on time series of *within individual* countries, the present approach exploits *inter-country* rather than intra-county variance, thereby probably allowing more general conclusions. As with GRANGER-causality, however, a problem with this approach is the determination of the lag. Since the model assumes causality to operate between t_1 and t_1, the lag is crucial. Hence, for a strict statistical test, the proper lag length should be derived from theory and then be specified a priori, before running the statistical test.

The general advice for two-wave models is that the lag should be 'long enough'. The data base allows lags to range from five to 20 years. Given the present state of our ignorance about the finance-development-nexus, however, I choose not to determine a fixed lag, but rather to run exploratory tests by trying out all possible lag lengths.

With this qualifications of the nature of the following tests, let us proceed to the results. Since the interest is directed toward causality issues rather than the magnitudes of the path coefficients, I report only the t-values and the significance levels for one-tailed tests of $\beta_1 > 0$ and $\alpha_1 > 0$, corresponding to path 1 (supply-leading finance) and path 2 (demand-following finance), respectively. Moreover, negative coefficients – not predicted by either of the two hypotheses – are indicated.

Table 1 Two-wave path model estimations

t_0	t_1	path 1	path 2
1970	1975	4.17**	2.20*
1970	1980	1.89*	2.48**
1970	1985	2.92**	1.86*
1970	1990	4.43**	1.52
1975	1980	2.70–	1.31
1975	1985	.04	1.02
1975	1990	2.63**	.87
1980	1985	2.45**	.33
1980	1990	5.24**	.41
1985	1990	5.28**	1.34

One-tailed significance (H_a: α_1, $\beta_1 > 0$) of path 1 and 2:
** $p < .01$, * $p < .05$
negative sign: —

An inspection of the results in table 1 reveals that β_1 (path 1) is highly significant in 7 of ten cases, and passes the 5%-test in an other case, while α_1 (path 2) is significant at the 1% level only in one case, and at the 5% level in two other cases. Consequently, The general picture is that though there are undoubtedly signs for mutual causation between finance and development, significance is mainly found in the supply-leading finance-column, hence, the most obvious line of causation is running from finance to development. Moreover, in no case do we find a pattern of significance for path 2 only. Thus, while there is evidence for mutual causation, the data do not give any indication for demand-following finance. These generalisation holds for all time lags (from five to twenty years) that could be tested in the panel data set.

These findings of the two-wave path model obviously do not support the demand-following finance hypothesis, and while the suspicion of mutual causation between finance and development cannot be rejected, my results clearly indicate that supply-leading finance prevailed.

However, some further qualifications, which are of special interest in the present context, are possible. Note first that the strongest signs of mutual (instead of unidirectional) causation from finance to development are found in the 1970s. Moreover, for the second half of the 1970s, the estimates indicate a strong departure from the usual quinquennial supply-leading pattern. If there is no severe measurement error in the data, the findings suggest that during this special period the level of financial activity was *detrimental* rather than beneficial to economic growth (corresponding to the sceptics' fear of financial activity disturbing rather then aiding real activity).

What follows is – at least – that the finance-growth nexus put forward in the literature is not a stable relationship. Specifically, some special circumstances in (such as the oil price shock induced turbulence in the international financial system, the severity of financial repression, or the of radical financial liberalisation induced by the MCKINNON/SHAW school) could be held responsible for the peculiar results in the 1975-80 period,[10] but more specific answers will require further substantial research.

Moreover, due to data availability, this framework presently does not allow statements about the 1990s. Though more evidence on the stability of the finance-growth nexus may be expected from new data allowing to conduct similar tests for the 1990-95 and following periods, with the data at hand, unfortunately, I cannot give any empirical evidence about possible shifts or reversals of causation that might be due to recent phenomena (globalisation of financial markets, growing numbers of active stock markets as well as the recent financial crises, to name just a few).

Conclusion

The empirical results presented here indicate that from about 1970-90 finance obviously mattered for growth. However, while causation ran mainly from financial to real development with only little evidence for mutual causation and no evidence at all for reverse causation (from real to financial development only), the estimations indicate that the finance-growth nexus is far from being a stable relationship. Specifically, during the second half of the 1970s it did not operate in the way expected by the proponents of financial development; on the contrary, in this period financial activity seems to have been detrimental to economic growth. In this respect, one can speculate whether some special circumstances in the 1975-80 period (such as the oil price shock, financial repression, or financial deregulation) are responsible for this finding.

---

10 For empirical evidence indicating that financial repression was a widely spread phenomenon during the late 70s, cf. FISCHER (1982: 87 ff).

Appendix: Data and sources

If not mentioned otherwise, data are from the PENN WORLD TABLES (Mark 5.6, revised December 1997).

Labour (L) is adjusted for capacity utilisation as described in GRAFF (2000).

The number of Banks and branches are counted from the 1970 to 1990 editions of the BANKERS' ALMANAC AND YEARBOOK, London: Thomas Skinner.

The share of labour employed in the financial system is taken from the ILO YEARBOOK OF LABOUR STATISTICS, Vols. 1971-1997, Geneva. The corresponding ISIC-2 ('international standard industrial classification of all economic activities', 1968) classification is 'major division 8' (financial institutions, insurance, real estate and business services)

The financial system's share of GDP is computed from various issues of the UN NATIONAL ACCOUNT STATISTICS, New York, referring to 'finance, insurance and business services'.

References

Cameron, Rondo, Crisp, Olga, Patrick, Hugh T. and Tilly, Richard (1967), Banking in the Early Stages of Industrialisation, New York: Oxford University Press.

Diamond, Douglas W. and Dybvig, Phillip H., (1983) Bank Runs, Deposit Insurance, and Liquidity, Journal of Political Economy, 91: 401-419.

Duncan, Otis Dudley (1966), Path Analysis: Sociological Examples, in: American Journal of Sociology, Vol. 72: 1-16.

Finkel, Steven E. (1995), Causal Analysis with Panel Data, Thousand Oaks: Sage.

Fischer, Bernhard (1982), Liberalisierung der Finanzmärkte und wirtschaftliches Wachstum in Entwicklungsländern, Tübingen: Mohr (Paul Siebeck)

Fry, Maxwell (1995), Money, Interest, and Banking in Economic Development, 2nd ed., Baltimore: Johns Hopkins University Press.

Goldsmith, Raymond W. (1969), Financial Structure and Development, New Haven: Yale University Press.

Goldsmith, Raymond W. (1987), Premodern Financial Systems. A Historical Comparative Study, Cambridge: Cambridge University Press.

Graff, Michael (2000), Finanzielle Entwicklung und reales Wirtschaftswachstum, Tübingen: Mohr Siebeck (Habilitationsschrift / post-doc thesis, Dresden University of Technology, August 1999, to appear shortly).

Harberger, Arnold C. (1998), A Vision of the Growth Process, American Economic Review, 88: 1-33.

Heise, David R. (1970), Causal Inference from Panel Data, in: Borgatta, Edgar F. (ed.), Sociological Methodology, San Francisco: Jossey Bass: 3-27

Keynes, John Maynard (1936), The General Theory of Employment, Interest, and Money, London: Harcourt Brace.

Krugman, Paul (1996), Cycles of Conventional Wisdom on Economic Development, International Affairs, 72: 717-732.

McKinnon, Ronald I. (1973), Money and Capital in Economic Development, Washington, D.C.: The Brookings Institution.

North, Douglass C. (1990), Institutions, Institutional Change and Economic Performance, Cambridge: Cambridge University Press.
Patrick, Hugh T. (1966), Financial Development and Economic Growth in Underdeveloped Countries, Economic Development and Cultural Change, 14: 174-199.
Shaw, Edward S. (1973), Financial Deepening in Economic Development, New York: Oxford University Press.
Singh, Ajit (1997), Financial Liberalisation, Stockmarkets and Economic Development, Economic Journal, 107: 771-782.
Sombart, Werner (1916), Der moderne Kapitalismus I: Die vorkapitalistische Wirtschaft, Der moderne Kapitalismus II: Das europäische Wirtschaftsleben im Zeitalter des Früh-kapitalismus", 2nd ed., München: Duncker & Humblot.
Sombart, Werner (1927), Der moderne Kapitalismus III: Das Wirtschaftsleben im Zeitalter des Hochkapitalismus, München: Duncker & Humblot.
Williamson, Oliver E. (1985), The Economic Institutions of Capitalism, New York: Free Press.

Sovereign risk, reserves, and implicit default probabilities: An option based spread analysis

Alexander Karmann[1]

Dresden University of Technology, Faculty of Economics, D-01062 Dresden, Germany

Abstract. As the Brady bond market indicates, USD bonds issued by different debtor nations show different interest rates. The conventional approach, to identify the spread as a compensation for default plus other market premia, lacks clear advices to infer default probabilities. Our arbitrage-oriented reasoning argues that the spread is the price of insurance against default, materialized by a put option on the sovereign's ability to pay back outstanding debt in foreign currency at the expiration date.

To identify the (lognormal) process of foreign reserves, we use spread data of bonds as well as fundamental economic data to infer μ and sigma .

Key Words: Sovereign Risk; Default Probability; Bond Spreads; International Lending

JEL Classification: F34, G15, G12

1 On the need to reconsider sovereign risk approaches

The most common definition of country risk is the risk of financial losses in foreign investment due to problems arising from macroeconomic and/or political events in the respective country. But as foreign investment is related to different aspects, like real investment, international bank credits and market based financial investment, assessing country risk in a systematic approach may differ according to a decision maker's own strategic goal attaching different weights to economic aspects (e.g. relating repayment ability to balance sheet data), institutional aspects (e.g. relating financial stability to financial deepness and economic integration) or socio-political aspects (e.g. relating willingness-to-pay to law systems, nepotism). In quantitative studies, until today "the fundamental difficulty ... is in defining ap-

[1] For valuable discussions, I would like to thank experts at banking places in Frankfurt and Zürich as well as participants of seminars at Dresden University of Technology, Daimler-Chrysler AG Research and Technology, Ulm, and Concordia University, Montreal and of the 8th symposium "Finance, Banking and Insurance" in Karlsruhe. I am grateful to Stefan Huschens for clarifying hints and to Dominik Maltritz for computational assistance. The usual disclaimer applies.

propriately the dependent variable" (EATON ET. AL.(1986), p. 506) which has to be explained by causing factors.

According to CANTOR AND PORTER (1996), commercial country risk ratings are shown to reflect, as a comprehensive summary statistics, economic, institutional as well as political aspects and are, on average, highly correlated to bond yield spreads (see also SCHOLTENS (1999)). Nevertheless, there are considerable objections against existing country risk ratings.

In contrast to corporate finance, country ratings differ considerably across agencies, which reflects the difficulty in evaluating and aggregating aspects of solvency, liquidity, willingness-to-pay of borrowers and contractual or political rights of creditors to inflict sanctions on a debtor nation. As the evaluation of default probabilities is more difficult in the context of sovereign bond (compared to corporate bond) analysis, basically because creditors are more helpless in their effective legal recourse, this fact may explain why, typically, sovereign bonds have higher yield spreads than corporate ones within the same commercial rating class (CANTOR AND PACKER (1995)). A second objection comes from the observation of biased country ratings. According to a study of SOMERVILLE AND TAFFLER (1995), experts assessing country risk typically fail to attribute powerful statistics for arrear versus non-arrear events. Running a test statistics for *Institutional Investor* rating to predict arrears, ratings had been shown to be biased towards an adverse view of creditworthiness producing high type-II forecasting errors of falsely predicting arrear events. This pessimistic view may be explained by concerns on unsystematic portfolio risk or by herding behavior of banking experts providing information for *Institutional Investor* ratings. On the other land, focusing on sovereigns' foreign currency bonds CANTOR AND PACKER (1996) show systematic differences between less pessimistic agency ratings by *Standard and Poor's* and *Moody's* and the market perception on sovereign risk as expressed by higher yield spreads. A third objection is drawn from high persistencies of commercial country ratings over time unless significant news occur, as found by HAQUE ET. AL. (1996). The example of Ukrainian Euro- and DM-bonds having experienced price discounts of up to 50% of their face value in secondary markets half a year before *Moody's* downgrade to Caal followed in January 2000, as a reaction to news on rescheduling negotiations initiated by the government, is an impressive illustration of rating persistency.

In this paper we concentrate on sovereign risk, i.e. the risk that the central bank has not acquired sufficient foreign reserves to fulfil current repayment obligations of the sovereign's public sector. Signals from the inherent debt status, as claimed by EATON ET AL. (1986, p. 506), will be derived by combining bond spreads, repayment obligations and the process of accumulating foreign exchange reserves in an option based approach. In section two, we summarize some theoretical findings on sovereign risk and report on the main shortcomings when evaluating sovereign credit risk. In section three, we present our option based approach to spread analysis within the context of sovereign bonds. We close by some numerical demonstrations on evaluating LDC default probabilities.

2 Review of existing studies

The discussion of sovereign default risk in the theoretical literature can be traced back to EATON AND GERSOVITZ (1981). Assuming future exclusion from capital markets as permanent after default, they show that the default probability increases cp. with increasing debt obligations. Lenders will establish credit ceilings increasing with the volatility of the proceeds enabling the debtor economy to repay its debts. This result conforms to our empirical approach in section 3.

One strand of literature, starting from the observation of debt overhang in the 1980‘s, focuses on debt relief Laffer curve, forgiveness, and disclosure policy like interest capitalization, debt equity swaps or foreign aid programmes (see ARMENDARIZ DE AGHION (1993) for a survey). The other strand concentrates on moral hazard and sanctions versus self-regulation. In this view, credit ceilings are seen to be time-inconsistent, and direct sanctions are pre-requisitory instruments for an LCD's reputation for repayment in order to preserve 'reputational collateral' needed in future borrowing (BULOW AND ROGOFF (1989)). Other institutional arrangements which help creditors to pursue their contractual rights are co-operation among lenders, FDI or country contributions to an international lending institution. More recently, ROGOFF (1999, p. 31) emphasizes the aspect of self-regulation as means to overcome moral hazard issues. Debtor nations could be concerned about their status as a member in good standing of the world economic community, facing – among others – the threat of interference in short-term trade credits by creditors in case of default. Debtor nations are forced by self-interest to signal future creditworthiness. And these signals of creditworthiness may even enter decisions on the IMF's Contingent Credit Lines, as established in 1999, by arguing that sovereign borrower moral hazard is substantially lower than investor moral hazard due to policy conditionality (see FISCHER (1999, p. 101).Whether or not borrower moral hazard is involved by offering contingent foreign aid, a sovereign debtor's ability to attract private international capital in the future is strongly influencing the market's perception of creditworthiness and repayment prospects. And building foreign reserves is one major determinant, therein.

A remark should be addressed to the dual role of capital inflows into debtor nations in the presence of shallow financial markets. On one hand, and in a medium-term perspective, capital infusions ease a debtor nation's attempt to stock its foreign reserve. On the other hand, they encourage maturity mismatch of short-term borrowing and long-term lending. In the presence of a shallow domestic financial sector, this exposition makes a debtor nation more vulnerable to suffer from international financial rumours leading to capital reversals (see e.g. WONG AND CARRANZA (1999)). This reasoning should be taken into account when analysing the empirical process of foreign reserve accumulation and its determinants.

Empirical studies on sovereign risk have concentrated for a long time on such observable events like rescheduling, arrears, or IMF programmes and their explanation in a macroeconometric setting (a comprehensive overview of earlier studies is given in SAINI AND BATES (1984), for a representative approach using a logit model see e. g. LLOYD-ELLIS ET. AL. (1989)). The fundamental criticism in dealing with event analysis of the above type is what really reports the present value of outstanding debt, a question in which an investor would basically be interested in (see EATON ET. AL. (1986, p. 506-07)). Rescheduling, for example, may be voluntary, rescheduling arrangements may be signed a long period of time after the first occurrence of default problems, foreign aid may prevent actual arrears, and so on. These examples illustrate the still unsolved difficulty in defining a reliable variable of debt status.

More recently, the increasing role of sovereign rating business in the process of sovereign lending has shifted interests in the field of country risk analysis to the question to which extent sovereign credit ratings can be attributed to economic fundamentals and/or to political factors (see BREWER AND RIVOLI (1990), ORAL ET. AL. (1992), SOMERVILLE AND TAFFLER (1995), HAQUE ET. AL. (1996) for an analysis of *Institutional Investor* ratings). Again, and as already outlined in the first section, there had been revealed considerable shortcomings in using business country risk ratings.

A third empirical approach focuses on the analysis of spreads. Here, instead of relying on subjective expert scoring expressed by rating figures the focus is on informationally efficient markets which produce spreads to signal the market's perception on sovereign risk. There are two different ways to explain the spread as the difference between the interest rate of a risky bond and the interest rate of a secure (default-free) bond: a cost-oriented way and an arbitrage-based way.

The first explains the spread as being equated to total costs for holding the risky asset. These costs include costs for the compensation of the expected losses in the case of default, risk premium, and other factors related to market competition or to liquidity. An early contribution to this approach is given by EDWARDS (1984) who analyses the differences of risky bond prices over LIBOR, while ALFORD AND LUSSIER (1993) look at (end-year) prices of loans and SCHOLTENS (1999) uses bond yield spreads by comparing with US-T bond yields.

The second, arbitrage-based approach explains the spread as the price of being insured against default. This interpretation, well known for corporate lending, cannot be applied directly to sovereign lending. In the case of corporate zero bonds (for coupon bonds, a similar but more elaborate argument applies; see BLACK AND SCHOLES (1973, p. 651)), the standard argument runs as follows: the corporation's stockholders being obliged to repay the face value of the bonds at the maturity time, may be viewed as having the equivalent of a call option C issued by the bond holders, on their company's assets. The call option's expiration date is equal to the maturity of the bonds, its strike price is the face value. And the common stock's net value will be the maximum of the value S of the company's assets minus the bonds' face value and zero. Accordingly, by subtracting the value of the bonds, which is described equivalently by $S - C$, from the value of the default-free bonds of the same maturity we get the so-called risk-neutral discount the corporate bonds should bear.

In the case of sovereign bonds, the primary objective is on the sovereign's ability to fulfil repayment obligations by having accumulated forex reserves (see CLAESSENS AND VAN WIJNBERGEN (1990)). Stated otherwise, the issue of sovereign risk is on illiquidity rather than insolvency. Methodologically, two different questions may be posed. Either, to calculate fair bond spreads by estimating solvency coefficients out of a cross-country logit model (see LICHTLEN (1997)). Or, to calculate default probabilities and expected losses by estimating the process S of the sovereign's reserve holdings. The latter will be taken up in the next section. The common criticism to sovereign bond spread analysis is, of course, whether observed bond spreads allow to infer the process of forex reserves and to separate between aspects of ability-to-pay (economic risk) and willingness-to-pay (political risk).

3 Option based approach to sovereign default

3.1 The basic idea

Our perspective is on repayment prospects of sovereign bonds traded in secondary markets at the end of some planning horizon T. For simplicity, we concentrate on zero bonds. This may be justified by arguing that the decision to default or not hinges on the principal rather than on the coupon payments.

Assumption 1: There are two types of zero bonds of identical maturities, equal to T, and of identical face value B_T. Both are denominated in one international currency, say US Dollar: risky bonds $B_{t,T}^{risk}$, issued by a foreign sovereign or sovereign institution ("governmentally guaranteed bonds"); and default-free bonds $B_{t,T}^{sec}$ ("US-T bonds") with interest rate r, i.e.

$$B_{t,T}^{sec} = B_T \exp(-r(T-t)).$$

Repayments in foreign currency will be performed by using the central bank's actual foreign exchange reserves. It is often argued that there may be seniorities involved in depleting a country's forex reserves: international trade credit may enjoy highest priority, followed by sovereign bonds, while private sector loans rank lowest. Assuming governments to have full access to their central bank's actual foreign exchange reserves (as will be the case for LDCs), we specify default to occur if the total sum of repayment obligations with priority higher or equal to sovereign bonds exceeds the volume of reserves. Hence, we disregard other aspects like unwillingness-to-pay (political risk). This may be justified especially in the case of sovereigns being integrated in the world community, which makes debt repudiation costly. For simplicity, we assume repayments to be done not prior to the time horizon T (which may be thought of as one year). Or,

Assumption 2: There will be no repayments prior to T. The total amount K of (net) repayment obligations at T with priority higher or equal to the sovereign bonds (and including them) is publicly observable (any other financial claims of the sovereign, denominated in foreign currency, may be netted with the repayment obligations). The sovereign's decision to default depends on the central bank's foreign exchange reserves S_t at time T: default occurs when $S_T < K$ holds.

Let us consider (S_t) as a stochastic process of forex reserves which, at any time t, represent the upper limit of the sovereign's repayment ability. Assume, there is one singular international lender holding all forex claims with face value $K = B_T$ at maturity T. Then the value P of an insurance the lender is willing to pay against sovereign default risk will not exceed the spread between the price of the risky and the secure investment having both identical face values. Hence, assuming non-arbitrage: $P = B^{sec} - B^{risk}$. If the lender holds only a part α of total claims, then P will be replaced by α P in this relation. The event to be insured is nothing else than the occurrence of (S_t) to fall short of K at time T, i.e. $S_T < K$. Hence, the price of this insurance can be materialized as the price of an European put option to sell financial claims of face value K, at expiration date t* equal to time of maturity T, against an economic entity whose market value is given by the process (S_t). The put price can be calculated by the well known put-call parity if the assumptions of the Black-Scholes mechanism on the process (S_t) hold (see HULL (1993, chap. 10) for a reference). Therefore, we formulate

Assumption 3: The process of foreign reserves is characterized by

$$dS_t = \mu\, S_t\, dt + \sigma\, S_t\, dW_t \tag{3.1}$$

where μ, σ are constant and W is Brownian notion.

Non-arbitrage between holding risky and secure financial claims holds. Hence, the price $P_{t,T}$ of a (European) put option to sell the total volume of risky claims with face value K at expiration date equal to maturity T fulfills the following condition to insure the fraction $\alpha := B_T/K$ of total claims: the price spread between risky and secure claims of identical face value B_T equals $\alpha\, P_{t,T}$, or

$$B_{t,T}^{sec} = B_{t,T}^{risk} + \alpha\, P_{t,T} \qquad (3.2).$$

Assumption 3 implies that S_t increments are lognormally distributed, or

$$\ln S_t - \ln S_{t-\Delta t} \sim N\left((\mu - \sigma^2/2)\,\Delta t,\ \sigma^2 \Delta t\right).$$

According to put-call parity, we have

$$P_{t,T} = K \exp(-r(T-t)) N(-d_2) - S_t N(-d_1), \tag{3.3}$$

where

$$d_1 = [\ln(S_t/K) + (r + \sigma^2/2)(T-t)]/(\sigma\sqrt{T-t})$$

and

$$d_2 = [\ln(S_t/K) + (r - \sigma^2/2)(T-t)]/(\sigma\sqrt{T-t}).$$

Observing bond spreads $B^{sec}_{t,T} - B^{risk}_{t,T}$ in secondary markets, for any level K of repayment obligations using (3.1) to (3.3) we derive at σ, the market's *implicit volatility* of the forex reserve process. To characterize S_t, we still need to estimate the drift μ of reserve accumulations. Thus, the spread alone measures only the volatility of the sovereign's ability to repay the bond and does not capture completely the (economic) risk of default.

To estimate the drift, we use balance sheet data to predict the volume of international reserves available at the end of the planning horizon. According to FISCHER (1999, p. 98), in building up foreign exchange reserves, the country may run a current account surplus, can borrow reserves but typically above the returns on reserves, or tries to be in favour of new international arrangements on lending programs. As long as there is no public information on additional private or public lending operations, we assume a country's reserves to be fully determined by its expected current account figures (see e.g. FRANK AND CLINE (1971) for an extensive discussion on predicted exports and non-compressible imports when analysing debt servicing difficulties) assuming to result in net reserves held by the sovereign's central bank. In general, net capital imports expected to occur within period have to be added, neglecting them expresses the more pessimistic view that a developing country may suffer absence of fresh capital import (see eq. 3.4 versus 3.4′ below). Hence, to derive expectations w.r.t. the drift of the reserves process we may use the following formulation.

Assumption 4: Expectations $E(S_T)$ on reserve holdings at time T will be equal to actual reserves plus expected current account, or

$$E(S_T) = S + E(CA_T)\,, \tag{3.4}$$

where S as a constant are the initial reserves at t, known to the public, and $E(CA_T)$ is the current account balance till time T, expected by the public at time t. To derive a lower bound of expected reserves accumulation, current account is expected to be determined only by net exports or

$$E(S_T) = S + E((Ex\text{-}Im)_T) \tag{3.4'}$$

where $E((Ex\text{-}Im)_T)$ is the corresponding value of exports minus imports.

Using eq. (3.2), we get S_T conditional on $S_t = S$ to have lognormal distribution (see e.g. HULL (1999, chap. 10.2)):

$$S_T = S\exp(\eta\,(T\text{-}t)) \text{ where } \eta \sim N(\mu - \sigma^2/2, \sigma^2/(T-t)). \tag{3.5}$$

Hence, $E(S_T) = S\exp(\mu\,(T\text{-}t))$, and inserting eq. (3.4) results in

$$\mu = \left(\ln \frac{S + E(CA)_T)}{S}\right)^{\frac{1}{T-t}}. \tag{3.6}$$

Eq. (3.6) allows to identify the *drift* or expected rate of return μ (in a short period of time) of the process S_T. The *default probability*, i.e. the probability that the sovereign's reserves S_t will fall short of repayment obligations K at time T, is given by $P(S_T < K)$. Using eq. (3.5), the probability to default at T can be calculated as

$$P(S_T < K) = P\big(S\exp(\eta(T-t)) < K\big) = \tag{3.7}$$

$$= P\left(\varepsilon < \frac{\ln(K/S) - (\mu - \sigma^2/2)(T-t)}{\sigma\sqrt{T-t}}\right) \quad \text{where } \varepsilon \sim N(0,1).$$

Eq. (3.7) represents the market's perception on the probability of the sovereign to default at time T. Similarly, by using the characteristics of the accumulation process S_T of reserves we can derive the *expected losses* $E(L_T)$ and, hence, the *exposure to risk.*

3.2 Extensions

Normalizing for differing maturities

Until now we have considered maturities to be equal to the period of asset holding, i.e. the option's expiration date. But, for a large number of countries there exist a few issues of USD- (or Euro-) governmental bonds, if any. And the time horizon an international investor is interested in for being insured against default, will typically be short- to medium-term, say one year. To overcome these problems, the following considerations will be useful.

First, yield curves are assumed to be available for the riskless bonds, say the USD-T bond yield curve, as well as for corporate bonds of any commercial rating class, using Bloomberg data e.g. Next, to compare different debtor nations i it will be useful to adjust the bonds of each debtor nation i with a maturity of T_i years to a common T-year maturity, say T = 5 years, by subtracting the difference between the average spread on T_i year and on T year corporate bonds of the same rating class R(i) as country i belongs to (see also PACKER AND CANTOR (1996, p. 40)).

Having executed this for all sovereign bonds under consideration, we end up with *maturity adjusted sovereign bond spreads*, say $B_i(T) - B^{sec}(T)$. Accounting for alternative expiration dates t*, say 6 month, 1 year, and so on, we calculate the effective interest rates $r_{e,i}$, r_e^{sec} resp., corresponding to $B_i(T)$, $B^{sec}(T)$ resp., by employing the formula

$$B(T) = (1 + r_e)^{-(T-t)}$$

and modify the bonds spread in eq. (3.1) in order to determine the put price of, say one, unit of international currency to be paid at t*, as follows:

$$(1 + r_e^{sec})^{-(t^*-t)} - (1 + r_{e,i})^{-(t^*-t)} = \mathrm{Put}(S/K, 1; t, t^*) \tag{3.1'}$$

where

$\mathrm{Put}(S, K; t, t^*) = P_{t,t^*}$, i.e. the put price w.r.t. K

for which holds

$$\text{Put}(S/K, 1; t, t^*) = 1/K \text{ Put}(S, K; t, t^*) = 1/K\, P_{t,t^*}, \qquad (3.8)$$

i.e. the put price w.r.t. one unit of the international currency.

Accounting for institutional features

The above reasoning is applicable straightforward in the case of floating exchange rate regimes. If the monetary authority of a debtor nation has committed to other exchange rate arrangements, like crawling peg, fixed exchange rate system, or currency board, we have to subtract strategic forex reserves in advance from the central bank's international reserves. In the Bulgarian case, for example, characterised by a currency board (of the second generation), one may identify S in eq. 3.4 with the "net government reserves", net exports may be inferred by some time series arguments, and additional capital inflow will be determined mainly by FDI replacement on a medium term perspective, as being suggested by the Vice Governor of BNB and taken up by *Moody's* in the upgrading procedure.

Similar arguments may hold for other institutional features. For example, the minimum reserve requirement to cover imports is commonly regarded as a two month time-span. The specification of these strategic reserves to be deducted from total reserves in advance may turn out to become a complex task. Heller and Khan (1978) have given some insight in the holdings of international reserves and the reactions following after the breakdown of the Bretton Woods fixed exchange rate system. As the authors have shown, offsetting effects resulting from perceived higher uncertainties hamper any straightforward identification of changes in the demand for international reserves caused by institutional rearrangements. On the other hand, the transition to the Euro System with a still ongoing process to reduce foreign currency holdings again demonstrates the importance of institutional arrangements for international reserve considerations.

A final remark should be addressed to the issue of political risk. As studies like HAQUE ET. AL. (1996) indicate, business country ratings are persistent and slowly adjusted to changes in economic fundamentals. Hence, business country ratings may primarily attribute to the aspect of political risk which in our context contributes more to the aspect of willingness-to-pay than to the aspect of ability-to-pay (economic risk). Accordingly, if political risk is understood as a more persistent phenomenon and being independent of economic risk, one may deduct part of the spread in equation (3.1') attributed to the aspect of political risk before calculating default probabilities attributed to economic risk.

4 The offsetting effect of volatility and drift: A numerical illustration

To demonstrate the offsetting effect between implicit volatility (spread resp.) and drift, we draw on an example of USD bonds issued by Argentina (ID#: 004785428) and by Ecuador (ID#: 007562128). We use the rates of 01/19/1999 as a convenient date where shocks had been absent. For simplicity, we disregard maturity normalization due to similar dates of maturity.

According to assumption 4, we assume that due to lack of public information decision makers, at the beginning of 1999, had zero expectations on additional capital inflows for the coming one-year period (T–t = 1) and had static expectations on exports and imports. Hence, the data of the bonds and the basic economic data of both nations are considered as following:

	Argentina	Ecuador
coupon	8.75	11.25
market price	90.0844	77.5000
maturity	12/20/2003	02/25/2002
risky interest rate $r_{e,i}$	11.04%	21.18%
secure interest rate r_e^{sec}	4.58%	4.58%
foreign debt	104,539 Mio. USD	15,941 Mio. USD
debt repayments	6,969 Mio. USD	638 Mio. USD
interest payments	6,454 Mio. USD	703 Mio. USD
total payments K	13,416 Mio. USD	1,341 Mio. USD
reserves of foreign currency S	25,470 Mio. USD	1,743 Mio. USD
exports EX	29,318 Mio. USD	5,700 Mio. USD
imports IM	34,899 Mio. USD	5,510 Mio. USD

The difference of the riskless and the risky one-year zero bonds with a face value of one USD has to be equal to the price of the put option on one USD foreign debt (see eq. (3.1')), which results in:

$$\text{Put}_{\text{Argentina}}(S/K,1) = \exp(-\ln(1+4{,}58\%)) - \exp(-\ln(1+11{,}04\%)) \quad = 0.0556$$

$$\text{Put}_{\text{Ecuador}}(S/K,1) = \exp(-\ln(1+4{,}58\%)) - \exp(-\ln(1+21{,}18\%)) \quad = 0.1311$$

The price of the put option on the total foreign debt that has to be repaid within the next year is (see eq. (3.8)):

$$\text{Put}_{\text{Argentina}}(S, K) \quad = 0.0556 * 13{,}416 \text{ Mio. USD} \quad = 746 \text{ Mio. USD}$$

$$\text{Put}_{\text{Ecuador}}(S, K) \quad = 0.1311 * 1{,}341 \text{ Mio. USD} \quad = 176 \text{ Mio. USD}$$

The prices of the put options in equation (3.3) are equal to the observed market prices if the implicit volatilities satisfy:

$\sigma_{\text{Argentina}}$ = <u>56.17%</u>

σ_{Ecuador} = <u>61.10%</u>.

The drift parameters μ in equation (3.6) can be computed as:

$$\mu_{\text{Argentina}} = \ln\left(\frac{25{,}470 + 29{,}318 - 34{,}899}{25{,}470}\right) = \underline{-24.73\%}$$

$$\mu_{\text{Ecuador}} = \ln\left(\frac{1{,}743 + 5{,}700 - 5{,}510}{1{,}743}\right) = \underline{+10.35\%}.$$

The probabilities that the debtor nations will not have sufficient foreign reserves to repay their foreign debts can be computed by using equation (3.7):

$$P(S_t < K)_{\text{Argentina}} = P\left(\varepsilon < \frac{\ln\left(\frac{13{,}416}{25{,}470}\right) - (-0.2473 - 0.562^2/2)}{0.5617}\right) \approx \underline{37\%}$$

$$P(S_t < K)_{\text{Ecuador}} = P\left(\varepsilon < \frac{\ln\left(\frac{1{,}341}{1{,}743}\right) - (+0.1035 - 0.611^2/2)}{0.6110}\right) \approx \underline{38\%}.$$

The model clearly shows in the case of Argentina and Ecuador in January 1999 that the spread is not a reliable indicator of a bond's default risk. In our example, the bond of Ecuador has a spread that is more than twice as high as the spread of the bond of Argentina. Nevertheless, the bond of Ecuador has a similar default risk due to the offsetting effect of a higher drift.

In the option-based model, the spreads indicate only the volatility of the foreign currency reserves, but not the default risk. Ecuador is a less developed economy with few, although diversified exports. Due to the small size of its economy Ecuador is exposed to a higher risk than Argentina. The experiences of the last decade (decrease of the oil-price, difficulties to export Ecuadorian bananas due to EC import restrictions) seem to have forced the government of Ecuador to insure against such external risks by accumulating foreign currency reserves considerably. In early 1999, Ecuador owned – as a percentage of GNP – about 30% more foreign reserves than Argentina. This decreased the default risk of the foreign debt of Ecuador to a level lower than the corresponding risk for Argentina despite of higher volatility. This example also highlights the importance to forecast the capital account correctly. In the case of Argentina, capital inflows favored repayment abilities in 1999, as being the result of, say, higher international reputation of Argentina's authorities, but had been unexpected for the public in the beginning, while Ecuador finally experienced actual debt servicing problems though reflected by a calculated default probability of approximately 40%.

5 Conclusion

Having identified the shortcomings of conventional methods to evaluate sovereign risk we propose an option-based analysis of foreign currency bonds where the underlying are the foreign reserves of a sovereign. Our option-based approach is, of course, valid only if the Black-Scholes mechanism of assumption 3 is applicable for computing the option price. The required data for the economic model (assumption 4) – especially the (expected) foreign currency reserves of the debtor nation – may be hard to get. Even if a debtor nation's actual foreign currency reserves are published officially, the figures may be questionable. Falsely reporting may occur when cheating on the data may be considered appropriate to hide solvency problems and/or to protect from speculative attacks. Second, expectations on future reserve accumulations are rarely derived on a sound macroeconomic data base. But all these informations are – among others – typically involved also in any of the standard indicator approaches to assess default risk. Besides a rather small set of reliable information, the advantage of our approach is to rely on spread signals which may reveal more relevant information on changes in certain fundamentals than any elaborate macro forecasting would do in evaluating sovereign risk.

References

Alford, A. and J. Lussier (1993), An Examination of the Price Discount on the External Debt of Developing Countries, World Economy 16, 713-724.

Armendariz de Aghion, B. (1993), Analytical Issues on LDC Debt: A Survey, World Economy 16, 467-482.

Black, F. and M. Scholes (1973), The Pricing of Options and Corporate Liabilities, Journal of Political Economy 81, 637-659.

Brewer,Th. L. and P. Rivoli (1990), Politics and Perceived Country Creditworthiness in International Banking, Journal of Money, Credit and Banking 22, 357-369.

Bulow, J. and K. Rogoff (1989), Sovereign Debt: Is to Forgive to Forget?, American Economic Review 79, 43-50.

Cantor, R. and F. Packer (1995), Sovereign Credit Ratings, FRBNY Current Issues in Economics and Finance 1, 1-6.

Cantor, R. and F. Packer (1996), Determinants and Impact of Sovereign Credit Ratings, FRBNY Economic Policy Review, 37-54.

Claessens, S. and S. van Wijnbergen (1990), Secondary Market Prices Under Alternative Debt Reduction Strategies: An Option Pricing Approach with an Application to Mexico , CEPR Discussion Paper No. 415.

Eaton, J. and M. Gersovitz (1981), Debt Repudiation: Theoretical and Empirical Analysis, Review of Economic Studies 48, 289-309.

Eaton, J.; Gersovitz, M. and J. E. Stiglitz (1986), The Pure Theory of Country Risk, European Economic Review 30, 481-513.

Edwards, S. (1984), LDC Borrowing and Default Risk: An Empirical Investigation, 1976-80, American Economic Review 74, 726-734.

Fischer, S. (1999), On the Need for an International Lender of Last Resort, Journal of Economic Perspectives 13, 85-104.

Frank, C. R. and W. R. Cline (1971), Measurement of Debt Servicing Capacity: An Application of Discriminant Analysis, Journal of International Economics 1, 327 – 344.

Heller, H. R. and M. S. Khan (1978), The Demand for International Reserves Under Fixed and Floating Exchange Rates, IMF Staff Papers 25, 623-649.

Haque, N. U.; Kumar, M. S.; Mark, N. and D. J. Mathieson (1996), The Economic Content of Indicators of Developing Country Creditworthiness, IMF Staff Papers 43, 688-724.

Hull, J. C. (1993), Options, Futures, and Other Derivative Securities, 2nd edition, Englewood Cliffs: Prentice Hall.

Lichtlen, M. F. (1997), Management von Länderrisiken, Bern: Haupt.

Lloyd-Ellis, H; McKenzie, G. W. and S. H. Thomas (1989), Using Country Balance Sheet Data to Predict Debt Rescheduling, Economic Letters 31, 173-177.

Oral, M.; Kettani, O.; Cosset, J.-C. and M. Daouas (1992), An Estimation Model for Country Risk Rating, International Journal of Forecasting 8, 583-593.

Rogoff, K. (1999), International Institutions for Reducing Global Financial Instability, Journal of Economic Perspectives 13, 21-41.

Saini, K. G. and P. S. Bates (1984), A Survey of the Quantitative Approaches to Country Risk Analysis, Journal of Banking and Finance 8, 341-356.

Scholtens, L. J. R. (1999), On the Co-Movement of Bond Yield Spreads and Country Risk Ratings, Journal of Fixed Income 8, 99-103.

Somerville, R. A. and R. J. Taffler (1995), Banker Judgement versus Formal Forecasting Models: The Case of Country Risk Assessment, Journal of Banking and Finance 19, 281-297.

Wong, C.-H. and L. Carranza (1999), Policy Responses to External Imbalances in Emerging Market Economies: Further Empirical Results, IMF Staff Papers 46, 225-237.

Notes on contributors

Prof. Timothy Devinney
Affiliation: Australian Graduate School of Management
Academic CV: BSc. Psychology and Applied Mathematics (Carnegie Mellon University), MA Public Policy Studies, MBA Economics and Statistics and PhD in Economics (University of Chicago)
Past affiliations: UCLA, Vanderbilt University
Visiting professorships: Universities of Trier, Hamburg, Ulm, Konstanz, Frankfurt, Hong Kong City University, Hong Kong University of Science and Technology

Prof. Dr. Bernhard Eckwert
Affiliation: Chemnitz University of Technology
Academic CV: Diploma in Economics 1981, PhD in Economics 1984 (University of Augsburg), Habilitation 1992 (University of Augsburg), Full Professor 1993 (University of Chemnitz, Department of Economics)
Past affiliations: University of Augsburg, University of Bonn
Memberships: Theoretischer Ausschuß im Verein für Socialpolitik, Ausschuß für Außenwirtschaftstheorie und -politik im Verein für Socialpolitik, Econometric Society

Chuluunbaatar Enkhzaya
Affiliation: Dresden University of Technology
Academic CV: Diploma in German Studies/Economics 1995 (National University of Mongolia)
Past affiliations: National University of Mongolia

Prof. David I. Fand
Affiliation: George Mason University
Academic CV: MA 1950, PhD 1954 (University of Chicago)
Past affiliations: Carnegie Institute of Technology, Brown University, University of Chicago, University of North Carolina, Southern Methodist University, University of Buffalo, Wayne State University
Visiting professorships: University of Uppsala, Cambridge University, University of Minnesota, Yale University, Hebrew University, University of Tokyo, Technical University of Chemnitz
Memberships: American Economic Association, Academy of Scholars of Wayne State University, National Association of Scholars

Prof. Dr. Wolfgang Filc
Affiliation: Trier University
Academic CV: Diploma of Economics 1970 (Free University of Berlin), Dr. rer. pol. 1974, Habilitation 1980 (Hannover University), Professor of Economics 1981 (Trier University)
Past affiliations: Director General and head of department "International Financial and Monetary Relations", German Ministry of Finance, 12/1998-06/1999
Visiting professorships: Clark University, Worcester, Mass. (USA)
Memberships: Verein für Socialpolitik, member of directorate of "Institut für Empirische Wirtschaftsforschung" (Berlin)

Prof. Dr. Michael Frenkel
Affiliation: WHU Koblenz
Academic CV: Doctorate 1980 (University of Mainz), Habiliation, Professor of Economics (WHU Koblenz) 1993
Past affiliations: International Monetary Fund
Visiting professorships: Konrad Adenauer Professor of Economics, Georgetown University, Brandes University, Emory University, Michigan University
Memberships: AEA, IAES, WEA, Verein für Socialpolitik (Ausschuß für Außenwirtschaftstheorie und –politik im Verein für Socialpolitik), Editorial Board "International Journal of Business" and "Global Finance Journal"

Prof. Dr. Wilfried Fuhrmann
Affiliation: University of Potsdam
Academic CV: Diploma in Economics 1971, PhD 1976, Habilitation 1986 (University of Kiel), Professor 1987 (University of Linz)
Past affiliations: University of Kiel, University of Linz, University of Paderborn

Prof. Gianandrea Goisis
Affiliation: Professor of Political Economy at the Università degli Studi di Milano
Academic CV: Laurea in Giurisprudenzia 1967 (University of Pavia), Research Student at LSE (1968-1969), Professor 1980 (University of Padova)
Past affiliations: University of Padova, University of Verona, University of Milan
Visiting professorships: University of Buckingham (U.K.), University of Berkeley (U.S.A.)
Memberships: Società Italiana degli Economisti, AEA, Ex Alumni LSE, Comitato di ricerche sanitarie (Università Cattolica di Milano), Comitato di ricerche sullo sviluppo dell'impresa (Università Biocca di Milano)

Dr. rer. pol. habil. Dipl. Soz. Michael Graff
Affiliation: Dresden University of Technology
Academic CV: Dipl. Soz. 1989 and Dr. rer. pol. 1994 (University of Hamburg), Habilitation in Economics 03/2000 (Dresden University of Technology)
Past affiliations: Institute of Medical Sociology, University of Hamburg, Faculty of Economics, University of Hamburg
Memberships: AEA, Deutscher Hochschulverband, IAES, Verein für Socialpolitik

Dr. Jens Hölscher
Affiliation: Senior Lecturer, University of Brighton, Business School
Academic CV: Dipl.-Volkswirt 1989, Dr. rer. pol. 1993 (FU Berlin)
Past affiliations: Freie Universität Berlin, University of Wales Swansea, University of Birmingham
Visiting professorships: Halle Institute for Economic Research, Chemnitz University of Technology
Memberships: Royal Economic Society, Verein für Socialpolitik

Prof. Dr. Hermann Locarek-Junge
Affiliation: Dresden University of Technology
Academic CV: Dipl. oec. 1983, Dr. rer. pol. 1987, Habilitation 1991 (University of Augsburg), Professor 1992 (University of Essen)
Past affiliations: University of Augsburg, University of Essen
Memberships: DVFA, DFG, GOR, SG, FMA, GFKl, GI Fachgruppe 5.4.1

Prof. Dr. Alexander Karmann
Affiliation: Dresden University of Technology
Academic CV: Diploma in Mathematics 1975, Dr. rer. pol. 1979, Habilitation 1983 (University of Karsruhe), Professor in Economics 1986 (University of Hamburg)
Past affiliations: University of Karlsruhe, University of Hamburg
Memberships: AEA, EEA, GOR, Verein für Socialpolitik (Ausschüsse für Industrieökonomik, Regionalwissenschaften, Umwelt/Ressorcenökonomie und Gesundheitspolitik)

Prof. Dr. Georg Milbradt
Affiliation: Minister of Finance, Free State of Saxony, professor of public finance, University of Münster
Academic CV: Diploma in Economics 1968, Dr. rer. pol. 1973, Habilitation 1980, Professor 1985 (University of Münster)
Past affiliations: Research Assistant 1973-1981 (Institute of Public Finance, Münster), Lectureship 1981-1983 (University of Mainz), Lectureship 1982-1983 (University of Osnabrück)

Prof. Dr. Doris Neuberger
Affiliation: University of Rostock
Academic CV: Diploma in Economics 1986, Dr. rer. pol. 1989, Habilitation 1993 (University of Erlangen-Nürnberg), Professor 1994 (University of Rostock)
Past affiliations: University of Erlangen-Nürnberg
Memberships: Verein für Socialpolitik (Industrial Organization Section), Thünen Society

Prof. Dr. Bernd Schips
Affiliation: Swiss Federal Institute of Technology (ETH) Zürich, Institute for Business Cycle Research (KOF)
Academic CV: Diploma in Economics 1966 (University of Karlsruhe), Dr. rer. pol. 1967 (University of Tübingen), Habilitation 1970, Professor 1970 (University of Bochum)
Past affiliations: University of Bochum, University of St. Gallen
Visiting professorships: Universities of Saarbrücken, Karlsruhe, Eichstätt/Ingolstadt, Zürich, Akademgorodok (Novosibirsk, USSR)
Memberships: Advisory Board of ifo-Institute (Munich), Advisory Board of ZEW (Mannheim), Head of Group of Experts "Revision Living Cost Index", President of Group of Experts "Economic Statistics", Swiss Commission for Vocational Training, Swiss Union of Commerce

Jan K. Solarz, Advisor to the President of the National Bank of Poland
Affiliation: Banking and Insurance University in Warszawa
Academic CV: MA Economics 1968, MA Sociology, PhD 1970, Habilitation 1997, Professor 1999 (Banking and Insurance University in Warszawa)
Past affiliations: Polish Academy of Science
Visiting professorships: Cornell University, International Management and Science Institute
Memberships: Polish Economist Association

Prof. Dr. Vincenz Timmermann
Affiliation: University of Hamburg
Academic CV: Diploma in Economics 1961 (University of Münster), Dr. rer. pol. 1965; Habilitation 1969 (University of Mannheim), Professor 1971 (University of Hamburg)
Past affiliations: Universities of Mannheim, Bonn and Heidelberg
Visiting professorships: University of East Anglia (Norwich, England), University of Southampton (England), University of Stellenbosch (RSA)

Prof. Dr. Helmut Wagner
Affiliation: University of Hagen
Academic CV: MA 1974, PhD 1976 (University of Regensburg), Habilitation 1981 (Technical University of Aachen), Professor 1982 (HWP, Hamburg)
Past affiliations: Technical University of Aachen, HWP Hamburg
Visiting professorships: University of California, MIT, Princeton University, Bank of Japan's Institute for Monetary and Economic Studies (Tokyo), Johns Hopkins University (Washington, DC), IMF Research Department (Washington, DC)
Memberships: AEA, EEA, WEA, Verein für Socialpolitik

Dr. Michael Weiss
Affiliation: Chairman of Executive Board, Giro Centre of Saxon Regional Bank
Academic CV: Bachelor of B.Sc./Economics 1971 (University of Bonn), Dr. sc. pol. 1975 (University of Kiel)
Past affiliations: Universities o Kiel, Giro Centre West German Regional Bank (Düsseldorf), Berlin Housing & Loan Corporation

Prof. Dr. Hans Wiesmeth
Affiliation: Dresden University of Technology
Academic CV: Diploma in Mathematics 1975 (University of Erlangen-Nürnberg), Dr. rer. pol. 1979, Habilitation 1980 (University of Hamburg), Professor 1992 (Dresden University of Technology)
Past affiliations: University of Bonn
Visiting professorships: University of Western Ontario (London, Canada), York University (Toronto, Canada)
Memberships: Econometric Society, Society for the Advancement of Economic Theory, Verein für Socialpolitik (Regionalwissenschaftlicher Ausschuß)

Contributions to Economics

Bruno Jeitziner
Political Economy of the Swiss National Bank
1999. ISBN 3-7908-1209-9

Irene Ring et al. (Eds.)
Regional Sustainability
1999. ISBN 3-7908-1233-1

Katharina Müller/Andreas Ryll/Hans-Jürgen Wagener (Eds.)
Transformation of Social Security: Pensions in Central-Eastern Europe
1999. ISBN 3-7908-1210-2

Stefan Traub
Framing Effects in Taxation
1999. ISBN 3-7908-1240-4

Pablo Coto-Millán
Utility and Production
1999. ISBN 3-7908-1153-X

Frank Riedel
Imperfect Information and Investor Heterogeneity in the Bond Market
2000. ISBN 3-7908-1247-1

Kirsten Ralf
Business Cycles
2000. ISBN 3-7908-1245-5

Michele Bagella/Leonardo Becchetti (Eds.)
The Competitive Advantage of Industrial Districts
2000. ISBN 3-7908-1254-4

Frank Bohn
Monetary Union and Fiscal Stability
2000. ISBN 3-7908-1266-8

Michael Malakellis
Integrated Macro-Micro-Modelling Under Rational Expectations
2000. ISBN 3-7908-1266-8

Stefan Baumgärtner
Ambivalent Joint Production and the Natural Environment
2000. ISBN 3-7908-1290-0

Henri Capron, Wim Meeusen (Eds.)
The National Innovation System of Belgium
2000. ISBN 3-7908-1308-7

Tobias Miarka
Financial Intermediation and Deregulation
2000. ISBN 3-7908-1307-9

Chisato Yoshida
Illegal Immigration and Economic Welfare
2000. ISBN 3-7908-1315-X

Nikolaus Thumm
Intellectual Property Rights
2000. ISBN 3-7908-1329-X

Max Keilbach
Spatial Knowledge Spillovers and the Dynamics of Agglomeration and Regional Growth
2000. ISBN 3-7908-1321-4

GPSR Compliance

The European Union's (EU) General Product Safety Regulation (GPSR) is a set of rules that requires consumer products to be safe and our obligations to ensure this.

If you have any concerns about our products, you can contact us on ProductSafety@springernature.com

In case Publisher is established outside the EU, the EU authorized representative is:

Springer Nature Customer Service Center GmbH
Europaplatz 3
69115 Heidelberg, Germany

Batch number: 10725973

Printed by Printforce, the Netherlands